IMAGES
*of America*

# WESLACO

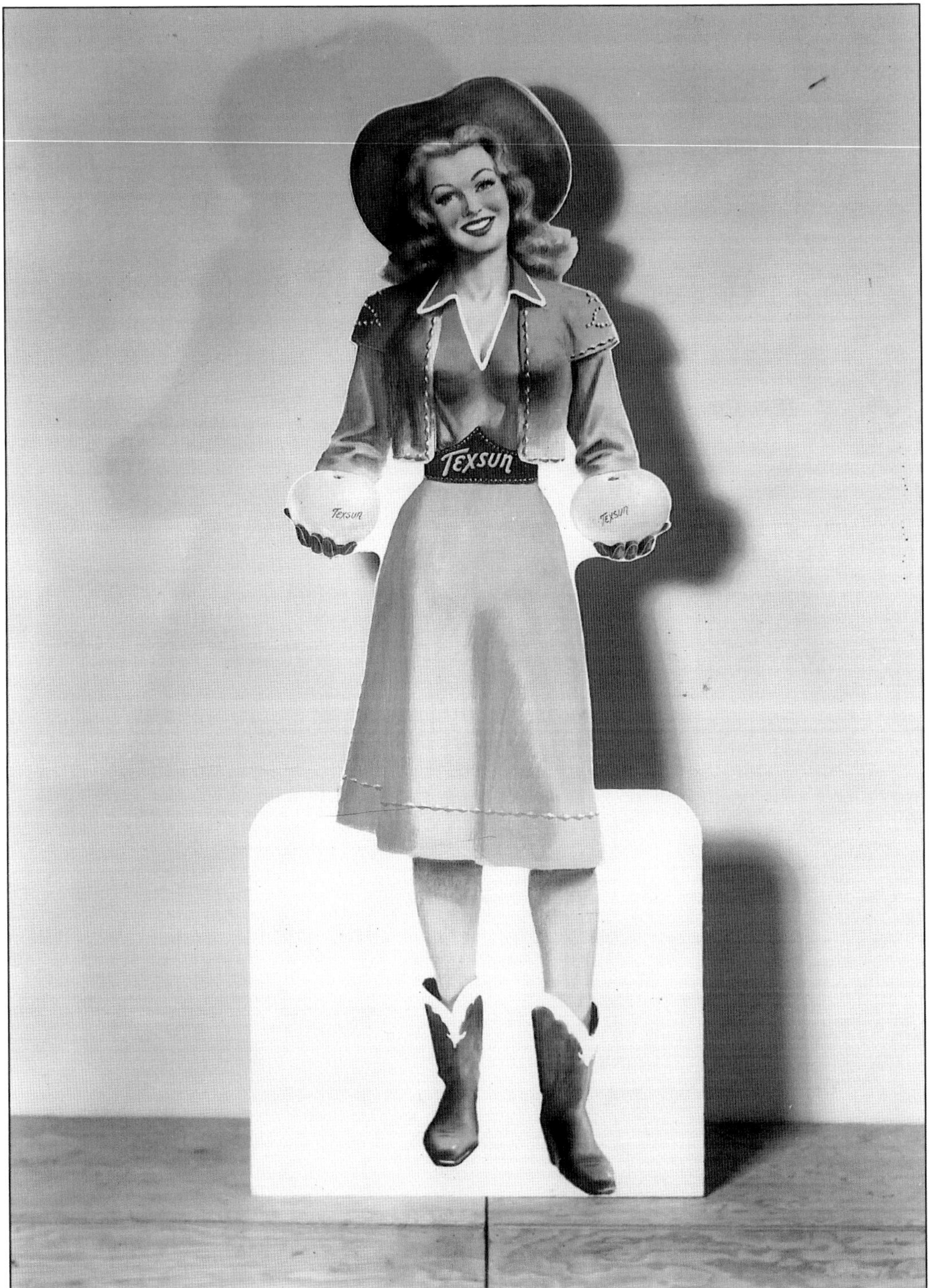

This grocery store counter card from the 1950s reminded housewives to buy fresh grapefruit from Texsun.

IMAGES
*of America*

# WESLACO

Karen Gerhardt and Blanca E. Tamez

ARCADIA
PUBLISHING

ISBN 978-0-7385-0305-9

Published by Arcadia Publishing
Charleston, South Carolina

Printed in the United States of America

Library of Congress Catalog Card Number: Applied for

For all general information contact Arcadia Publishing at:
Telephone 843-853-2070
Fax 843-853-0044
E-mail sales@arcadiapublishing.com
For customer service and orders:
Toll-Free 1-888-313-2665

Visit us on the Internet at www.arcadiapublishing.com

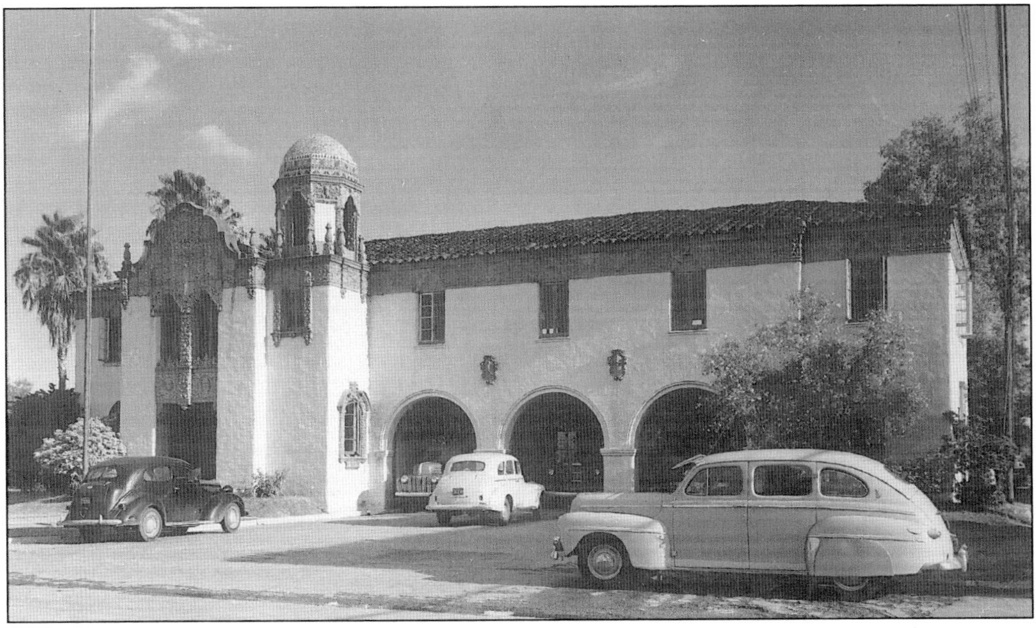

The two-story Weslaco City Hall, built in 1928, contained city offices and the fire station. Remodeled in 1951, the building continues to serve both functions.

# Contents

# Acknowledgments

This book would not have been possible without the help of many individuals. I would like to thank Pauline Whitaker, Marge Johnson, Golda Roberts, Loretta Barbee, Ruben Cardenas, Reeves and Margaret Russell, Weldon and Dorothy Blackwell, and Fran Isbell. The Weslaco Bicultural Museum Society, Inc. gave me permission to use the photographs for publication, for which I am grateful. Editor Allison Carpenter of Arcadia Publishing provided expertise, which saved much time and effort. I would most especially like to thank Blanca E. Tamez for her calmness and dedication in the midst of chaos. And finally, I would like to acknowledge the work of the Weslaco Bicultural Museum Guild and Anne Jorgensen, my predecessor, who served as the volunteer director of the museum from 1981 until 1997 and recognized the importance of the photographs.

Karen Gerhardt

I would like to thank the following individuals: Dr. Shelia Pozorski, Department of Anthropology, University of Texas-Pan American in Edinburg, Texas, for her guidance and advice towards my career choices; Ms. Karen Gerhardt, director of the Weslaco Bicultural Museum, for giving me a once-in-a-lifetime opportunity and for allowing me to enrich my museum experience; and Mrs. Pauline Whitaker for her notes and hard work on the Texsun collection. In addition, I would like to thank Mrs. Golda Roberts, Mrs. Marge Johnson, Mrs. Loretta Barbee, Ms. Fran Isbell, Mr. and Mrs. Reeves Russell, and Mr. and Mrs. Weldon Blackwell for all the extra information and revising. I am especially grateful to Arcadia Publishing and our editor, Allison Carpenter, for making this happen. Finally, I thank my parents, Mr. Cipriano Tamez Sr. and Mrs. Yolanda H. Tamez. I appreciate everything you have ever done for me. I love you. To my sister Belen and my brother Cipi, I thank you for your humor and for your sense of adventure.

Blanca E. Tamez

# INTRODUCTION

In 1747, Spanish settlers led by Gov. José de Escandón, a military officer, merchant, and rancher, began to colonize the region along both sides of the Rio Grande known as Nuevo Santander. Some of Escandón's colonists acquired large tracts of land and became ranchers. They also grew a few citrus trees for a supply of fresh fruit.

During the 19th century, due to changes in families and governments, the forces of nature, and the whims of fortune, many of the ranchers began subdividing their grants into sections called porciones. By the turn of the 20th century, the sections were too small to support large herds of cattle. Ranchers and their descendants sold their land to hardy newcomers determined to make the rich river delta soil produce commercial citrus crops.

Soon after the first train reached the town of Harlingen in July 1904, men wielding shovels and guiding horse-drawn scrapers called "fresnos" cut irrigation canals. Pump stations powered by steam engines provided a steady supply of water from the Rio Grande to experimental farms with small groves of oranges and grapefruit.

Between 1910 and 1920, land companies bought large tracts of brush country, cut roads, and built showcase hotels. The companies advertised in Midwestern cities and brought prospective land owners to the Rio Grande Valley from as far away as Chicago. The new homesteaders purchased small tracts, cleared the brush, and planted citrus trees.

W.E. Stewart, a land developer from Kansas City, Missouri, chose a townsite on a portion of the former Llano Grande land grant. He sold the first lots at auction on December 10, 1919. The new town was named Weslaco, an acronym for W.E. Stewart Land Company.

While most pioneering today is accomplished in outer space, it is helpful to remember that only 80 years ago equally inspired adventurers sought new territory and staked a claim on the future. This album of photographs tells their story between 1915 and 1950.

# *Photography Credits*

The photographs in this album of Weslaco history are a portion of the photograph collection held by the Weslaco Bicultural Museum. An attempt has been made to link each photographer with the city where he or she was located, but in some cases, that has not been possible. In those instances we have credited the photographer without the location.

Abdoo; Tom W. Collins of Dallas, Texas; Dickey Foto; Dickey and Moore Photographers; George Dorill of St. Louis, Missouri; Edrington Studio, Portrait & Commercial Photography of Weslaco, Texas; Eskildsen Photo of McAllen, Texas; Parker Griffith, Commercial & Illustrative Photography of Dallas, Texas; Hall Studio of Weslaco, Texas; Hidalgo County Historical Commission of Hidalgo, Texas; Hidalgo County Historical Museum of Edinburg, Texas; J. Gilbert Hill of Oklahoma City, Oklahoma; Holbrook Studio of Harlingen, Texas; James F. Laughead of Dallas, Texas; Moore Photo; Shell Oil Company of Houston, Texas; Smith of Weslaco, Texas; Brad Smith of Weslaco, Texas; Ken Snyder, Industrial & Illustrative Photography and Ken Snyder & Associates of Donna, Texas; Thomas D. Solether of Weslaco, Texas; Texas Citriculture; Woody Tullis of Mercedes, Texas; Yoder Studio of Weslaco, Texas.

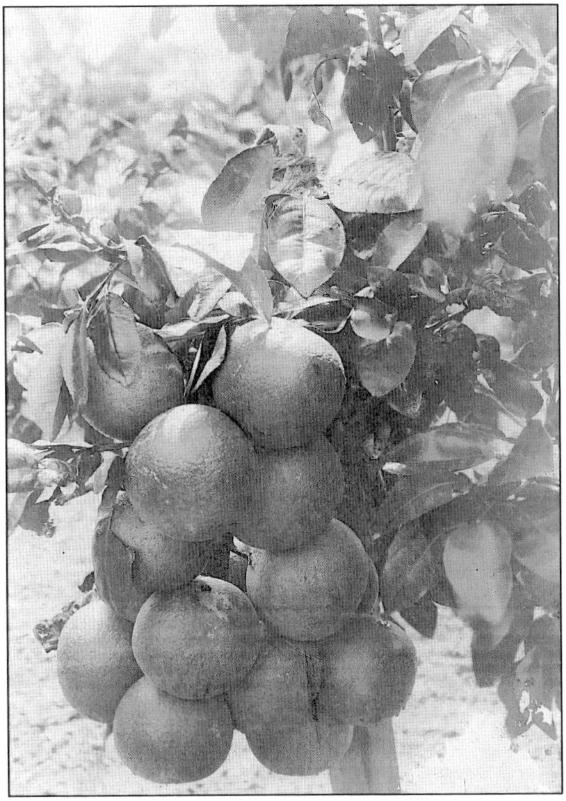

Grapefruit from the Rio Grande Valley became known and desired all over the United States.

# One

# Early Days

*We had the howling of wolves for company at night.*

—Mrs. Almeda Couch Reeves.

When the first 20th-century homesteaders arrived in the Rio Grande Valley, they faced danger on every side. An unfamiliar climate, wild animals, attacks by bandits from across the river, isolation, and distance from loved ones heightened the risks involved in moving to a new land and gambling on the successful outcome of new agricultural pursuits. They fought the risks with hard work and the dangers with hope.

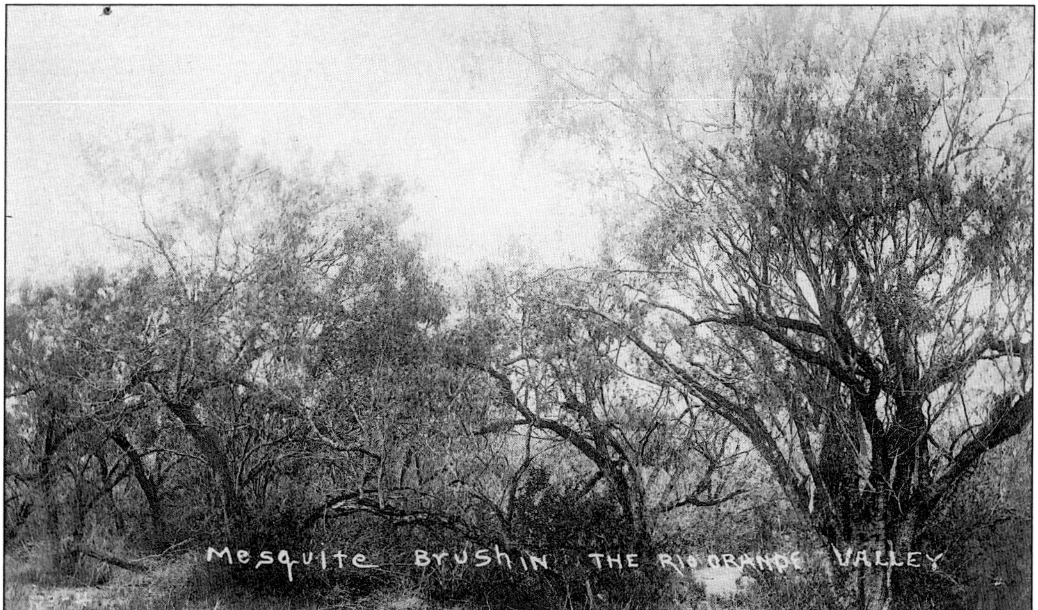


When the first 20th-century pioneers arrived in the Rio Grande Valley, they found mesquite, cat-claw, ebony, and a dense wilderness of brush. The land had to be cleared before towns could be built. (Thomas D. Solether.)

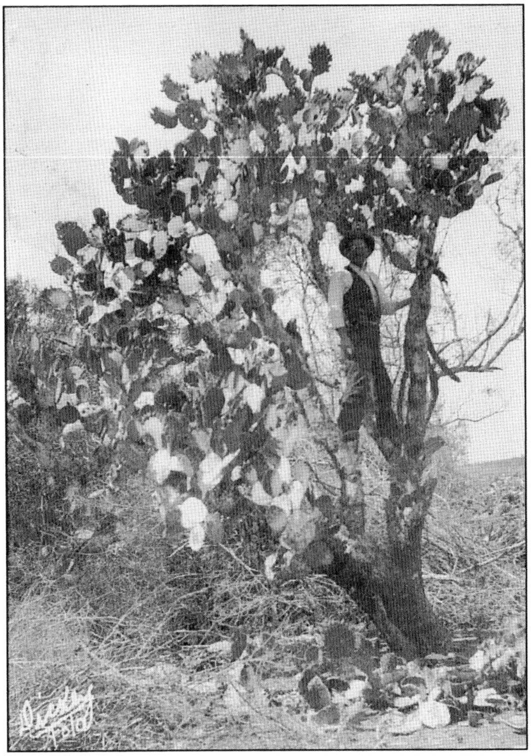

Prickly pear cactus flourished in the Valley, and giants like this one dotted the landscape. Note the man standing within the plant. (Dickey Foto.)

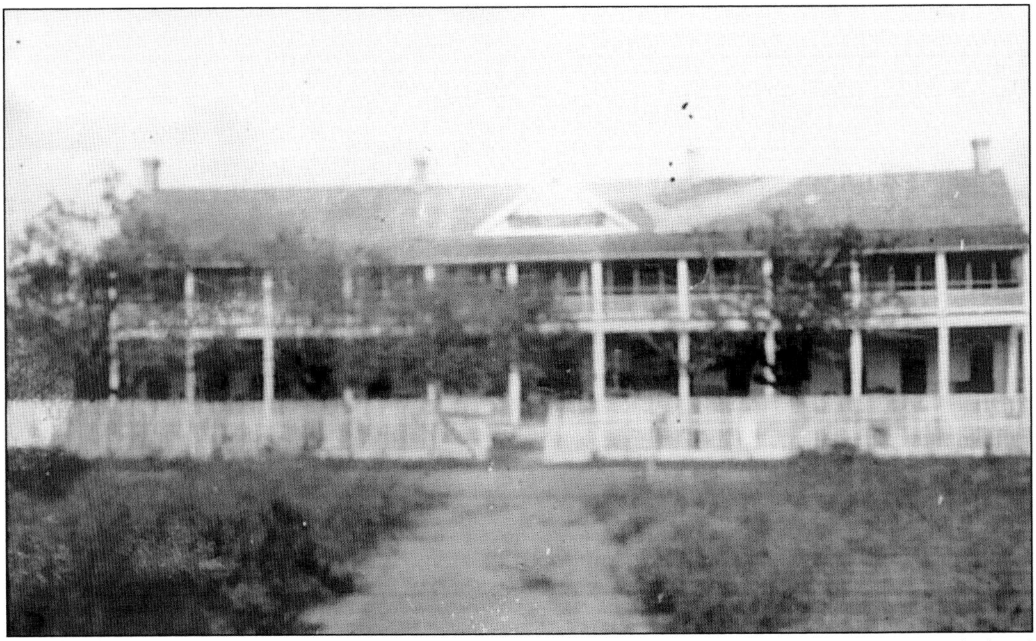

Land developer John P. Withers of Chicago bought a portion of the former Spanish land grant called Llano Grande (big plain). He built the Casa Blanca Hotel to house and entertain potential buyers of farmland. Salesmen in automobiles drove land excursion parties of visitors from the Midwest to see cultivated land and citrus groves. The land they bought, however, turned out to be uncleared brushland.

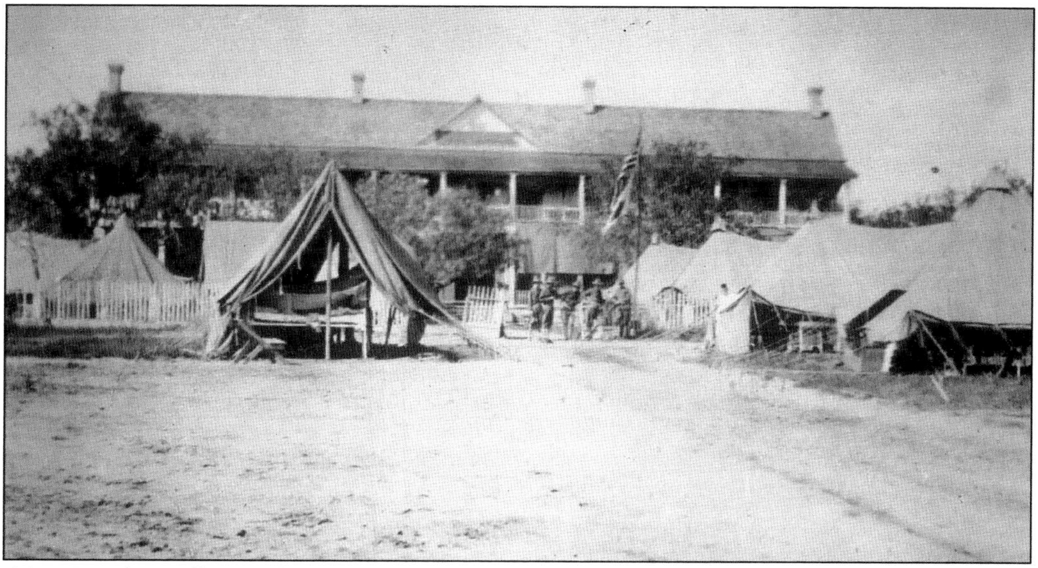

After Pancho Villa's raid on Columbus, New Mexico, in 1916, bandits from across the Rio Grande raided the growing number of Valley farms and towns on almost a daily basis. Due to repeated calls for help, the U.S. Cavalry commanded by Gen. John J. Pershing came to protect Valley residents. In July 1916, National Guard units from Indiana, Nebraska, Minnesota, and North Dakota arrived as reinforcements and set up camp at Llano Grande.

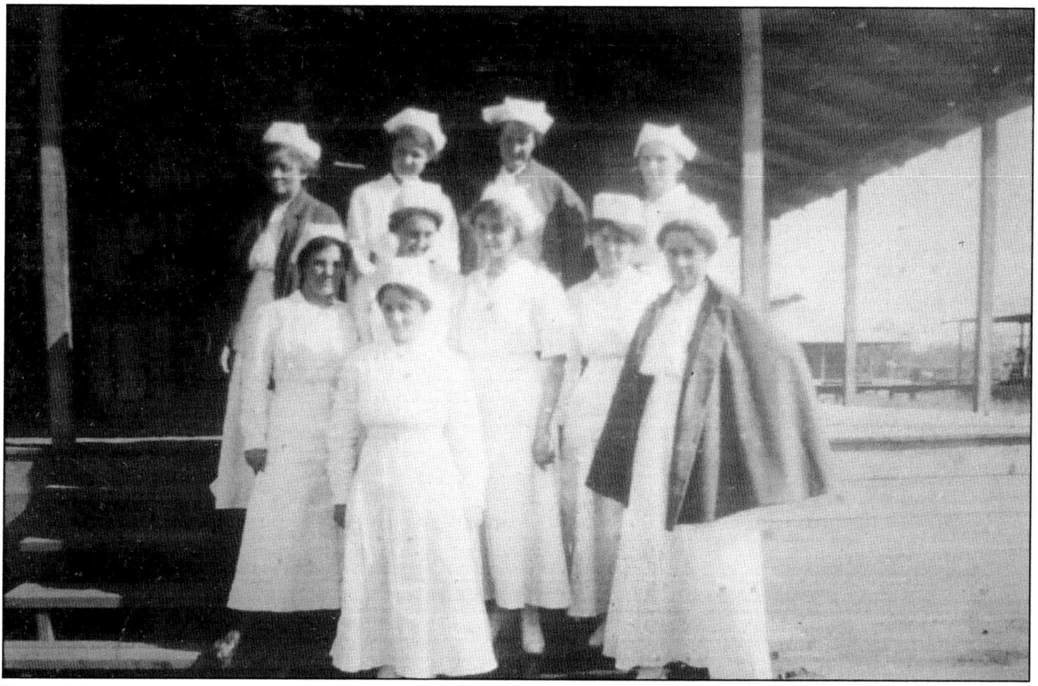

In 1916, the Casa Blanca Hotel was converted to a hospital to serve the National Guardsmen. About thirty Red Cross nurses, who were also from the Midwest, treated the soldiers. Heat, insects, contaminated water, and diseases such as pneumonia and measles caused much illness among the guardsmen, who were not accustomed to such a hostile environment.

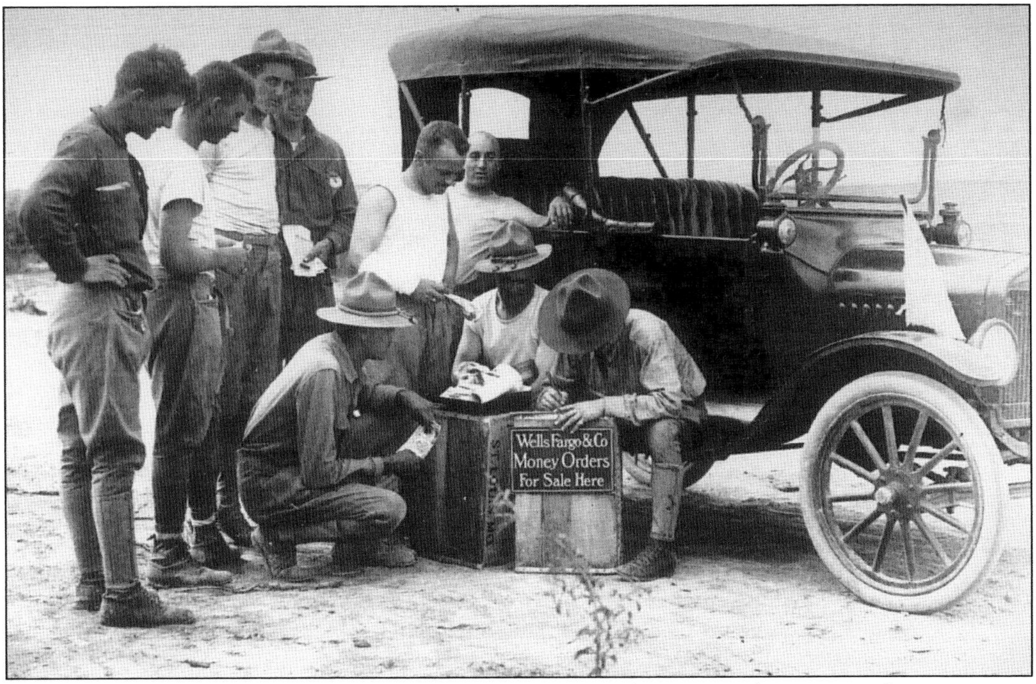


Tradesmen from Donna and Mercedes visited Camp Llano Grande to provide services to the guardsmen. This typical scene represents the informal way in which business had to be conducted. Here, soldiers buy money orders to send home.

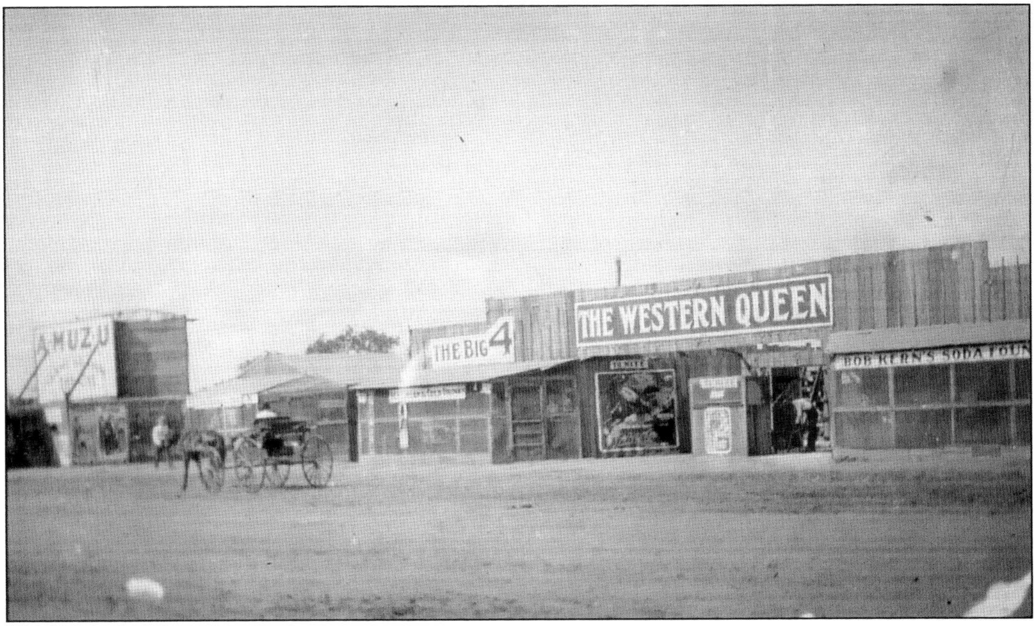


Soldiers enjoyed "Broadway"-type recreation facilities at Camp Llano Grande. The Western Queen was an open-air theater owned by Bob Kern of Mercedes. The A-Muz-U theater showed such movies as *Will a Woman Tell?*. Band music accompanied the silent pictures. Movie stars from Mexico sometimes performed in the theater to entertain the troops.

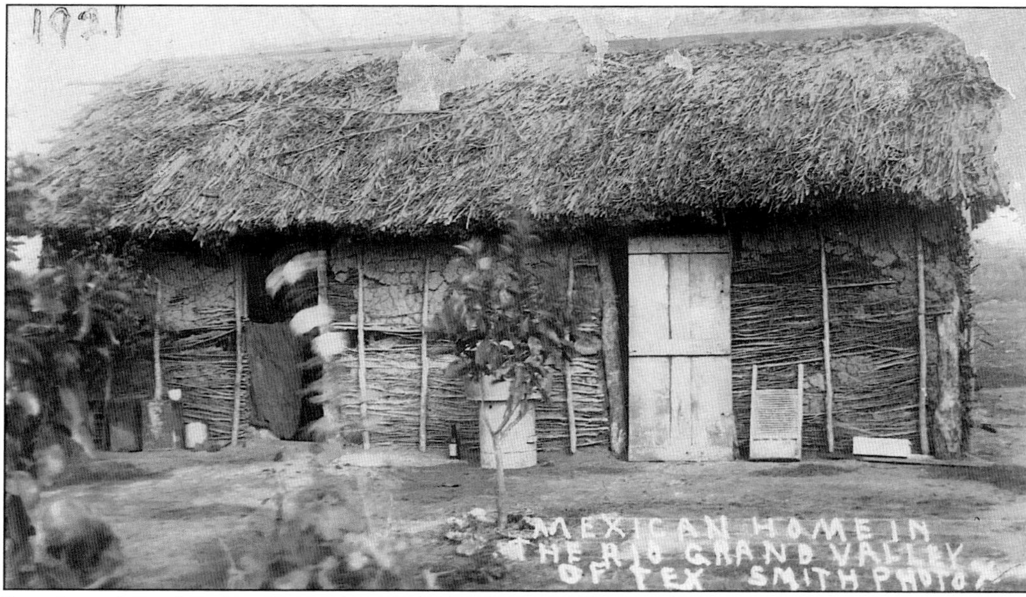


Local residents lived in huts of mud daubed onto willow stakes with roofs thatched with tule (cattail). These homes, called jacales, were a very old type of construction that made use of available materials. Boards nailed together formed doors. Note the washboard leaning against the wall. (Smith Photo.) [Authors' note: Most of the jacales disappeared after the 1933 hurricane.]

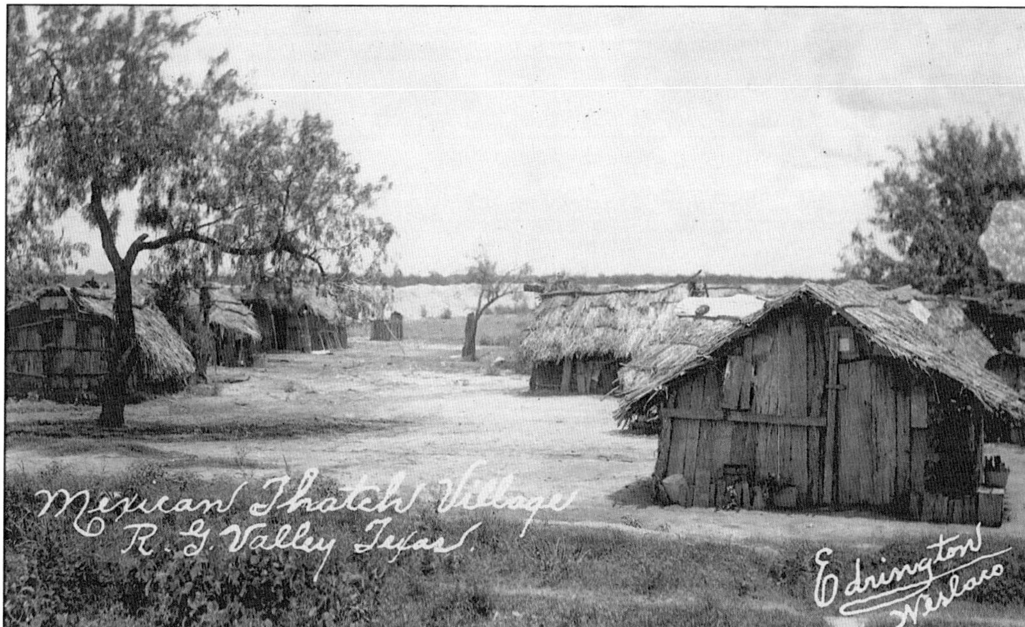


Early Valley residents lived in small communities. The 20th-century settlers lived in tents while constructing their permanent frame homes. (Edrington Studio.)

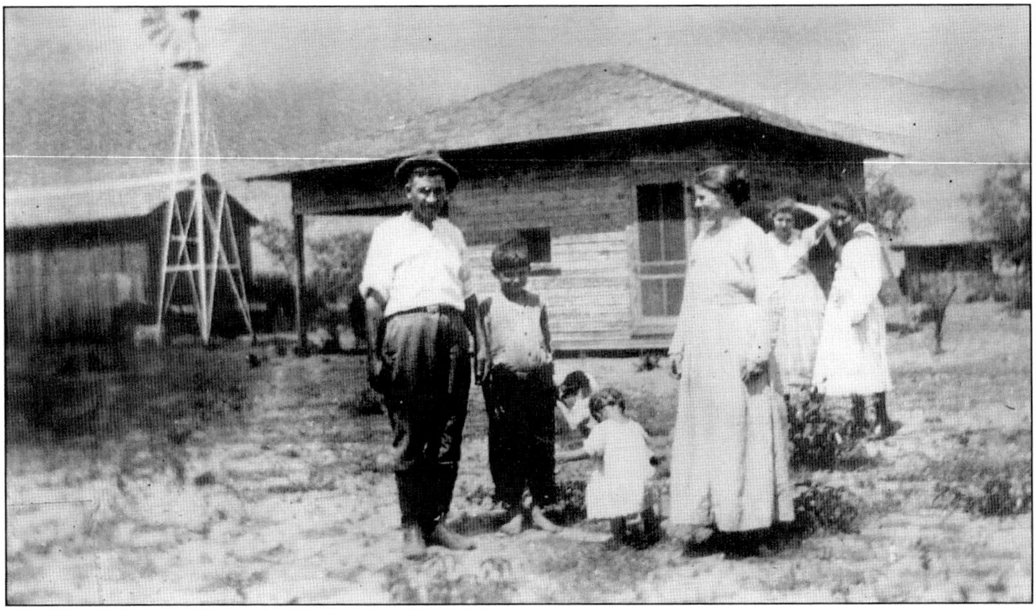

After the St. Louis, Brownsville and Mexican Railroad reached the Valley in 1904, land developers like John P. Withers attempted to establish permanent towns. His Llano Grande, located at a railroad stop west of Mercedes, lasted only a few years.

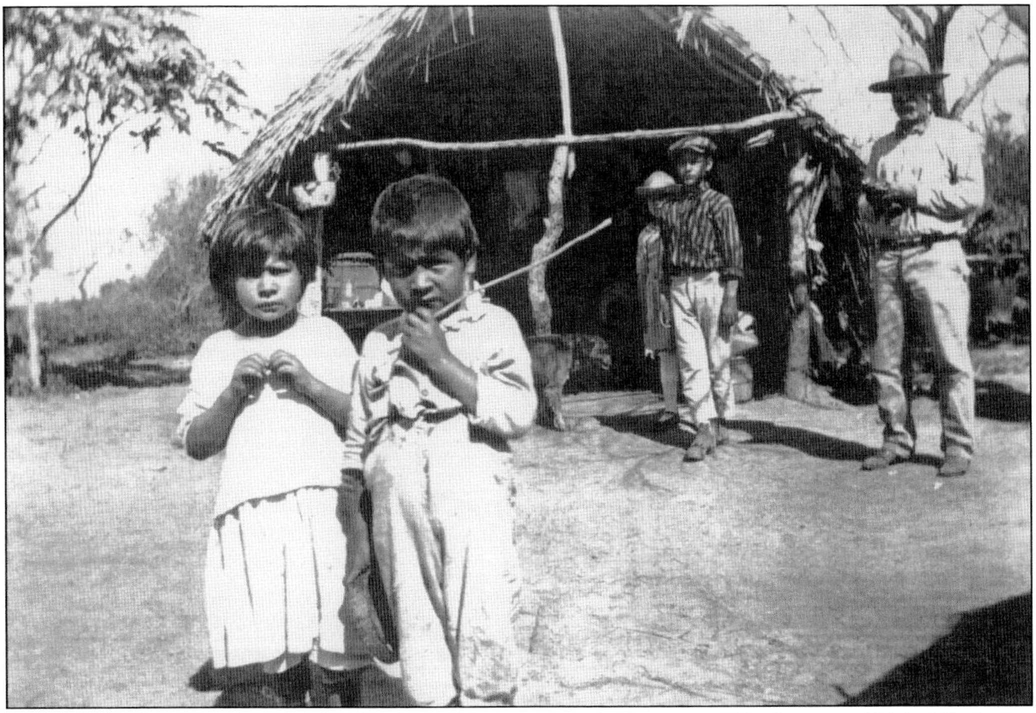

The first settler bought land and began farming in what is now Weslaco in 1912. With the arrival of new homesteaders, more land had to be cleared of brush and cactus. Clearing crews from Mexico earned $12 per acre. This thatched home, common in northern Mexico, had an open front view.

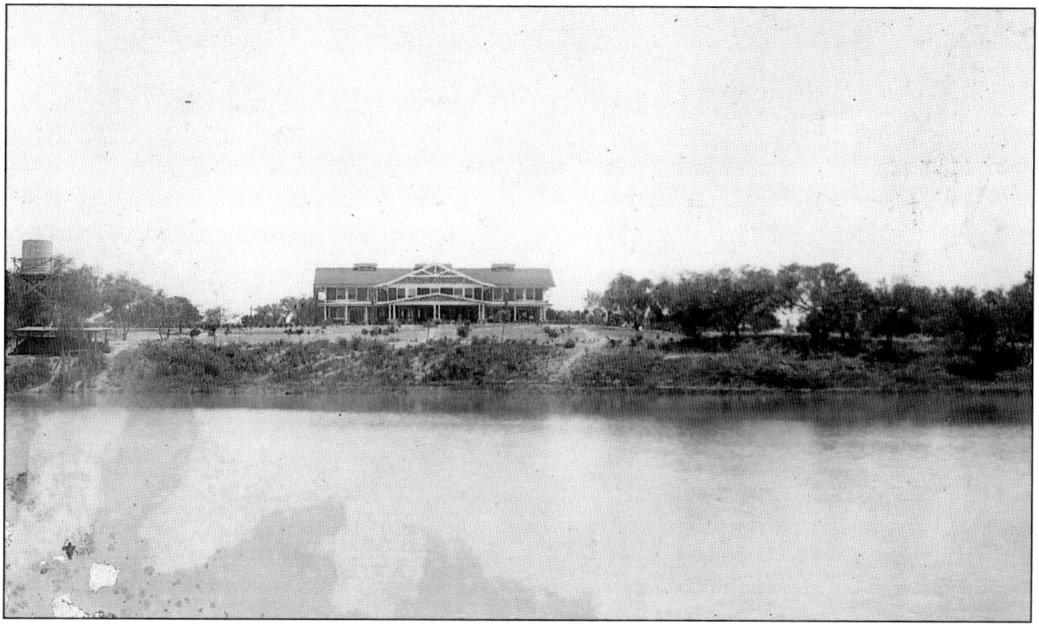

In 1919, a Tyler-born developer named W.E. Stewart, who owned a land company in Kansas City, Missouri, bought a large block in the west tract of the Llano Grande land grant. He built a beautiful clubhouse on Llano Grande Lake, south of what is now Weslaco, to house and entertain land excursion parties.

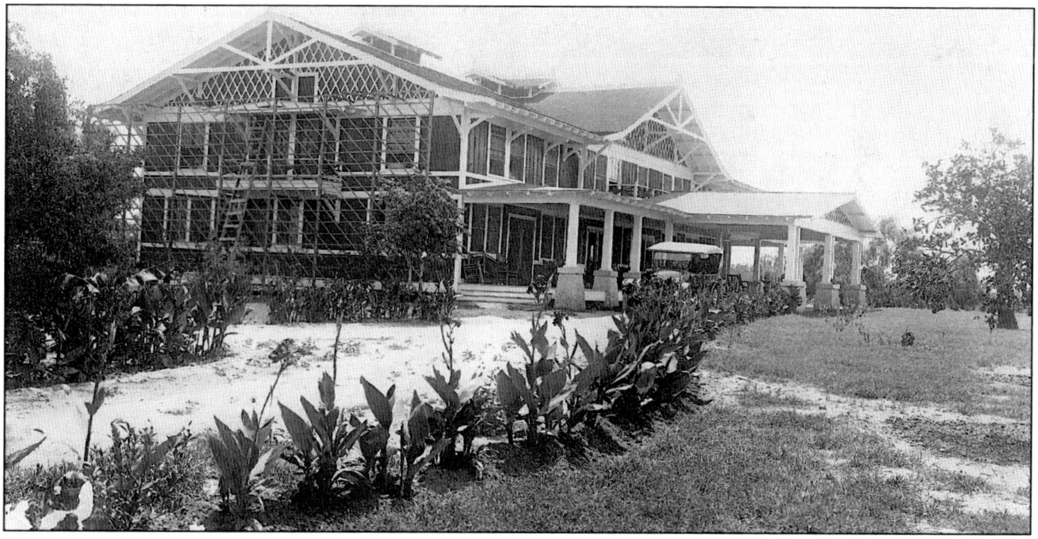

The W.E. Stewart Clubhouse served as background for panoramic photographs of the excursion parties. In September 1919, four men approached Stewart and offered to purchase a section of his land for a townsite. Ed C. Couch, his two brothers Dan R. and R.C. Couch, and Ed Couch's brother-in-law Robert L. Reeves, bought 320 acres of the West Tract Subdivision for $250,000. Ed Couch's brothers changed their minds and withdrew, but Ed Couch and R.L. Reeves maintained their faith in the future of the town. "Weslaco" is an acronym for the W.E. Stewart Land Company.

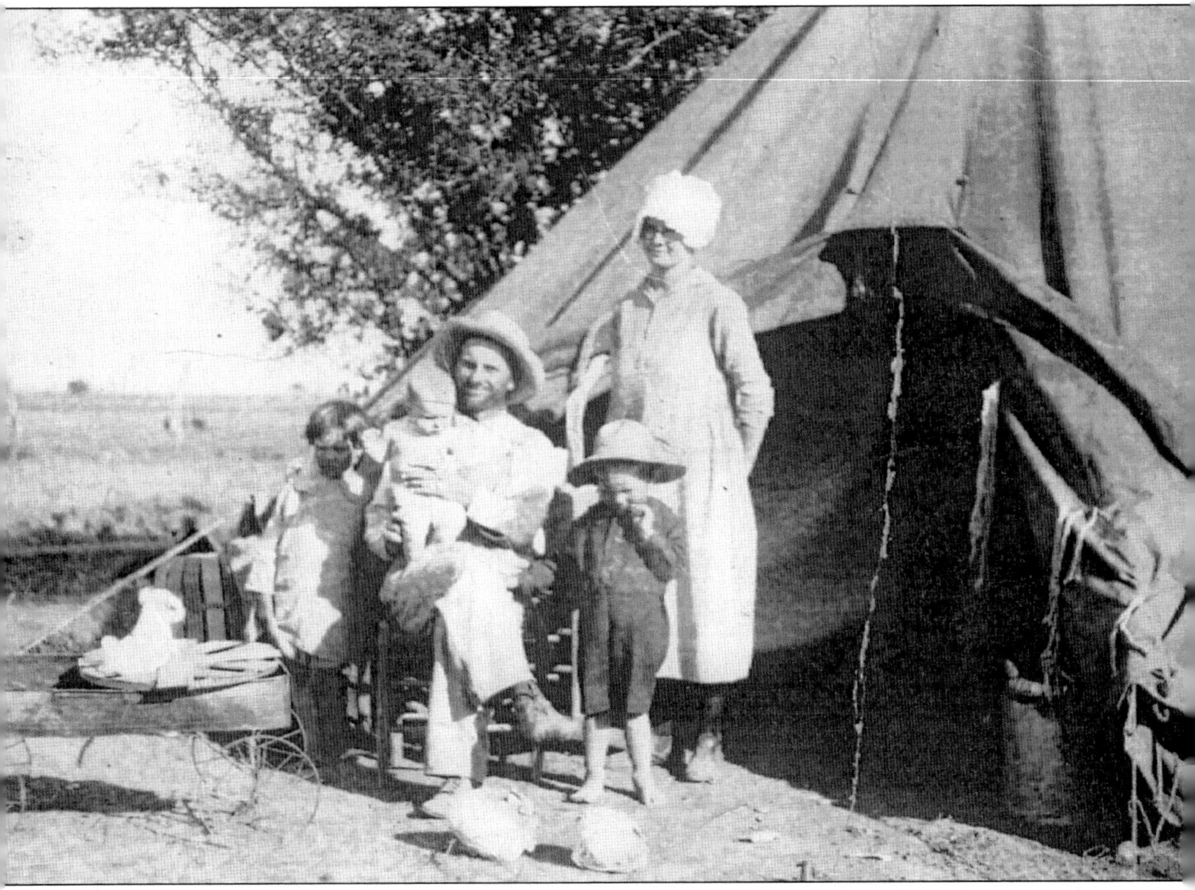

Weslaco pioneers Harvey and Mary Cleckler lived in a tent while their frame home was being built during the spring of 1925. The children, from left to right, are Lila, Glen, and Doyce. The Clecklers' frame home was located north of Memorial Elementary School at the canal and South Border Street. The Cleckler family remains prominent in the community. (Courtesy of the Cleckler family.)

Robert L. Reeves (1871–1938) was a co-founder of Weslaco and secretary of the Weslaco Townsite Company. He was a partner in the Reeves and Langford Real Estate Co. and later, with his son-in-law Robert Compere, in the Reeves and Compere Insurance Agency.

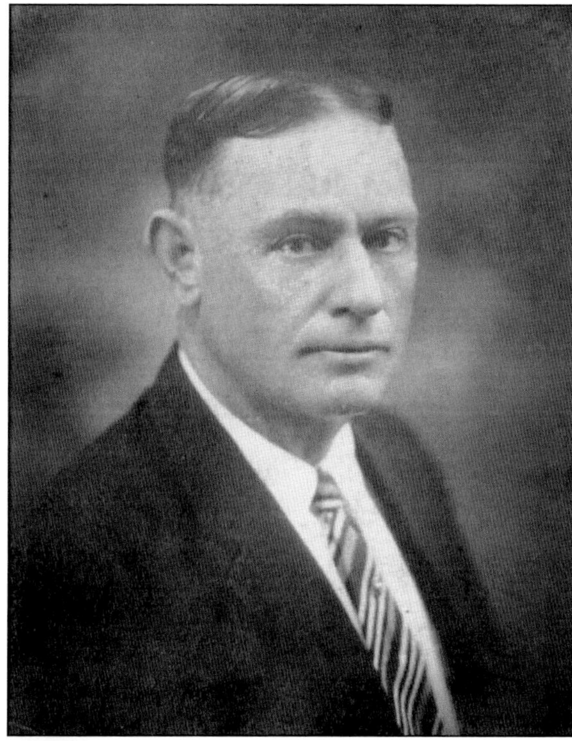

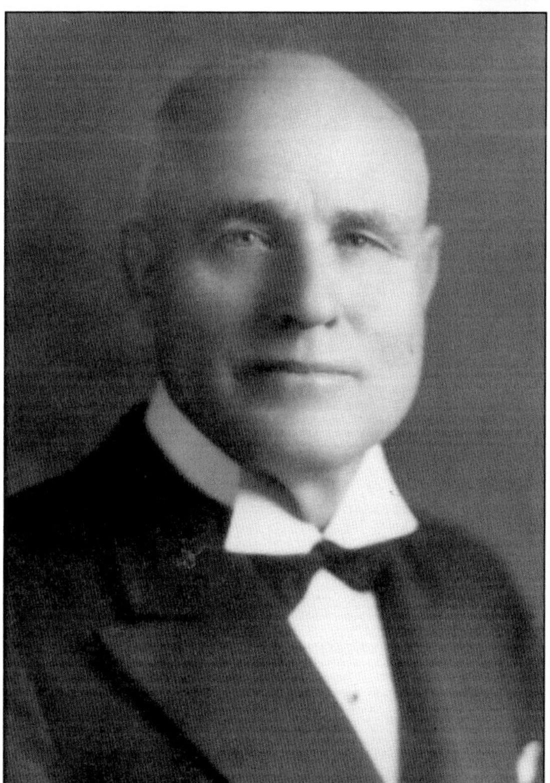

Banker Ed C. Couch and R.L. Reeves hired civil engineer H.E. Bennett to survey and plat the town streets on both sides of the railroad from First to Eighth with Main Street being what is now Fifth Street. Bennett filed the survey on September 18, 1919. Couch and Reeves posted announcements that an auction of townsite lots would be held on December 10, 1919. Lots varied in price from $50 to about $400. To attract settlers, Couch and Reeves gave away three automobiles during the land sale.

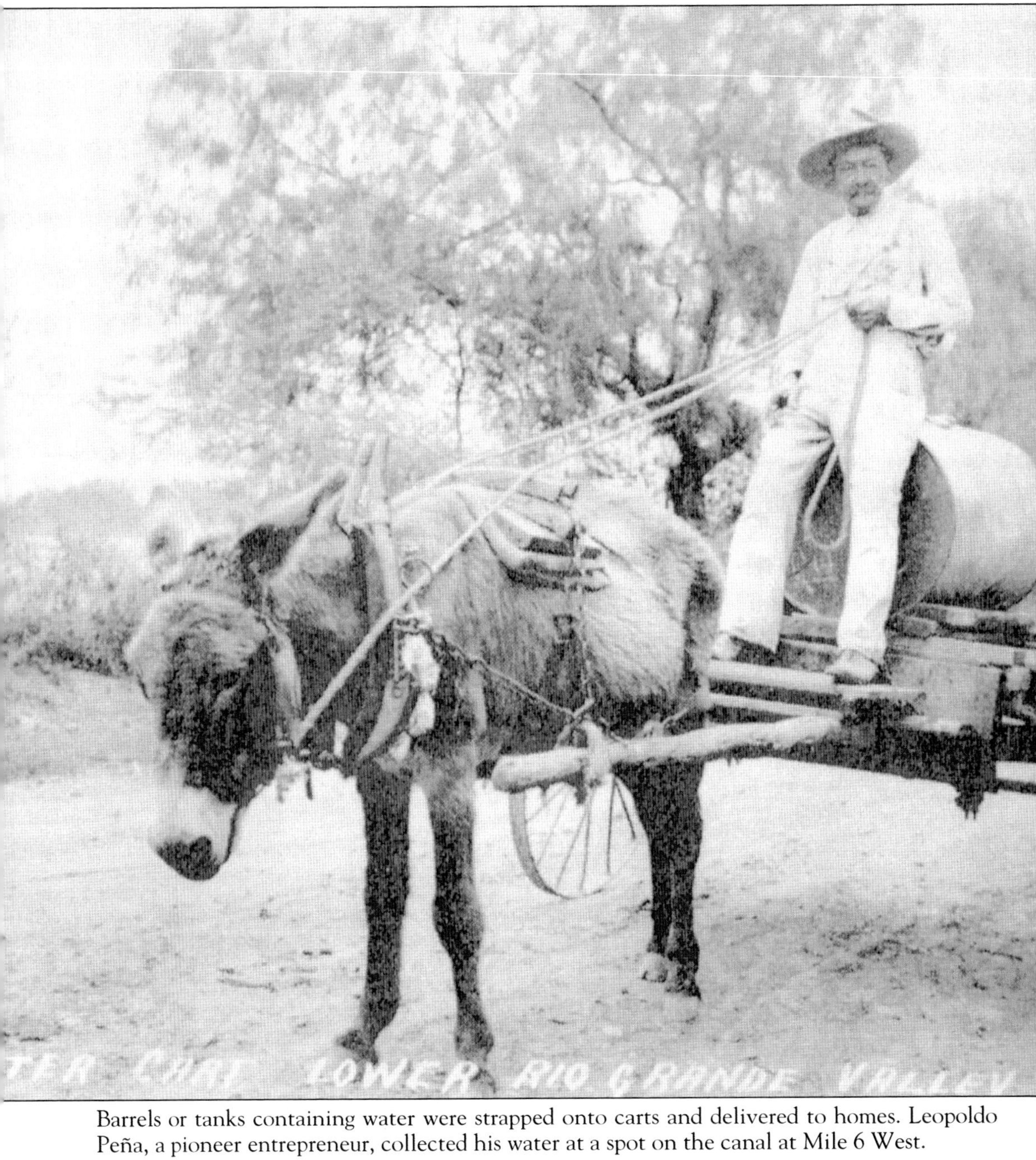


Barrels or tanks containing water were strapped onto carts and delivered to homes. Leopoldo Peña, a pioneer entrepreneur, collected his water at a spot on the canal at Mile 6 West.

Before city services became available, residents of the new town bought water from men hauling water on burro-drawn tank carts. They filled the tanks at canals and delivered the water to homes, where it was boiled and strained. Some residents placed water barrels on the running boards of their automobiles and filled them at the second lift pump north of Weslaco.

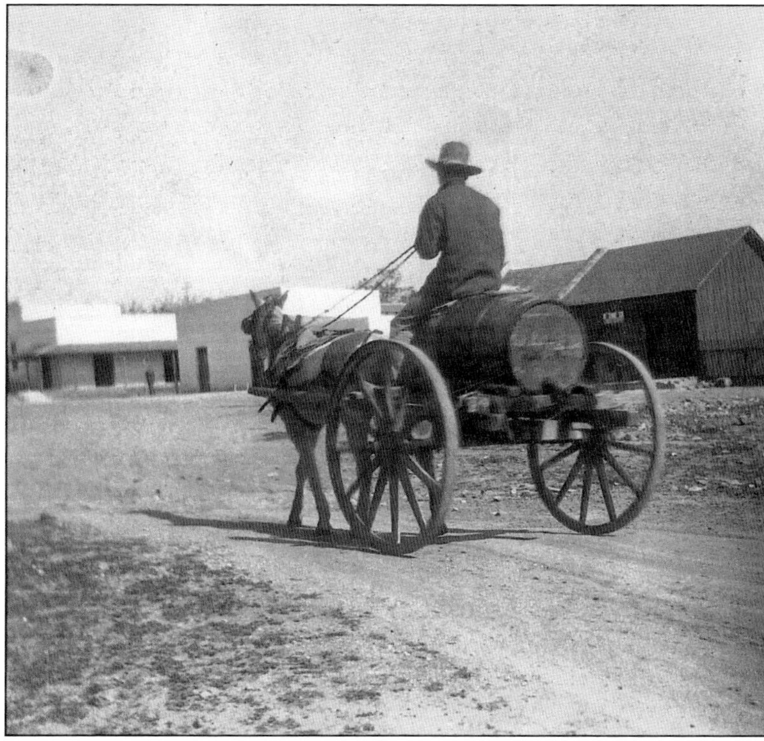

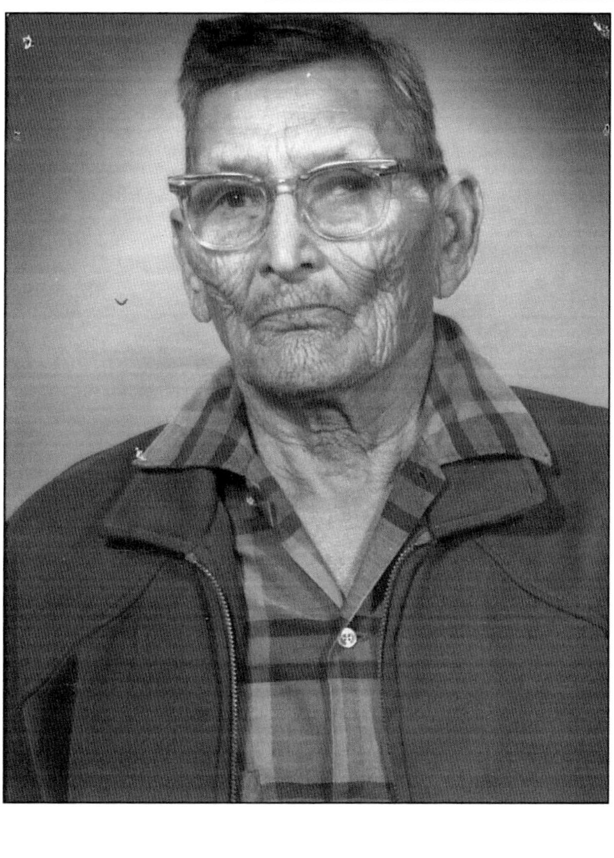

Leopoldo Peña came to Weslaco in 1919 and lived for a while in a tent on Republica Street. The price of water ranged from 10¢ to 40¢ per barrel, and the water had to be boiled before it could be drunk or used for cooking.

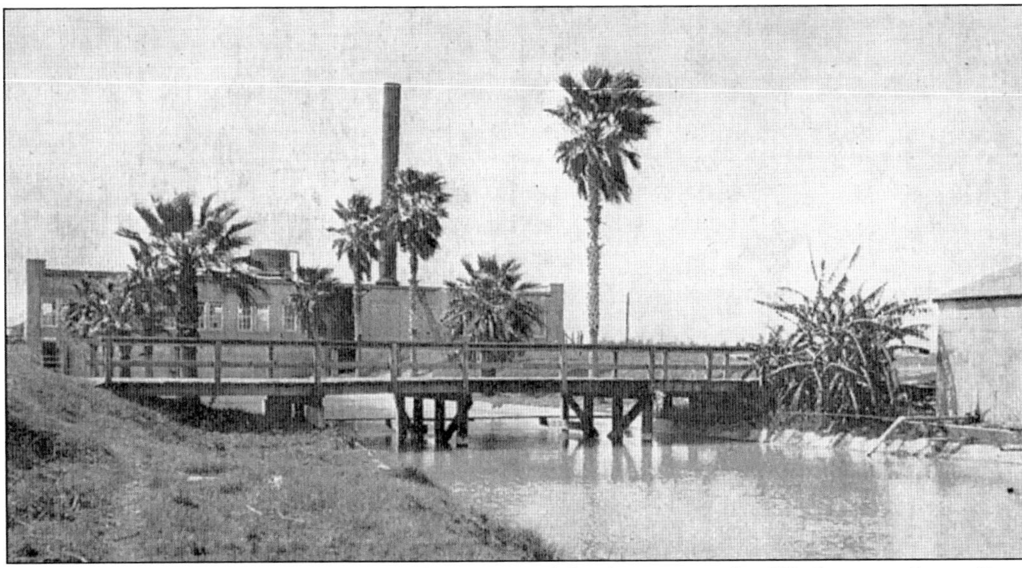

The second lift pump on a canal was the source of drinking water for Weslaco residents. Pipes made of redwood and wrapped with copper wire soon carried water into Weslaco. The wooden pipes were gradually replaced with cast iron pipes.

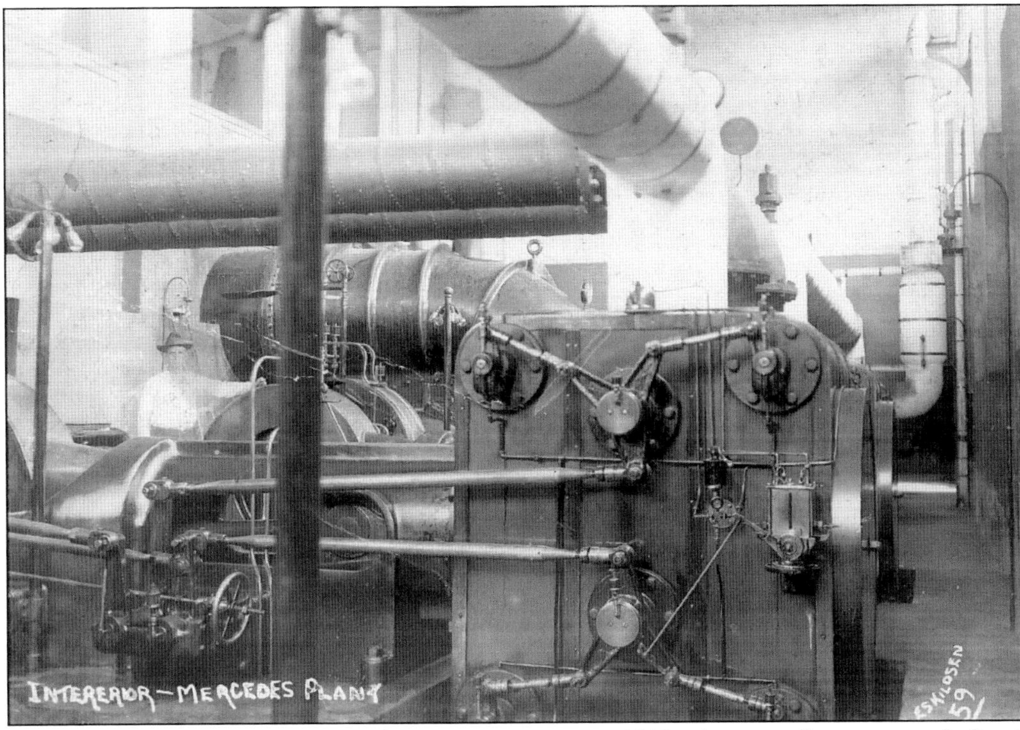


This interior view of the Mercedes pump station, c. 1920, shows well-maintained diesel-powered machinery of extremely high quality and efficiency. The station, built in 1906, pumped water from the Rio Grande River into a reservoir known as the Mercedes Settling Basin. Water flowed by gravity from the reservoir through the main canal and into the branch canals. (Eskildsen Photo.)

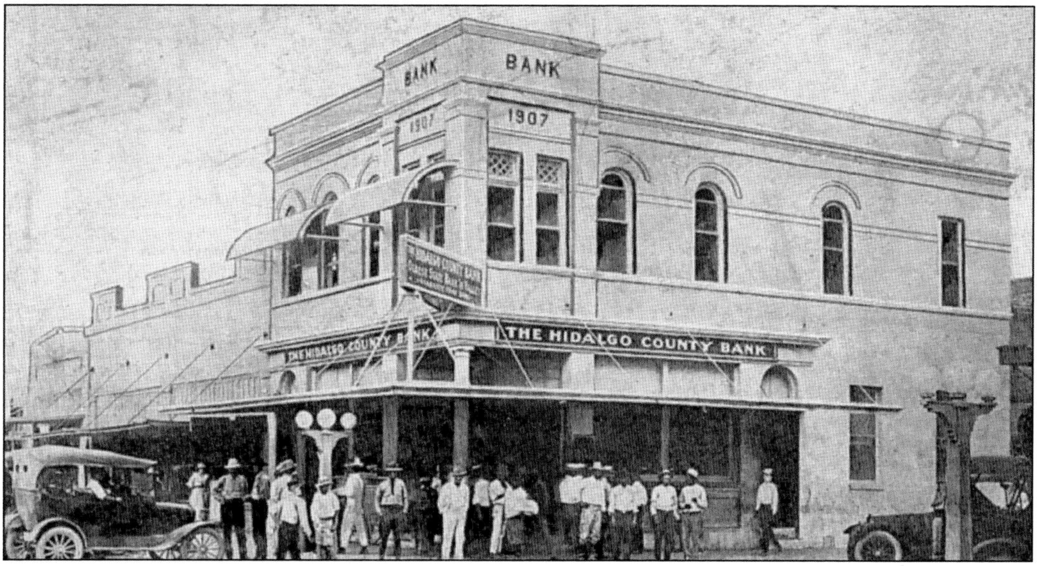


Mercedes, Texas, incorporated in 1909, is Weslaco's neighbor to the east. The original town was called Lonsboro, in honor of its founder, Lon C. Hill. The town site was later moved 2 miles west on Capisallo Ranch and renamed Mercedes, probably by its developer, the American & Rio Grande Land and Irrigation Company. This is a view of the busiest corner of Mercedes in 1907. The Hidalgo County Bank is shown adjacent to the post office. [Authors' note: The origin of the name Mercedes is unknown, but it is certainly not that of one of Porfirio Diaz's two wives, as erroneously reported.]

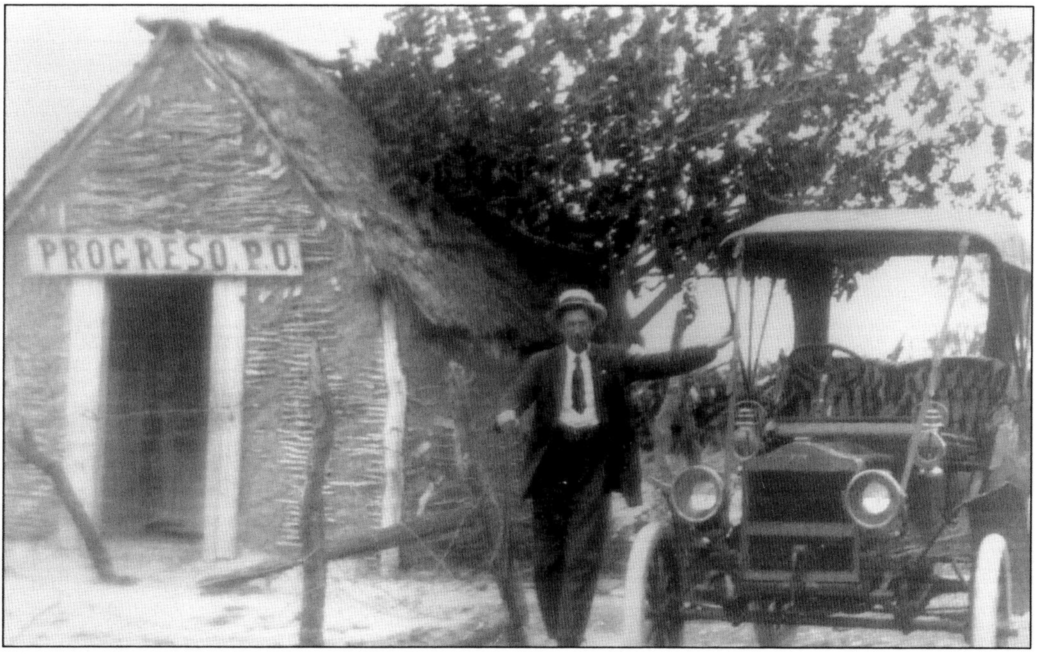


The Progreso post office (1903–1910) was constructed like many contemporary Mexican thatched homes. The postmaster was A. Newman Smith. The post office was located on Toluca Ranch, close to the Rio Grande, but was razed because of potential attacks during the bandit wars. Later, it was reestablished in the town of Progreso.

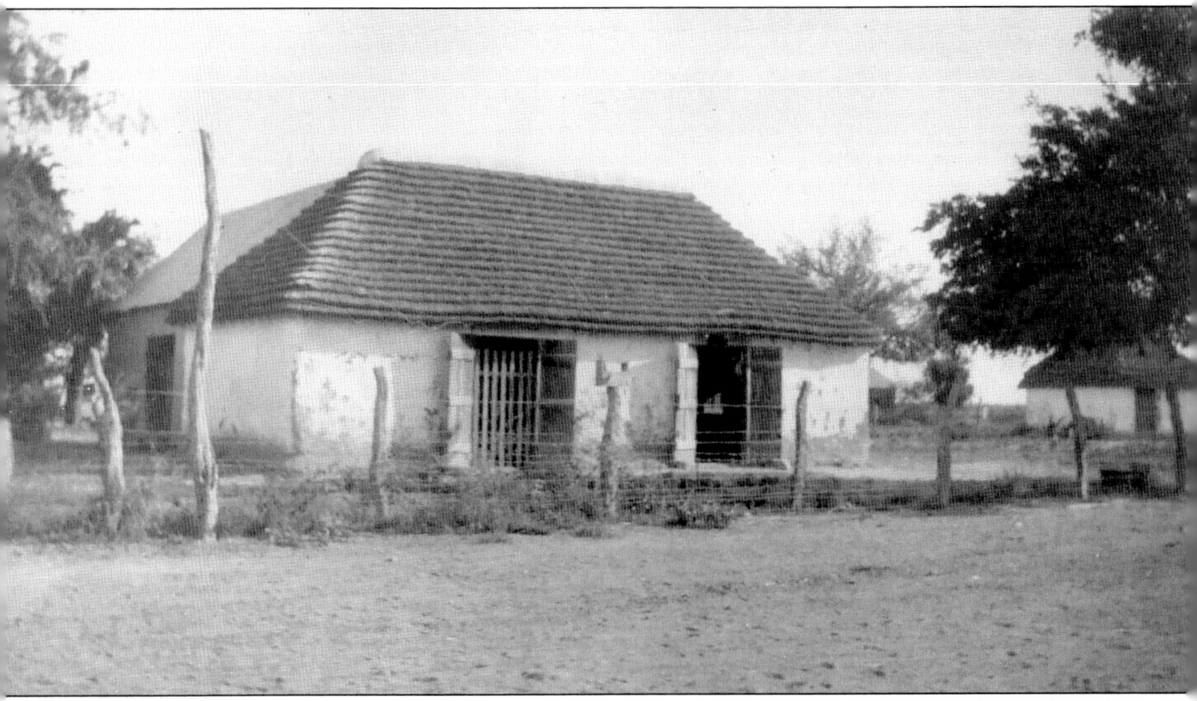

This is the Champion store and post office in Run, Texas, in 1909. The town is located on the old military road in southern Hidalgo County. Run, frequently misspelled Runn, was named for early storekeeper Ed Ruthven. Andrew Champion, a former Texas Ranger, served as a justice of the peace and operated the store and post office in 1909. Schools and businesses opened in Run, but after the disastrous flood of 1909, residents moved to higher ground at Donna. The town is sometimes called "Old Donna."

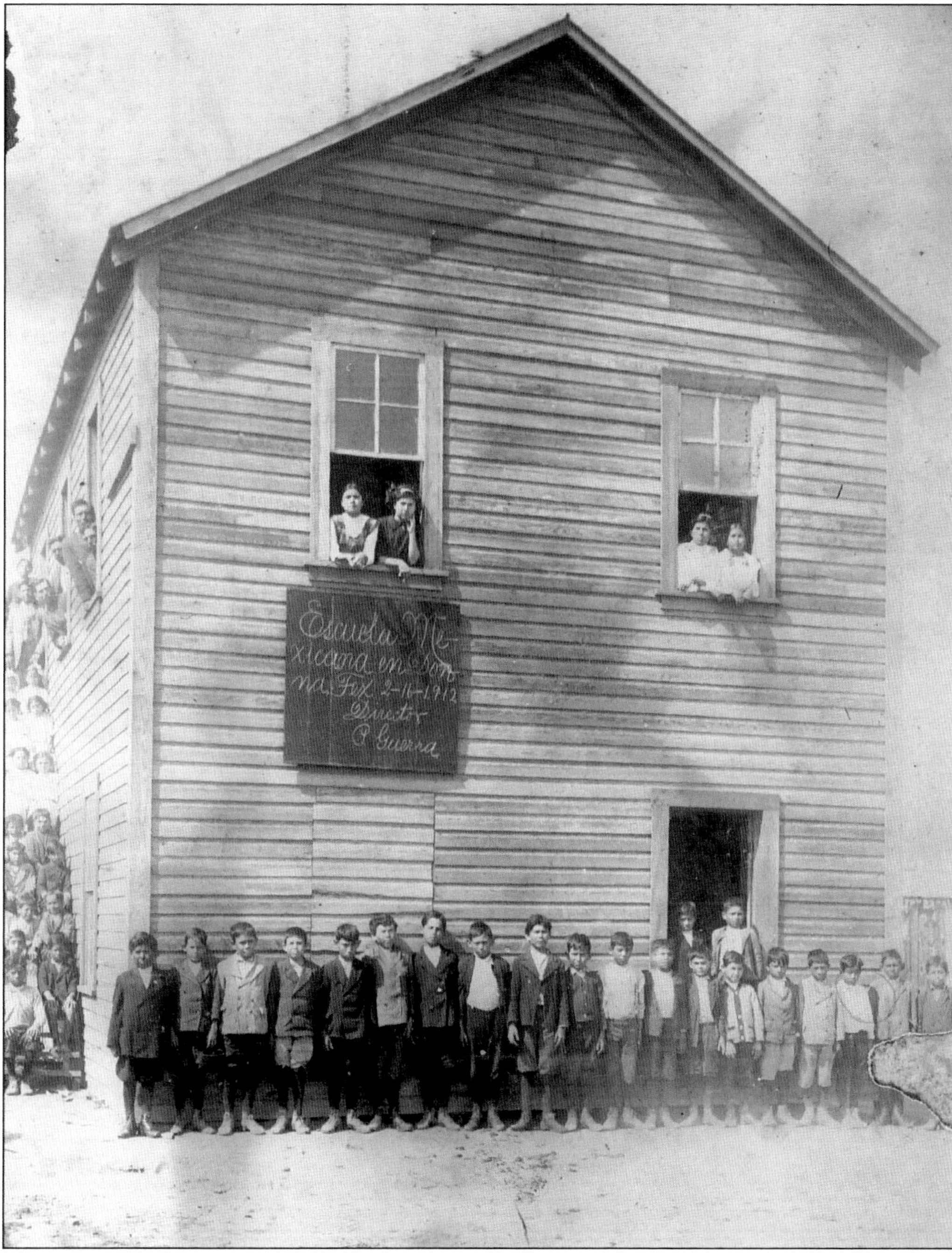


Spanish-speaking children attended classes at the Escuela Mexicana (Mexican School) in Donna to receive their education. The school building was a two-story wooden house. P. Guerra was the director of the school. This class picture was taken on February 16, 1912. Donna, Weslaco's neighbor to the west, was established in 1904 and named for Donna Hooks Fletcher, daughter of T.J. Hooks, one of the town's founders.

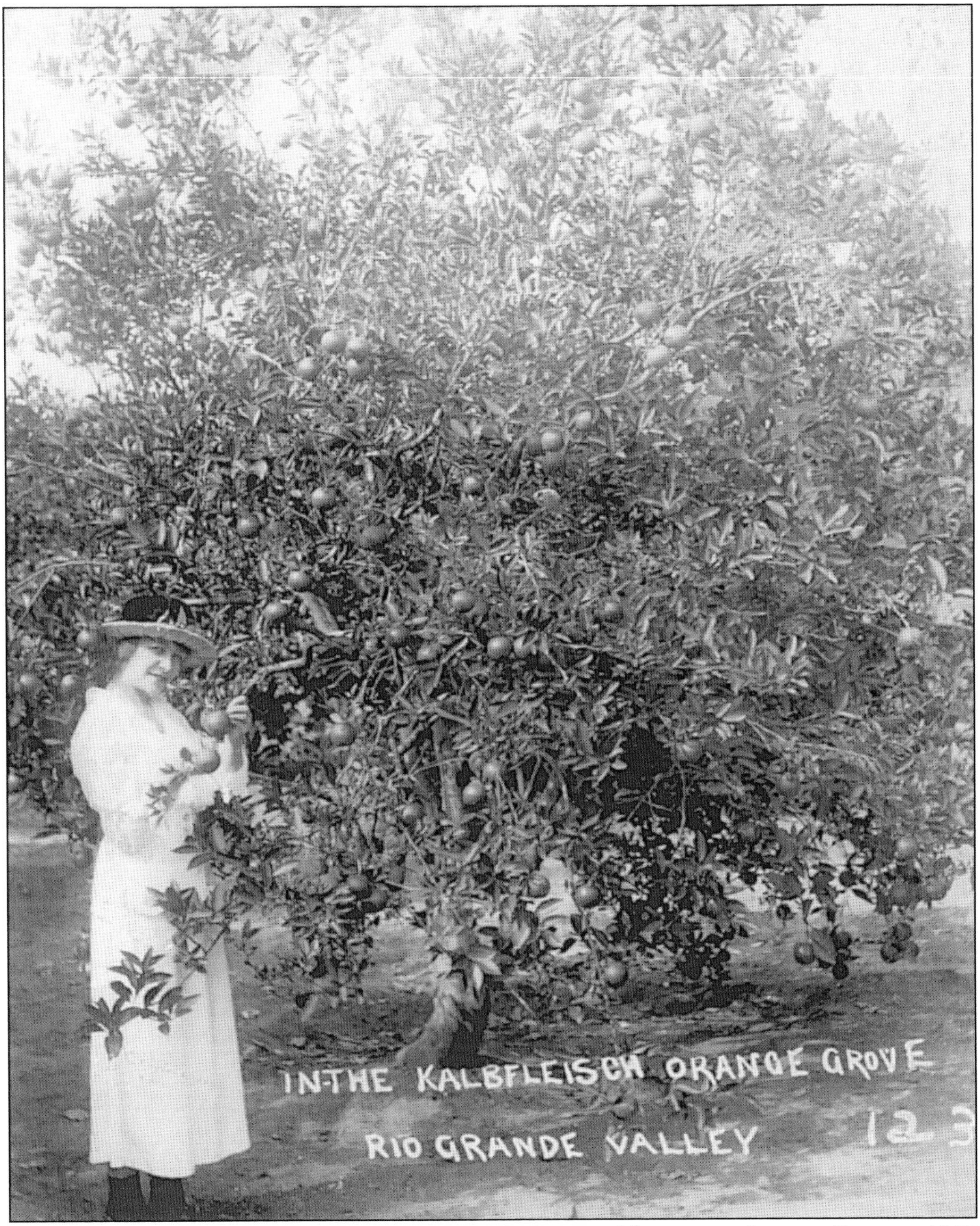


The Kalbfleisch orange grove, c. 1920, was typical of successful citrus production. Between 1900 and 1920, citrus production grew from a small, experimental crop, providing fresh fruit for gift baskets and local markets, to a major industry comprised of thousands of acres of groves, large industrial canning and shipping facilities, and worldwide markets.

# *Two*

# ENTREPRENEURS

The new town of Weslaco developed rapidly. The founders had reserved land for churches and parks, schools, and a city hall. Almost overnight, the town lost its frontier aspect and became a settled community.

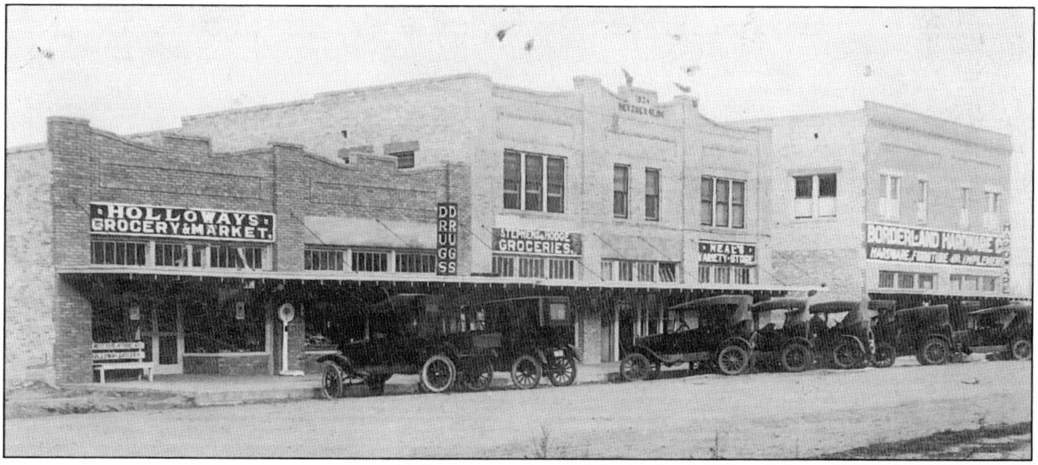


Part of Weslaco's business district on Texas Boulevard consisted of Holloway's Grocery, a drug store, Stephens-Hodge Groceries, Neal's Variety Store, and Borderland Hardware. Originally laid out on an east-west axis on what is now Fifth Street, the business district was re-oriented north-south on what is now Texas Boulevard after a fire on October 10, 1921, destroyed six businesses and the post office. (Smith Photo.)

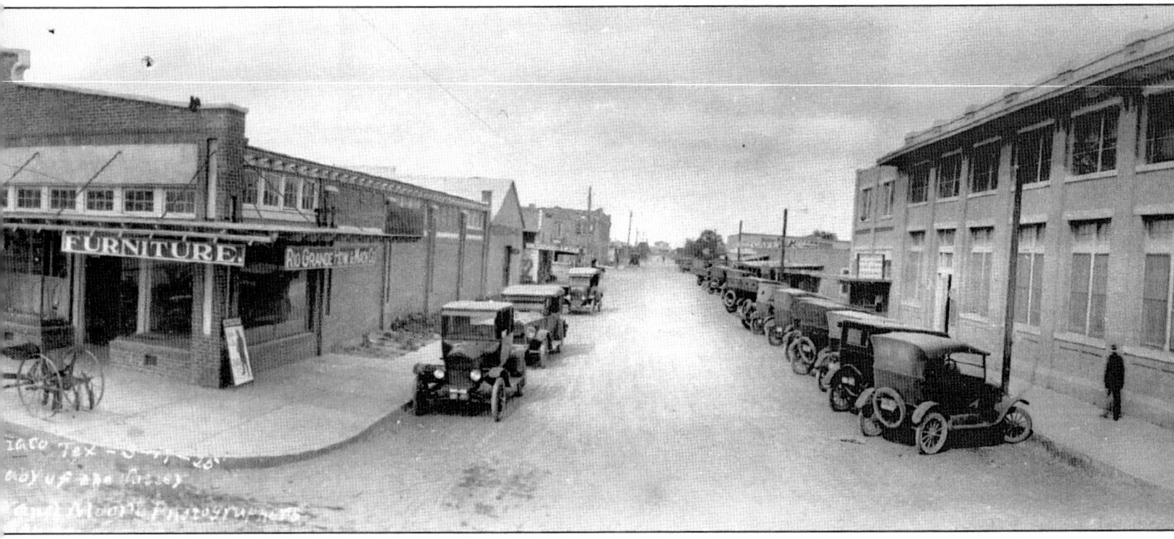


This was Weslaco in May 1923, looking west on Fifth Street and north on Texas Boulevard. The first trades day, staged by Weslaco merchants on May 7, 1923, brought crowds

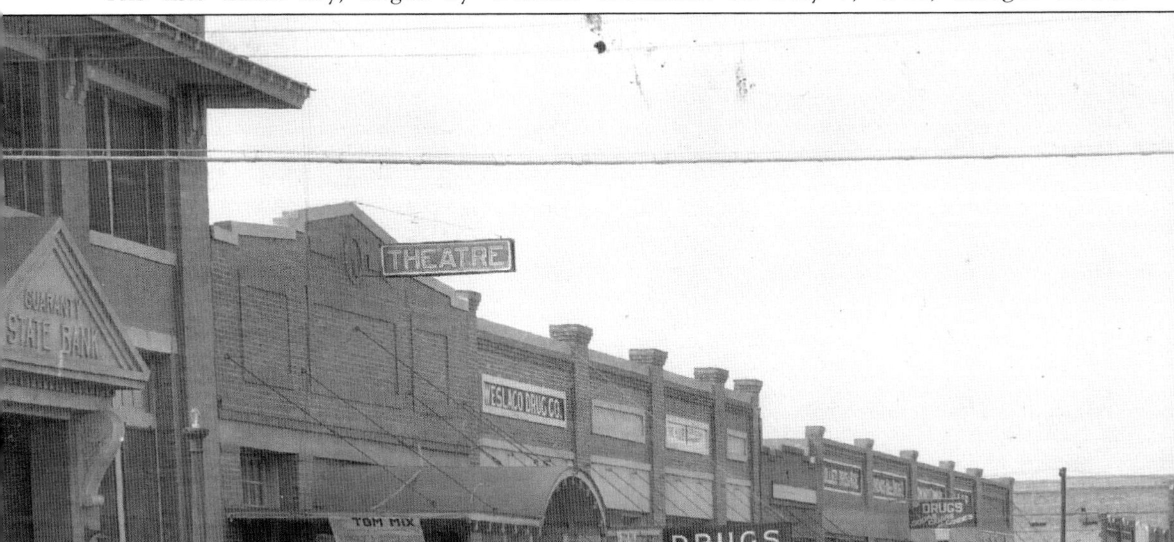


This Weslaco street scene, c. 1926, shows Texas Boulevard looking north. On the left are Guaranty State Bank, a movie theater, Weslaco Drug Co., which contained the post office, and Ladies Supply Company. On the right corner is the Weslaco Mercantile Company, which

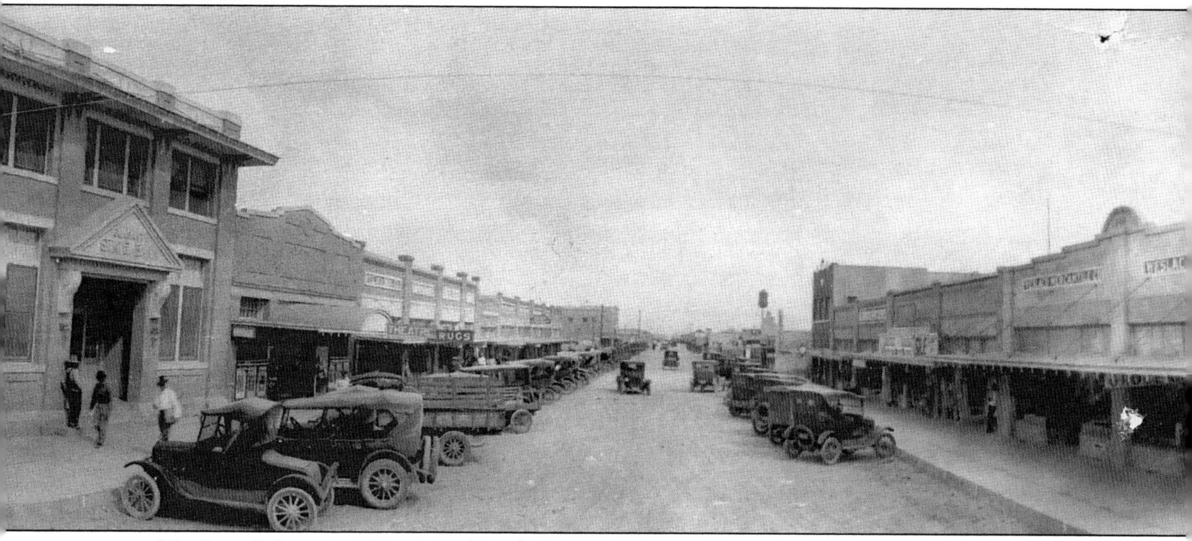

to town. (Dickey & Moore Photographers.)

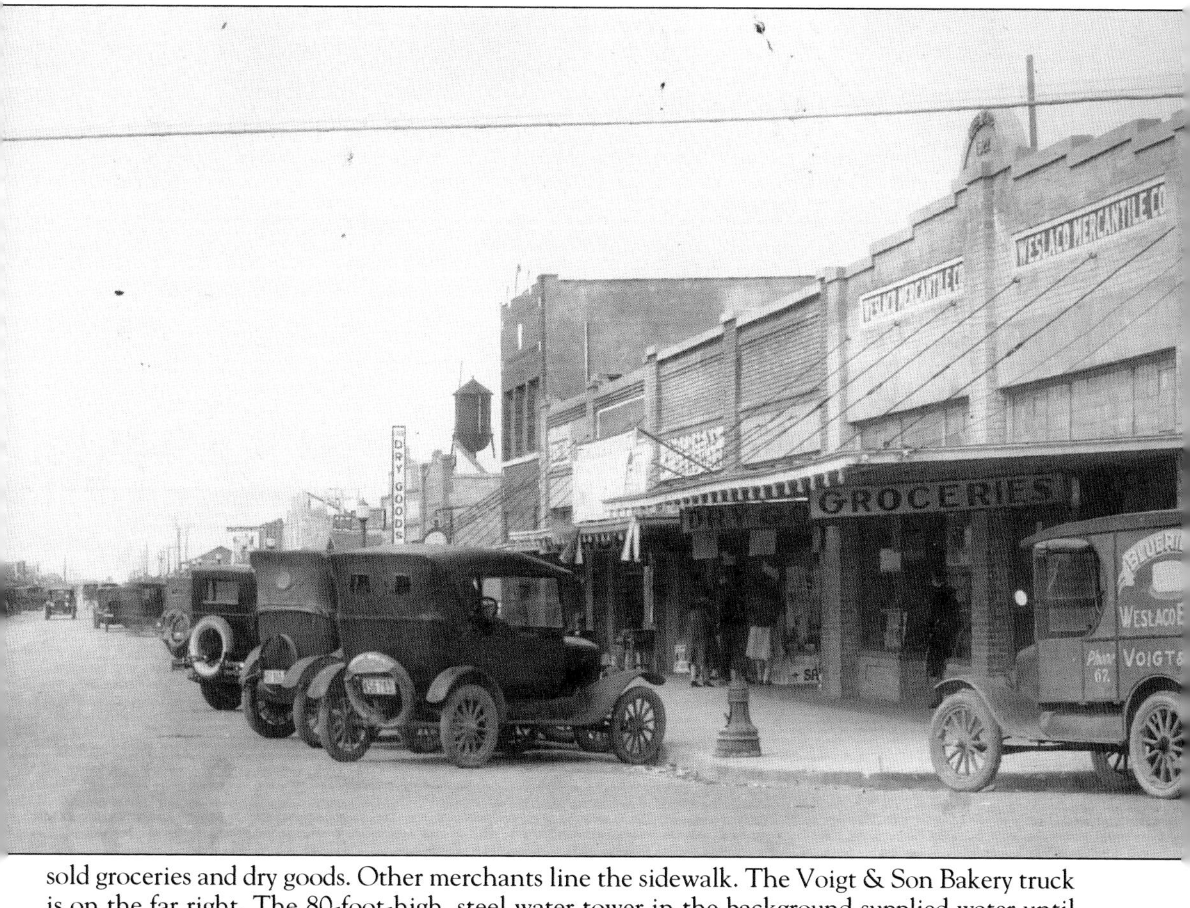


sold groceries and dry goods. Other merchants line the sidewalk. The Voigt & Son Bakery truck is on the far right. The 80-foot-high, steel water tower in the background supplied water until 1941, when it was replaced by a 140-foot-high concrete tank. (Edrington Studio.)

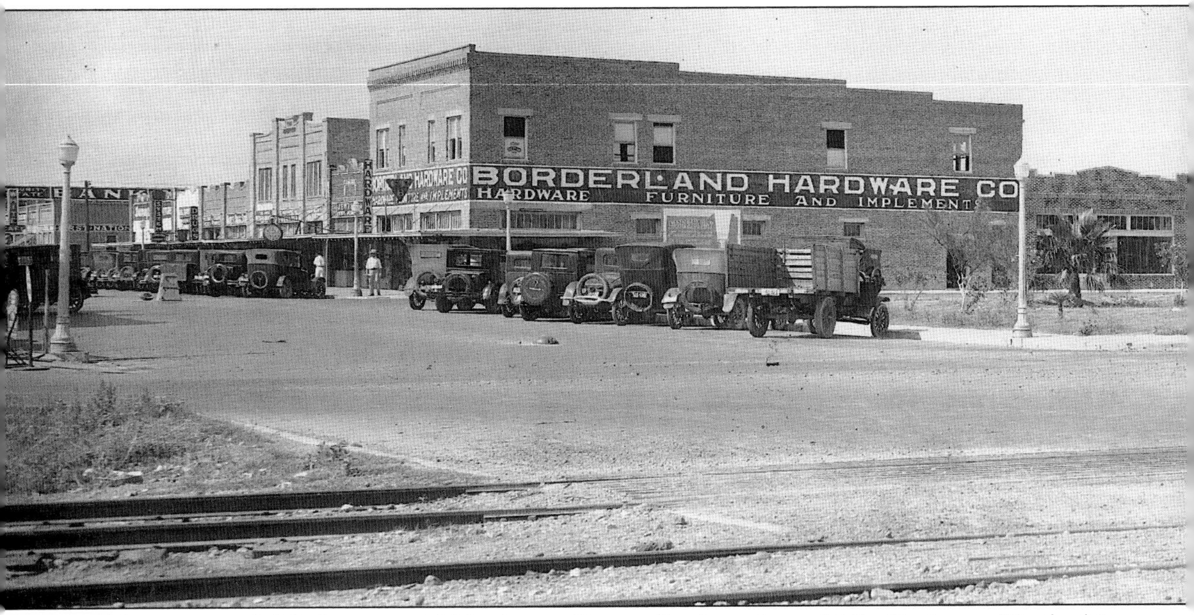


This view of Weslaco in 1926 shows Texas Boulevard at U.S. Business 83, looking south. The corner lot on the right served as a city park until the Cortez Hotel was built. (Edrinton Studio.)

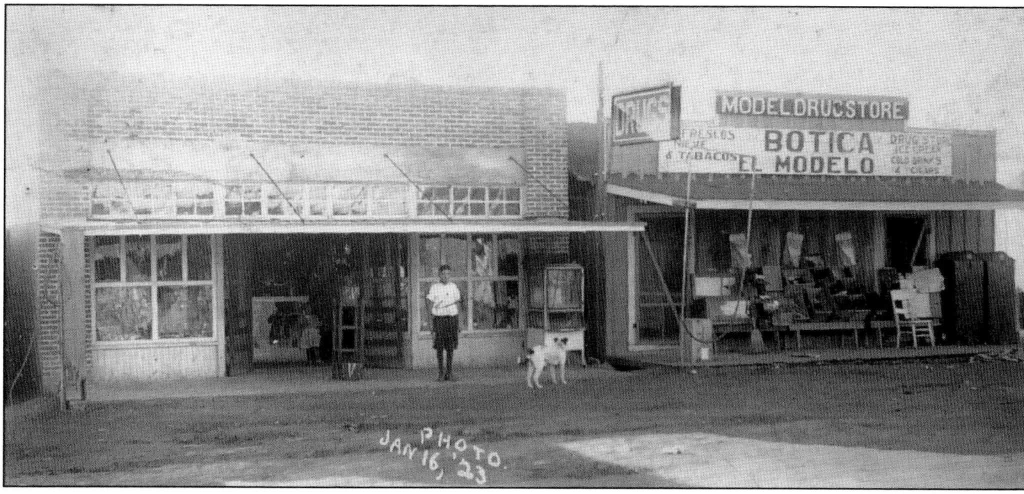


The Model Drug Store, located at Texas Boulevard and Second Street, was one of the first businesses in Weslaco. Pharmacist and owner A.G. "Tony" Valdez Sr., a University of Arkansas graduate, opened the store in December 1920 with an inventory of drugs and supplies, candy, and fruit amounting to $99. His first day's sales totaled $150. Three years later, on January 16, 1923, the drug store required extra space.

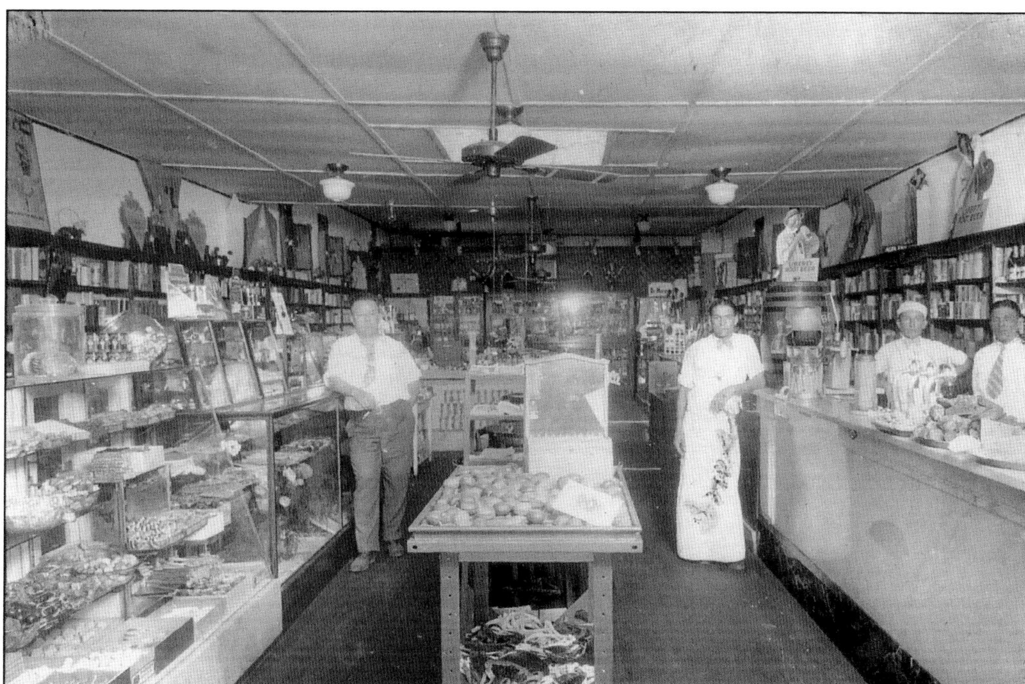

The interior of the Model Drug Store in 1925 shows that, in addition to medicine, the store also offered candy, ice cream, cold drinks, cigars, tobacco, and other favorites. From left to right are Tony Valdez, owner; Ines Escobar (in the white apron); Lorenzo Aguilar (in the white cap); and Fernando Avalos (in the striped tie). Today, Hector "Buddy" de la Rosa, grandson of Tony Valdez, owns and operates the de la Rosa Pharmacy in Weslaco.

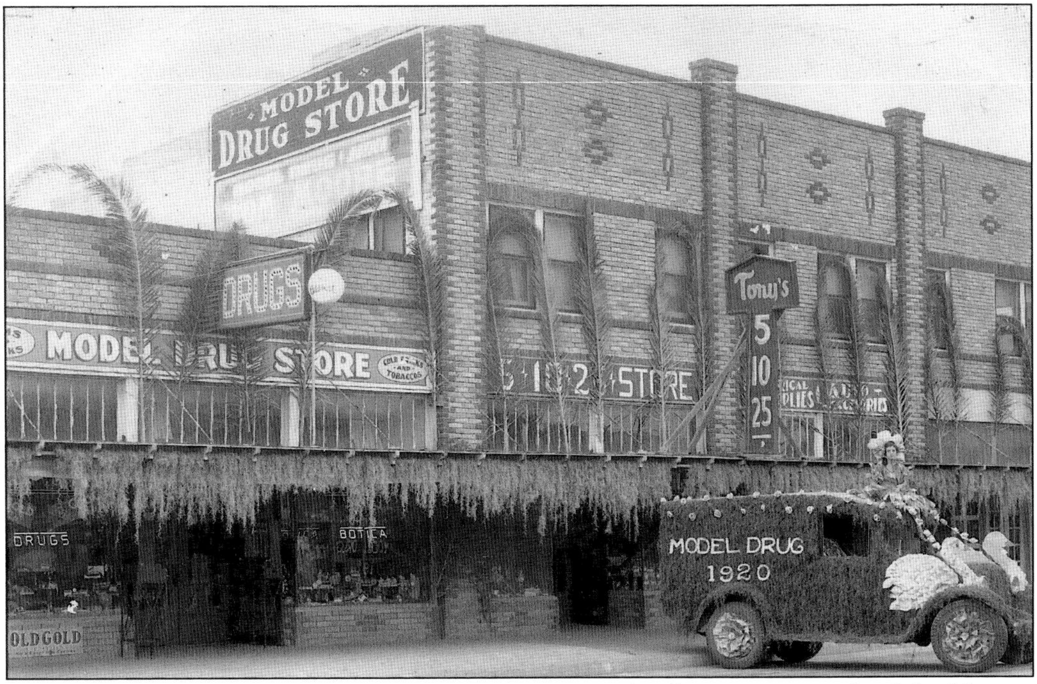


In 1925, Tony Valdez replaced the wooden structure with a large, attractive brick building at the same location. He operated the store for more than 40 years. The business was a joint effort between Valdez's and his wife's families. Later, the Valdez Pharmacy, owned and operated by Tony's son Lupe, opened up next to the Keno Café. The family business has now spread to other Valley towns such as Mercedes, Donna, and Pharr. Here, the truck and drug store are decorated for the Weslaco Birthday Party parade of 1932. The young lady posing on the front of the truck is Tony's daughter, Viola Valdez (de la Rosa). (Edrington Studio.)

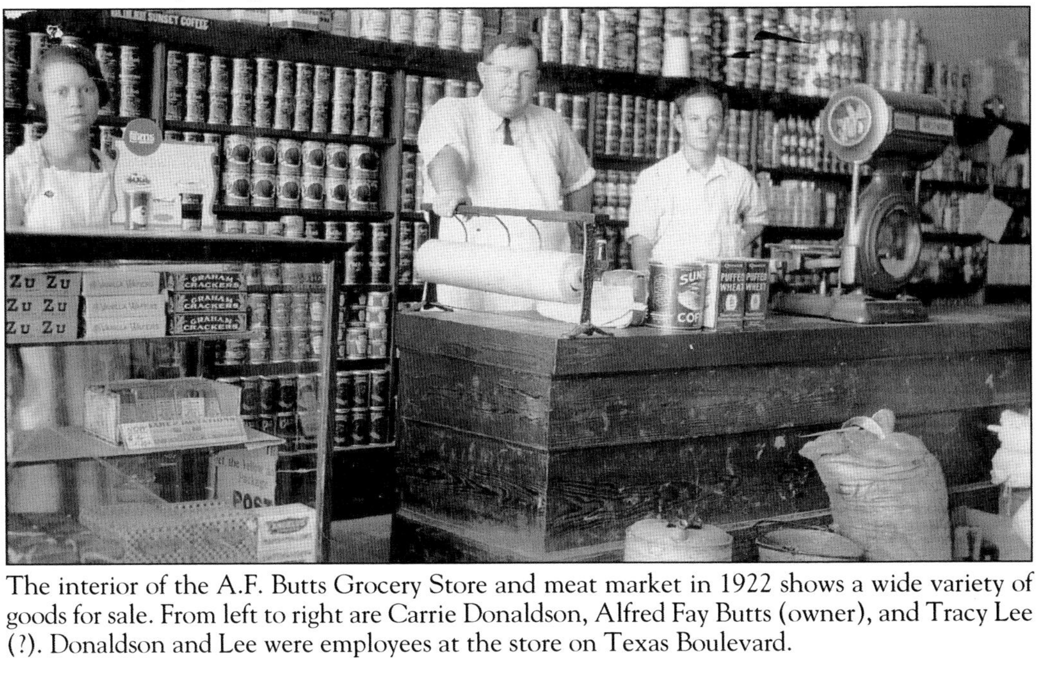


The interior of the A.F. Butts Grocery Store and meat market in 1922 shows a wide variety of goods for sale. From left to right are Carrie Donaldson, Alfred Fay Butts (owner), and Tracy Lee (?). Donaldson and Lee were employees at the store on Texas Boulevard.

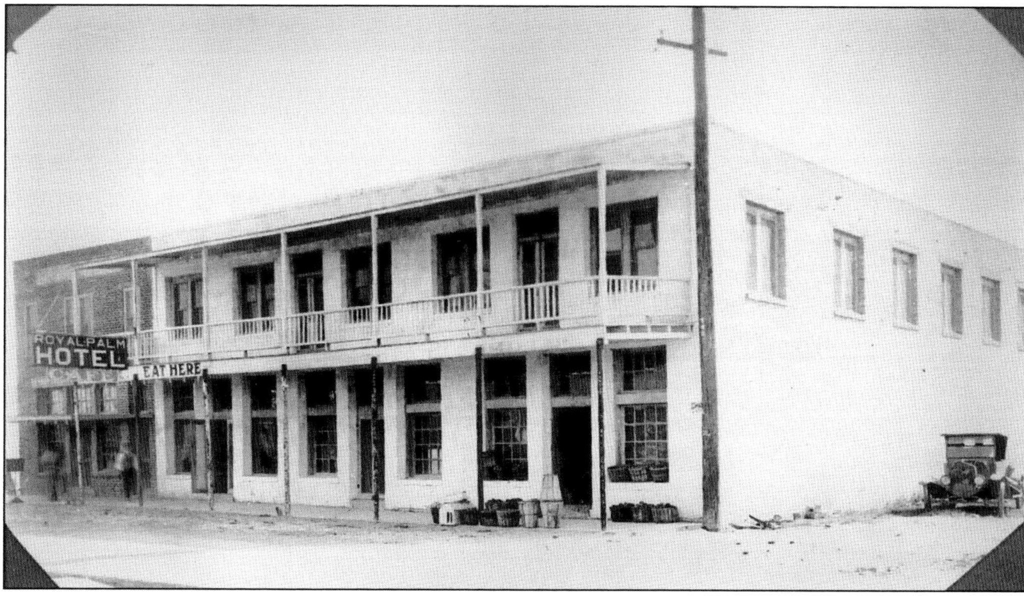

The Royal Palm Hotel, built by developer F.O. Richcreek in 1920, was one of the first hotels in Weslaco.

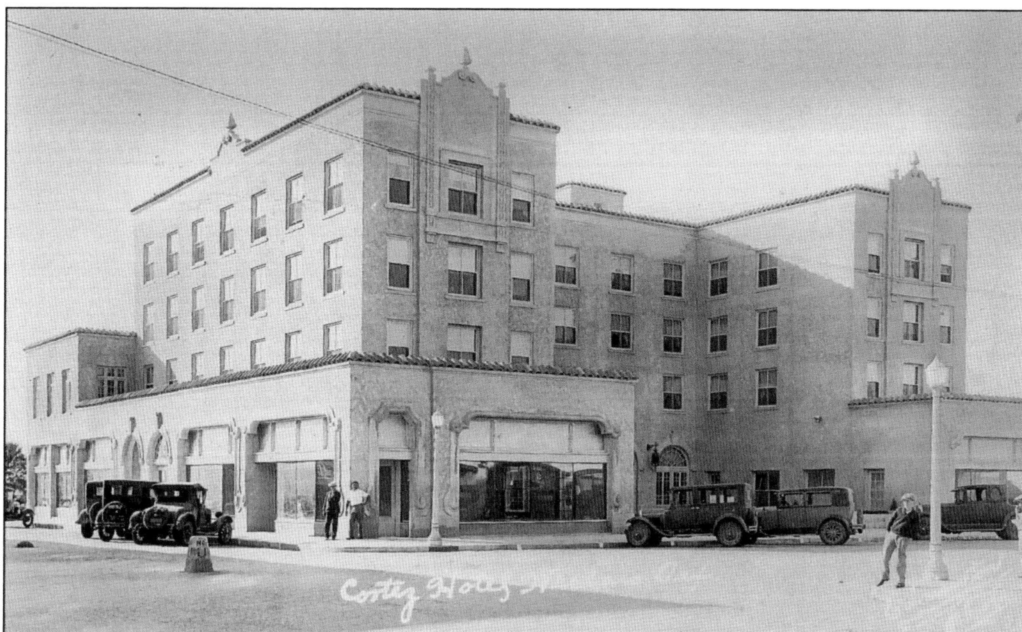
The Cortez Hotel, designed by San Antonio architect Paul Silber in the popular Spanish Colonial Revival style, cost about $250,000 to build. In addition to 65 guest rooms, the hotel contained office space, a barber shop, and a large banquet and dining hall. The Cortez opened its doors on December 31, 1928, with a New Year's Eve banquet and dance. For many years, the Cortez served as the favorite social gathering place in Weslaco. Radio personality Moulton "Ty" Cobb broadcast his program from an office on the ground floor. During 1997 and 1998, owners Patti and Larry Dittburner restored the hotel, now known as the Villa de Cortez, to its former beauty and elegance. (Edrington Studio.)

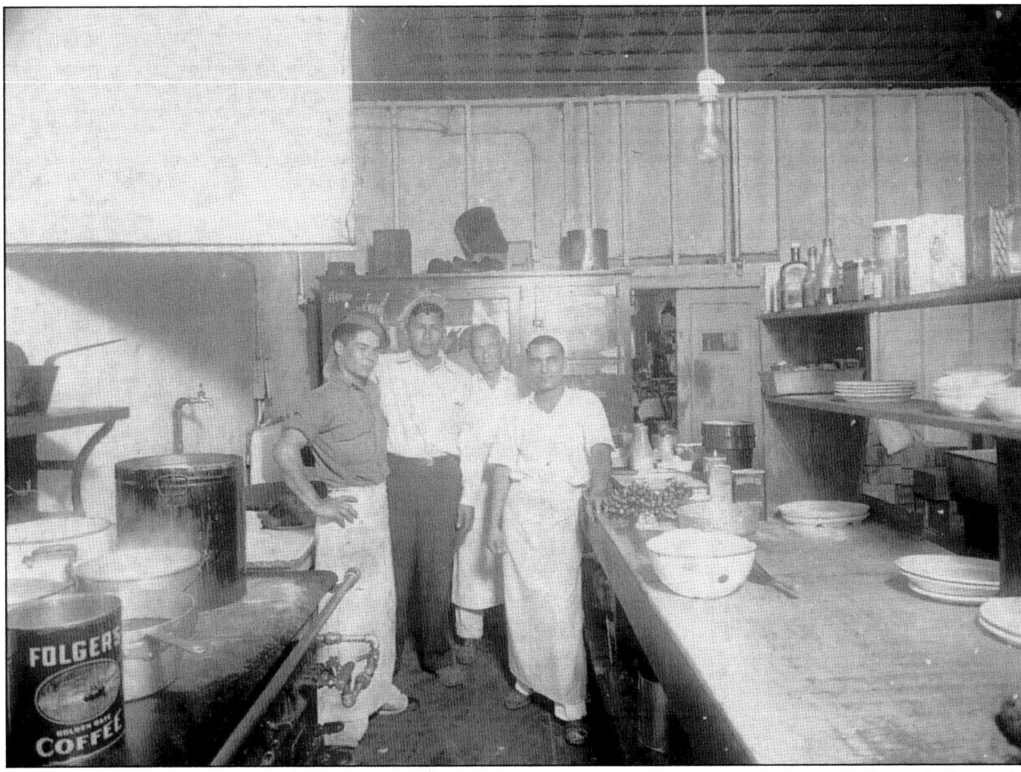


Shown here is the busy kitchen crew at the Cortez Hotel. Pictured second from left is the chef at the hotel, Santos Galván, who was the father of Dr. Amparo Galván Cardenas, a Weslaco educator.

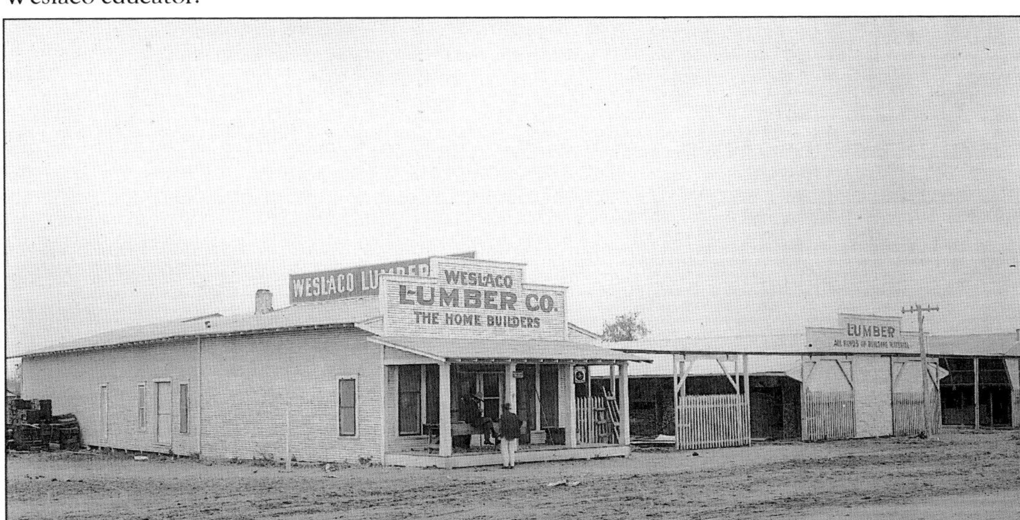


Founded in the earliest days of the city's growth, the Weslaco Lumber Company remained a landmark for many years. As soon as land became available for sale at the new town, the A.B. Spencer Lumber Company, owner of Weslaco Lumber Co., bought a site and moved in a supply of lumber. T.E. Stone was the first manager of the business, and C.M. Sherrill Sr. was the second manager.

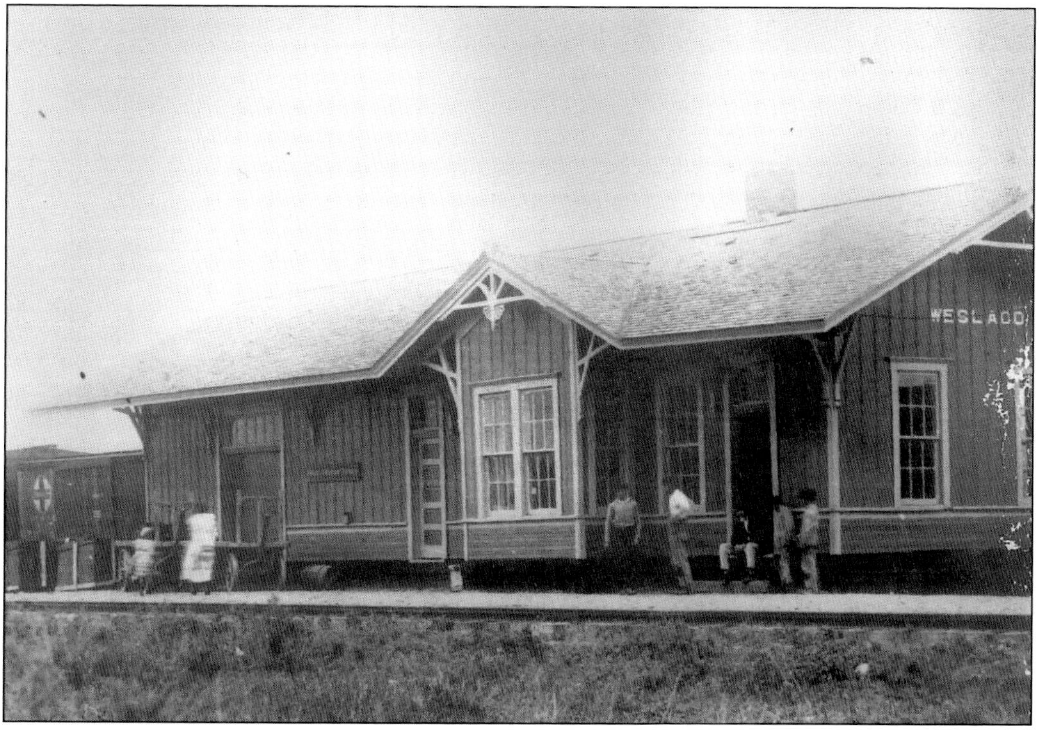


This is the first Weslaco train depot as it appeared in 1920. The depot stood south of the railroad track.

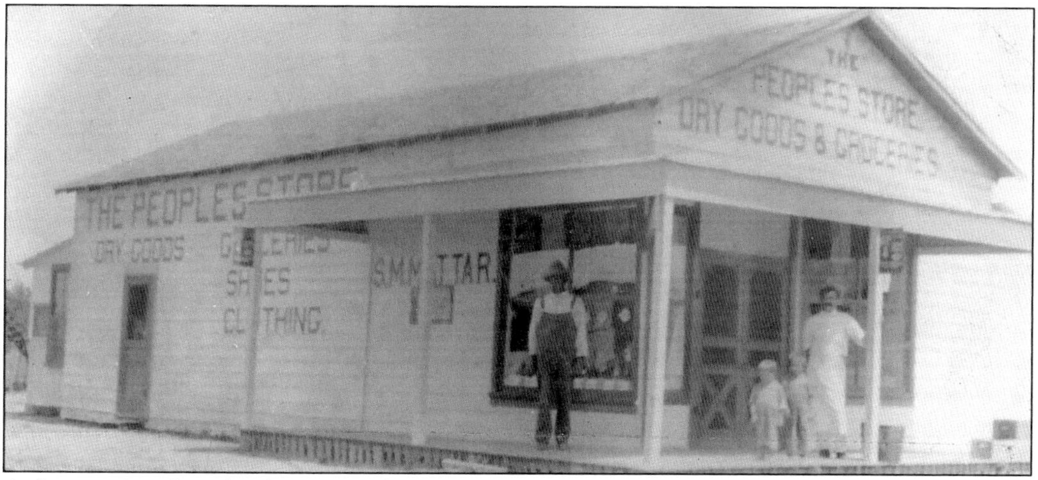


A few weeks after the first town lots were sold, the S.M. Mattar family bought property at Third and Missouri Streets. At the time, the family lived in Mission where they operated a general store. Mr. Mattar drove from Mission to Weslaco each day to bring fresh bread, meat, and all kinds of supplies to the homesteaders who had no way of buying them unless they went to Donna or Mercedes. The trip from Mission took at least three hours one way. The family soon built a store on their Weslaco site and named it The People's Store. The small-frame building housed groceries, dry goods, and the Mattar family, who lived in the back of the building for 26 years.

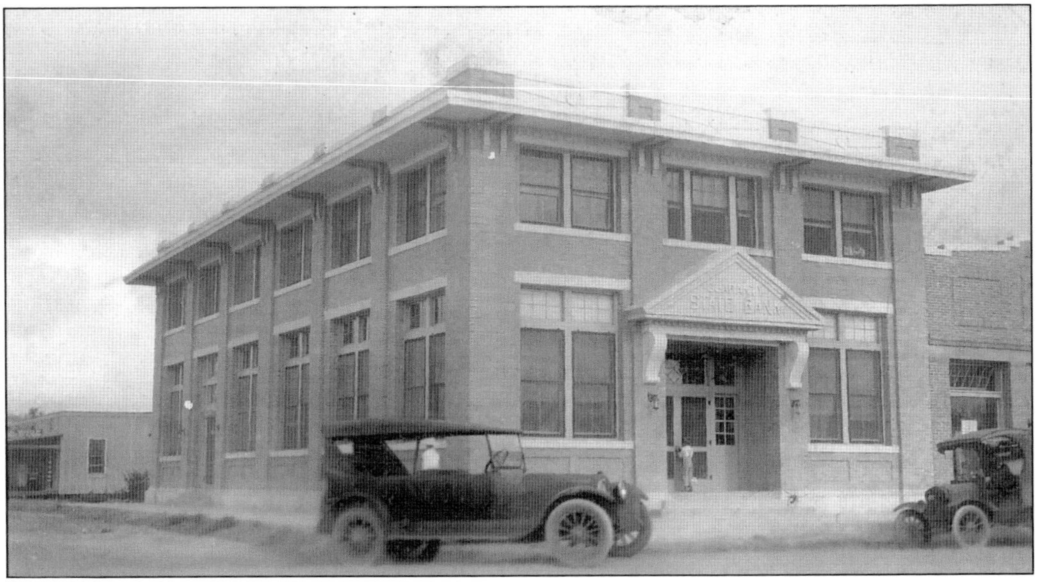

The Guaranty State Bank, built on the corner of Fifth Street and Texas Boulevard, opened for business on July 15, 1920, with a capital stock of $25,000. Ed C. Couch was the president, and L.H. Nix was cashier. Four months later, deposits amounted to $217,000.

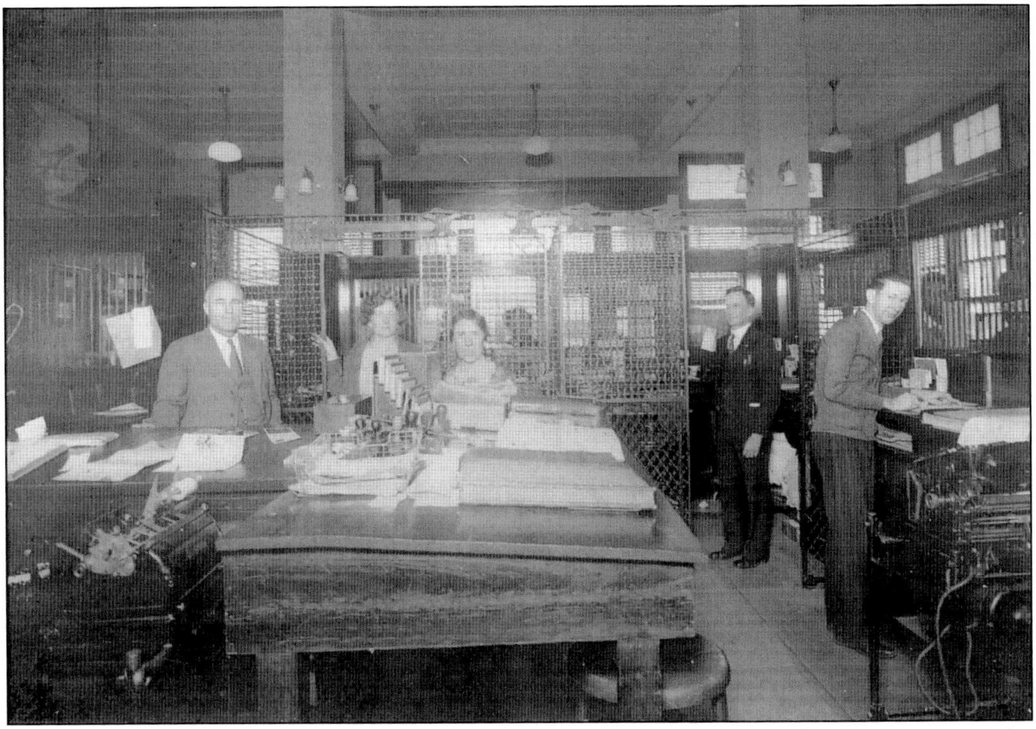

This interior view of the Security State Bank, c. 1925, presents a behind-the-scenes view of the employees' side of the bank. From left to right are President Ed C. Couch, Mrs. Alma Fort, Mrs. Della Crowley, A.C. LaDuke, and Charles Warren. (Courtesy of Mrs. Charles Warren.)

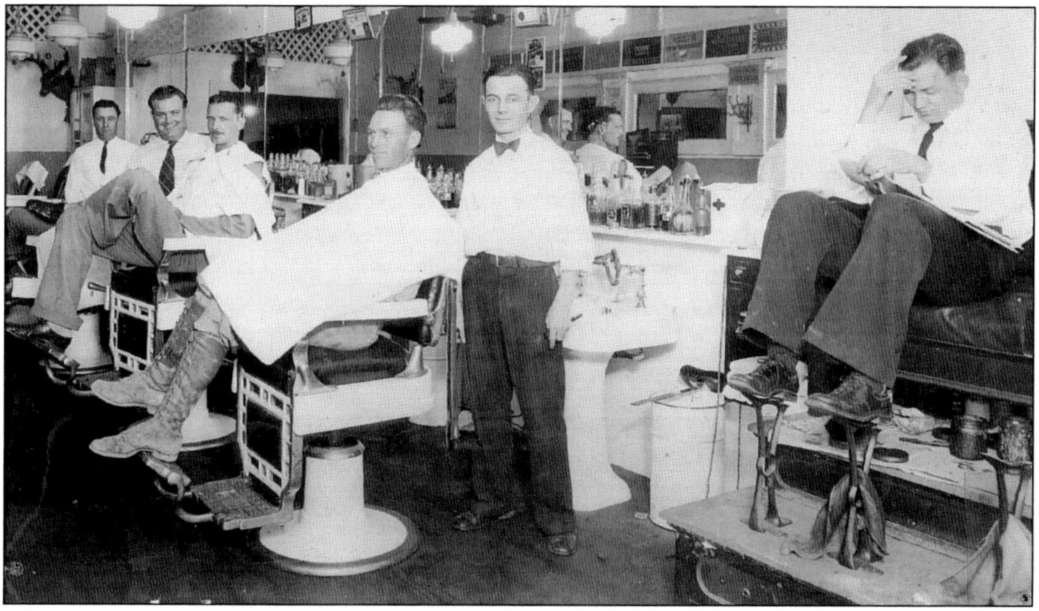

John Petty opened the Petty Barber Shop in 1925 and later added a partner. This photograph shows the Petty and Curlee Barber Shop in 1927. From left to right are ? Madden, John Petty, Chester Logan, unidentified, ? Curlee, and unidentified.

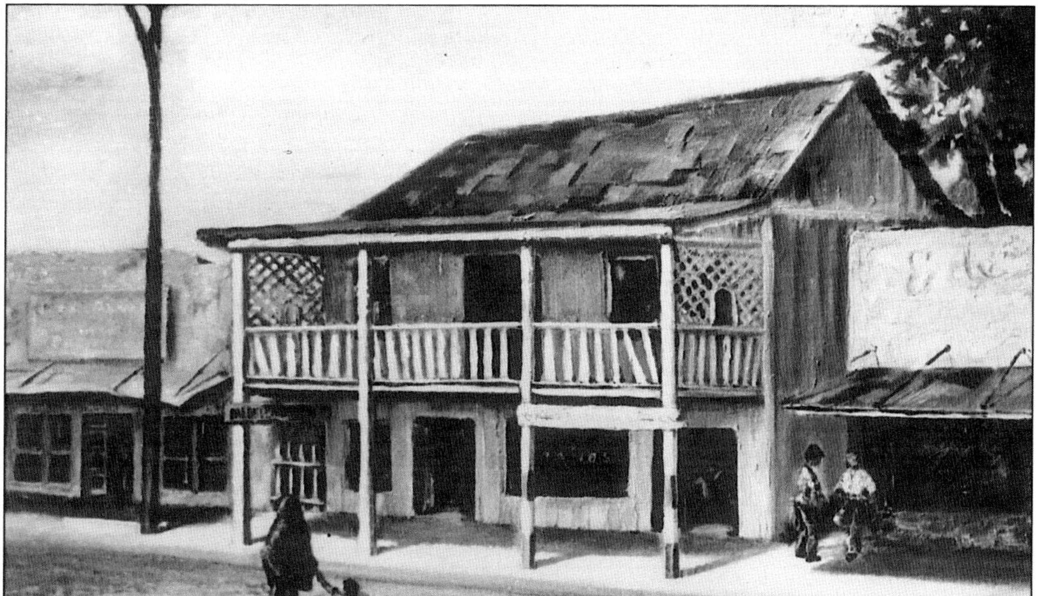

In 1923, a group of church women organized Weslaco's first Well Baby Clinic. For almost 30 years, the Federated Church Women of Weslaco, Weslaco physicians, other community members, and Hidalgo County, through a public health nurse, operated the clinic in Weslaco, although in a different building. The high infant death rate, due to malnutrition and diarrhea, plus the high tuberculosis rate in the community, made the clinic a necessity. Services for babies and expectant mothers were available for any indigent mother or baby. (Painting by Virginia Lehman.)

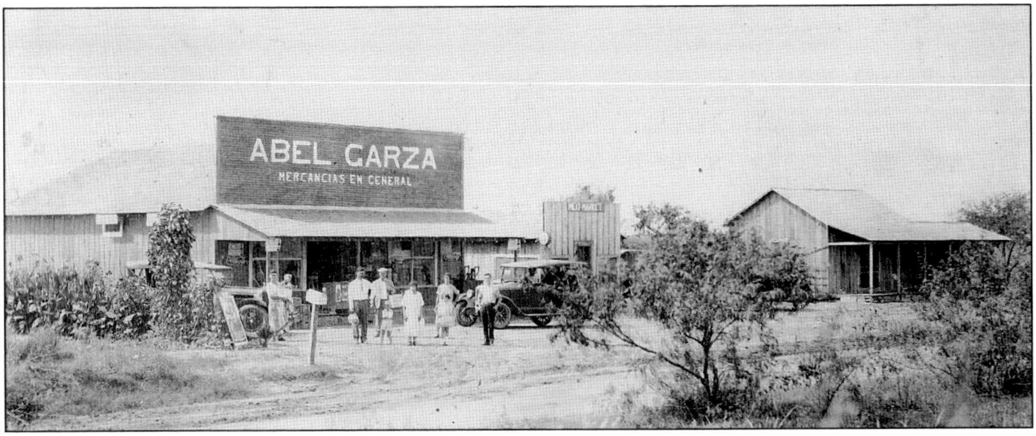


Owned by Abel Garza, the Garza General Mercantile store, seen here *c.* 1926, was another of Weslaco's first businesses.

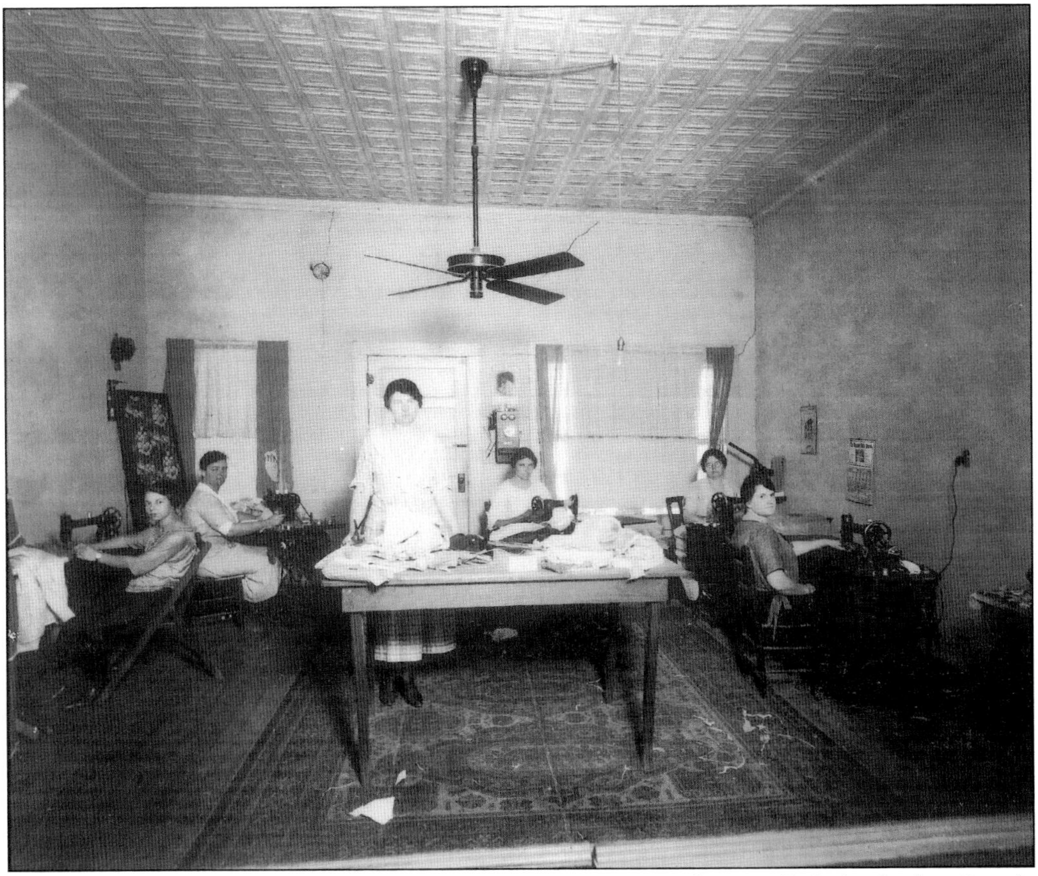

Zoe Brasher opened the first women's clothing store in Weslaco, called the Ladies Supply Company, in 1921.

John Wagner bought several lots from the Weslaco Townsite Company and built a bottling works for sarsaparilla in what is now downtown Weslaco.

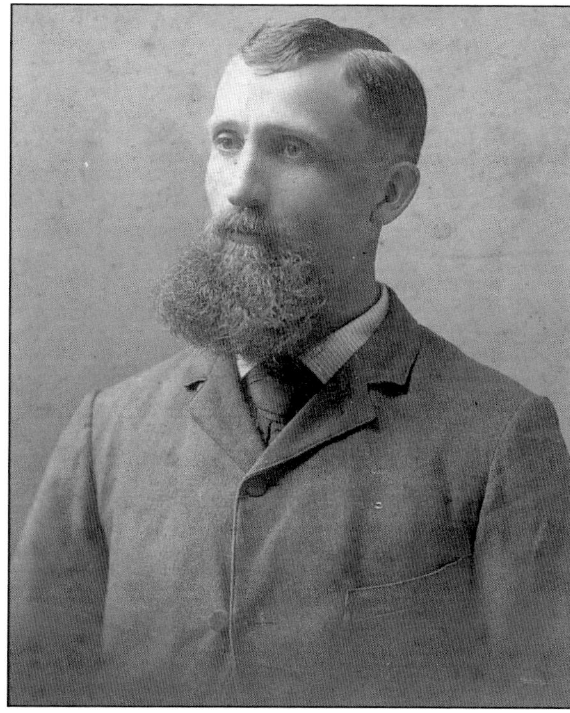

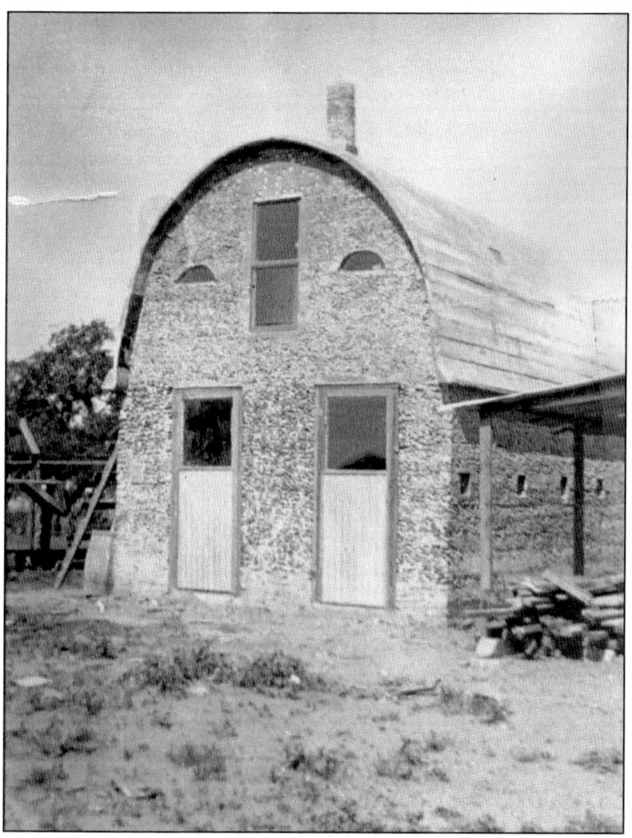

Wagner constructed this Dutch barn-style building on Missouri Avenue as a prototype to test the roof design before constructing the much larger bottling plant. The walls were made of native pebbles, and the roof was a solid concrete oval. Wagner built the larger plant but demolished it after a few years. During the 1960s, the unique structure became a landmark known as "The World's Smallest Museum." Because of the small size of the building, visitors to the museum had to look at exhibits through barred windows. The bars on the door of the museum came from Weslaco's first jail.

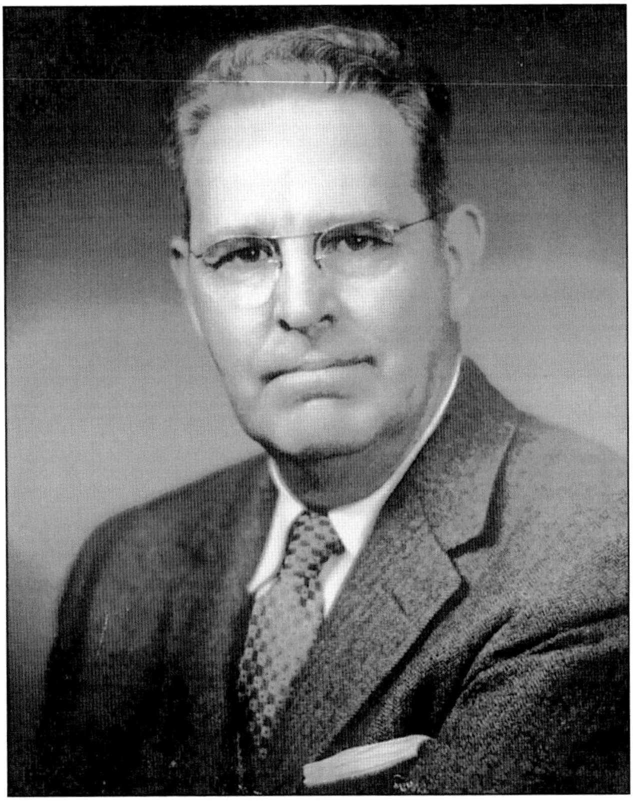

R. Newell Waters (1899–1979), a native of San Angelo, came to Weslaco to join his father, R.C. Waters, a partner in Kirgan and Waters Land Development Company of Edinburg, Texas. A 1923 graduate of the Massachusetts Institute of Technology, Waters opened his architectural practice in Weslaco in 1924 and remained in business, designing many Valley buildings, until 1962.

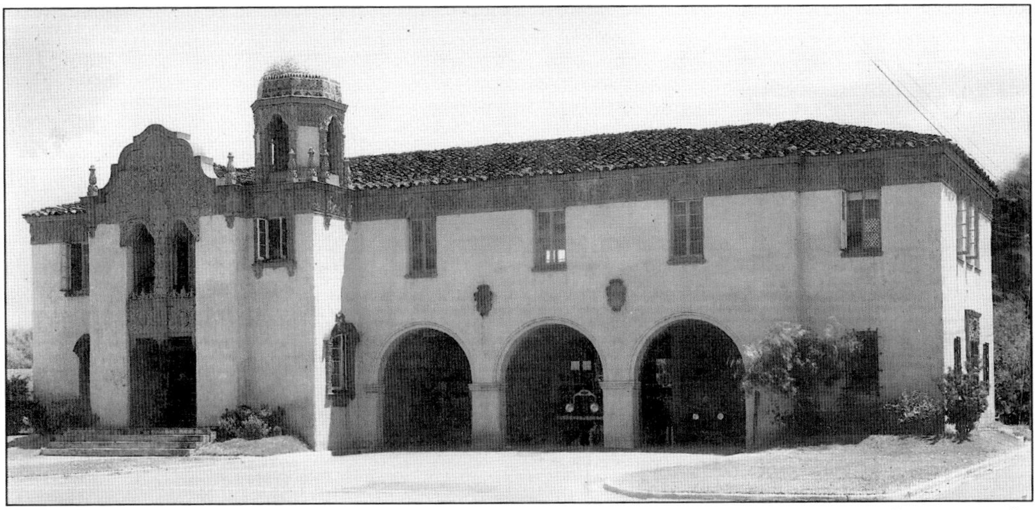

City fathers commissioned R. Newell Waters to design the Weslaco City Hall. Originally built in 1928, the city hall contained city offices, an auditorium, a dormitory for four firemen, a storage room for fire truck apparatus, a garage for the fire trucks, and a jail. Influenced by the architecture of Seville, Spain, Waters used ornamentation cast by the Delta Art Stone Company of Mercedes, a domed cupola for the fire bell, decorative tiles imported from Spain on the roof and stair risers, leaded stained-glass windows, and heavily carved doors. The building was commissioned an Official Texas Historic Landmark on March 25, 1979. (Edrington Studio.)

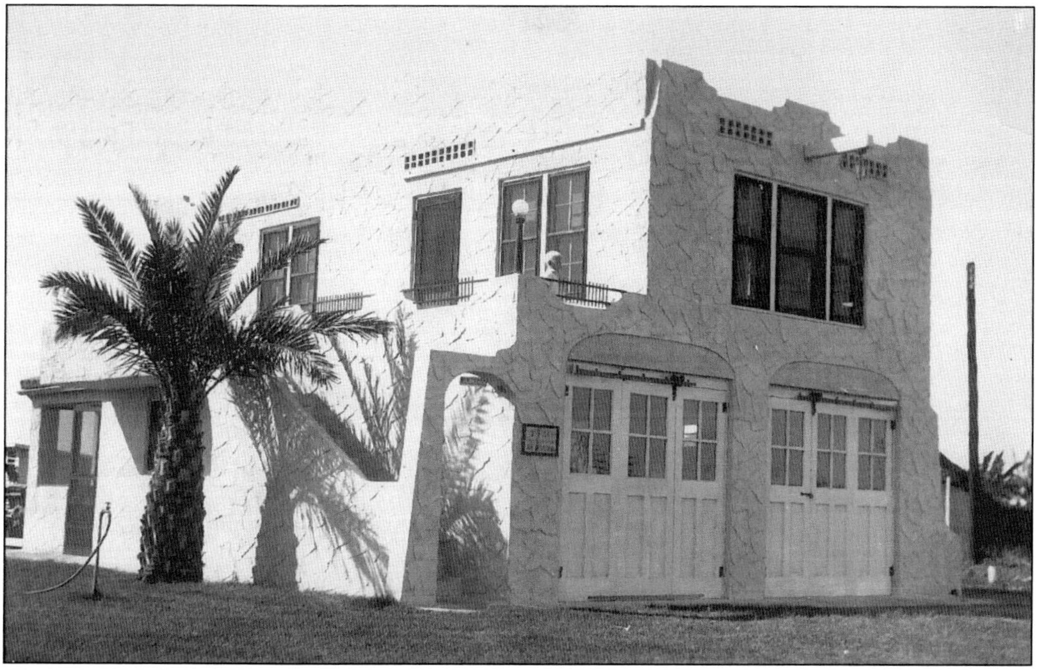

The Jorgensen home, built from 1924 to 1925 in the popular Spanish Colonial Revival design, was located in the 600 block of East-West Highway 83, now U.S. Business 83. (Edrington Studio.)

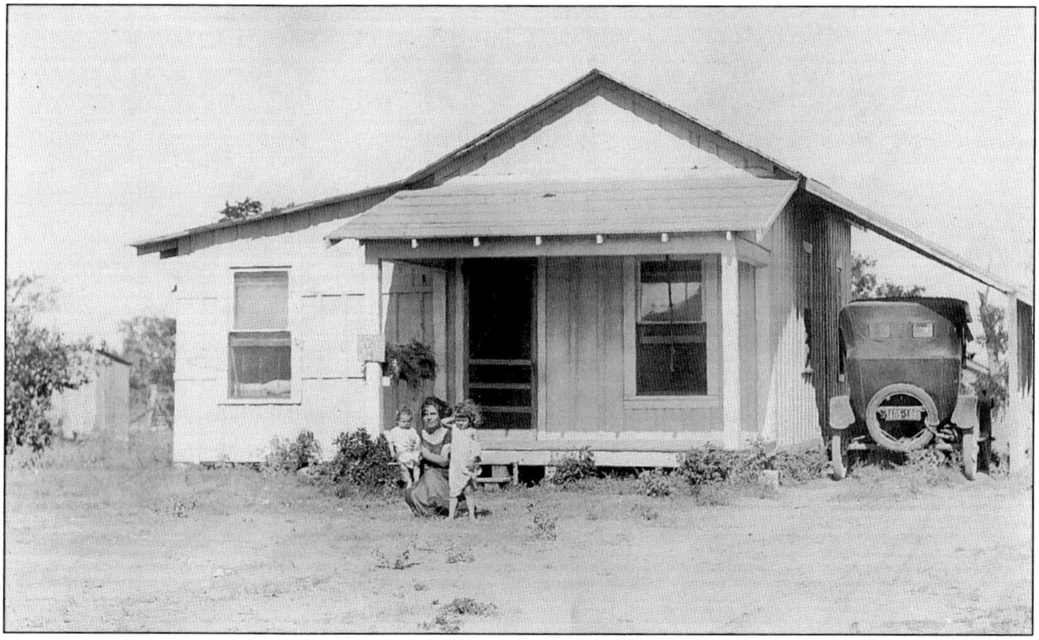

The Pete Miller home, built in the 1920s, was a wooden structure on North Iowa Street. Mrs. Willie Miller is pictured with her daughters, Marjorie and Dorothy.

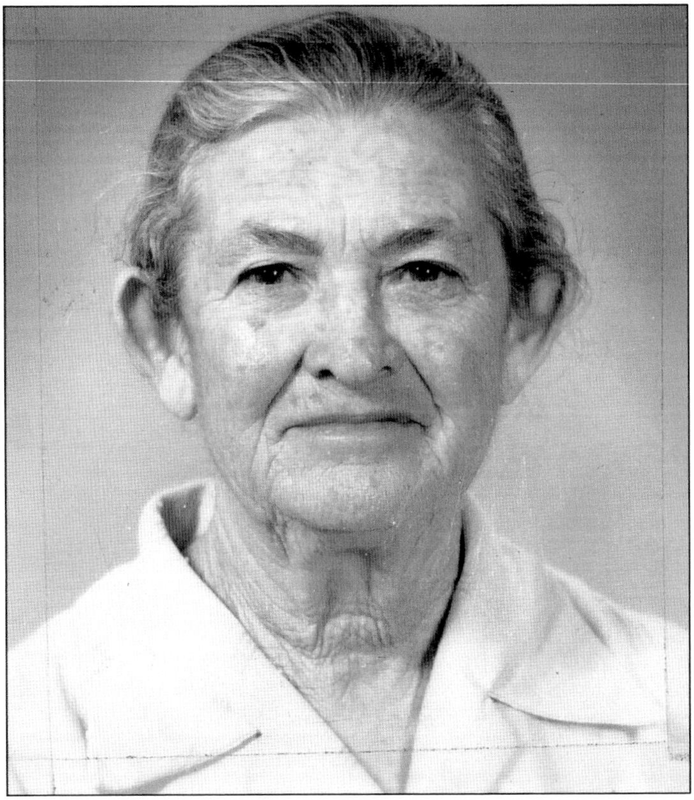

Francisca De Leon Robles came to Weslaco as a newlywed in 1924. Her husband, G.G. Robles of Burgos in northern Mexico, had come to the Weslaco area in 1918 to clear brush. He first worked for his brother José, who ran a food market, then opened his own grocery in 1925. In 1926, Robles moved the store to the 100 block of Texas Boulevard and added a slaughterhouse around 1940 so that he could offer fresh meat to his customers. Mrs. Robles worked in the store, and she also made and laundered the aprons worn by the men at the counter.

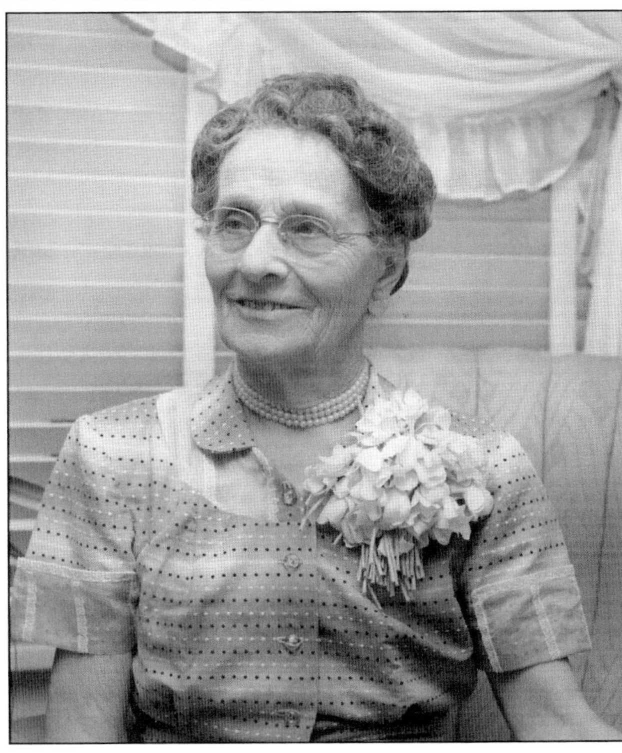

Almeda Couch Reeves (1871–1964), originally from Abilene, was the wife of Weslaco co-founder Robert L. Reeves. Considered Weslaco's first resident, she filled a much-needed role as Weslaco's first postmistress. She also created the first beautification project by planting palm trees, shrubs, and flowers in the city park where the Villa de Cortez now stands. (Yoder Studio.)

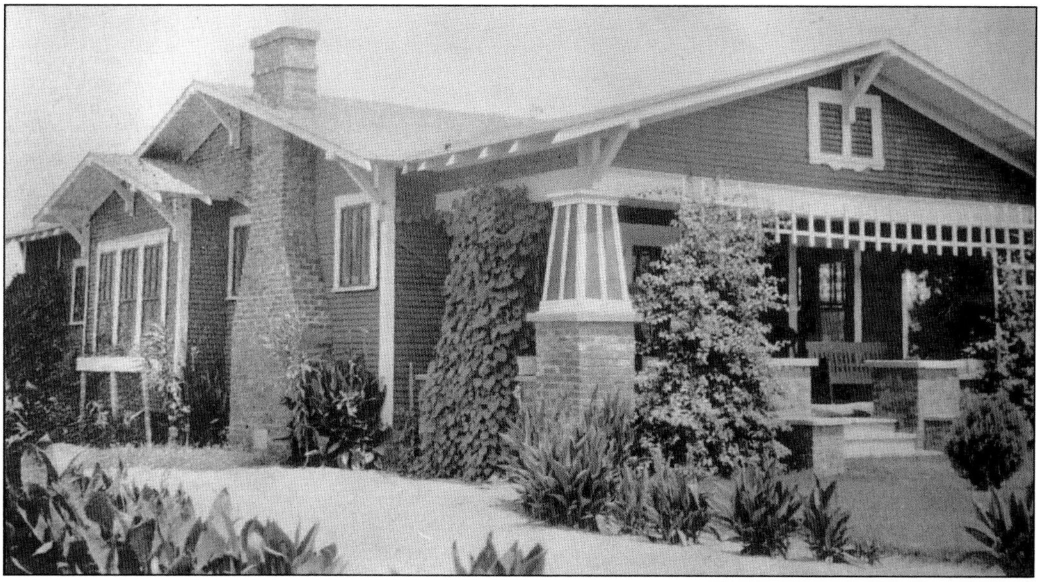

The Richcreek home, built in 1923 on South Kansas Avenue, was designed by Ruby Richcreek in California bungalow style and built by her father, developer F.O. Richcreek.

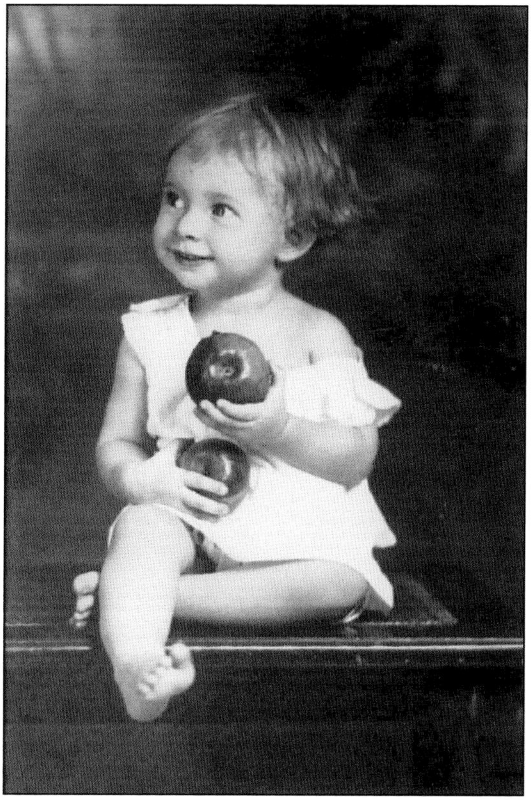

Elaine Walker, age 14 months on October 12, 1926, was the daughter of Monte Walker and Florence Richcreek and the granddaughter of F.O. Richcreek.

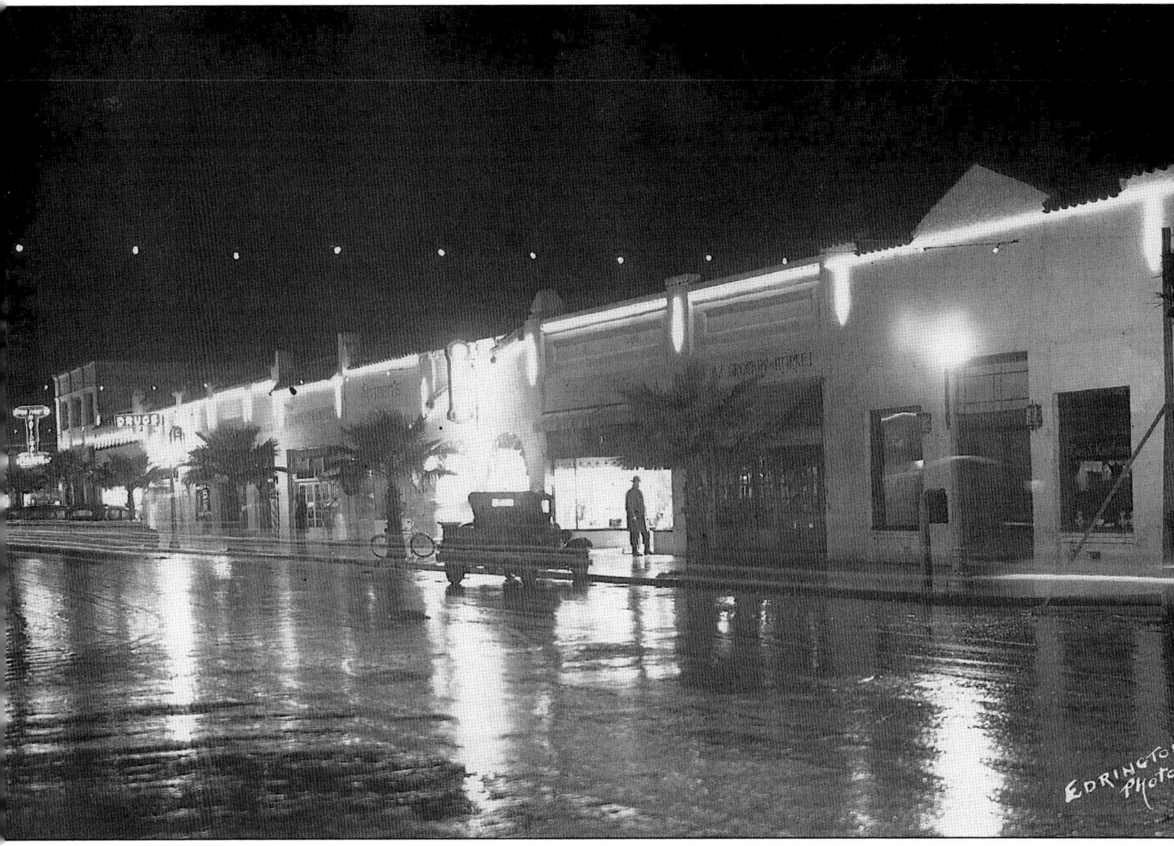


Weslaco businessmen, having coffee in Cressner's Drug Store, discussed a way to improve the town despite the constraints of the Great Depression. Soon, sketches by architect R. Newell Waters were displayed downtown. On January 27, 1936, T.D. Cressner began the project by remodeling his store. By December 1936, two blocks of Texas Boulevard between Third and Fifth Streets were dressed in the white-stuccoed Spanish architectural style. In addition to improving the facades of their buildings, Weslaco businessmen added neon lights at roof height to create a unique identity for the city. Weslaco became known as "the town that lifted its face" and "the city with the neon skyline" because of the renovations. (Edrington Studio.)

# *Three*

# FRAMEWORK OF COMMUNITY

In the first years, few Weslaco residents grew wealthy, but all became rich in community pride and spirit. Many institutions founded during those early times remain active today.

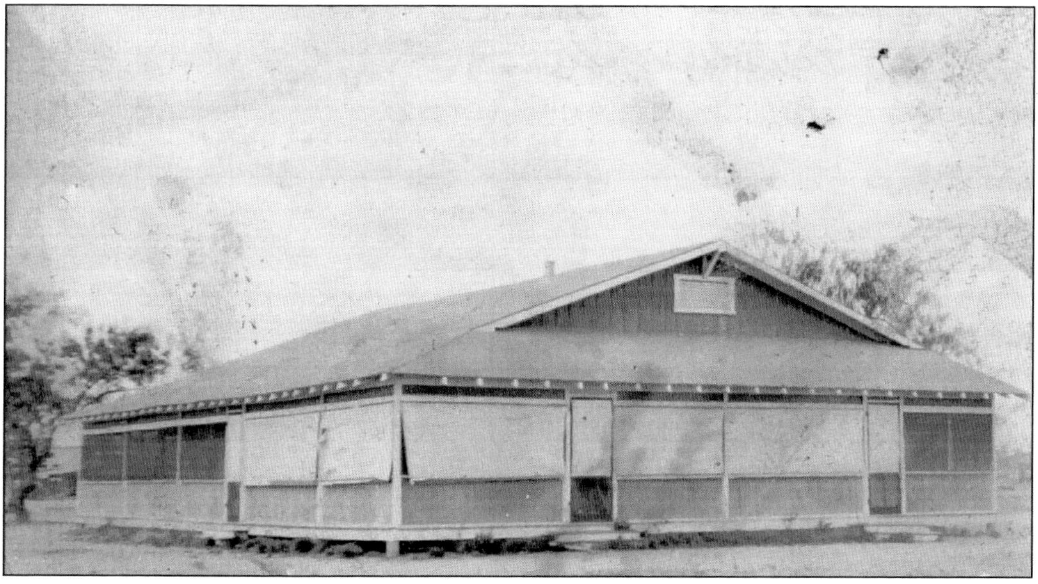

The community building served Weslaco residents as an all-purpose structure for meetings of city officials, church services, and classes for high school students until permanent buildings were constructed.

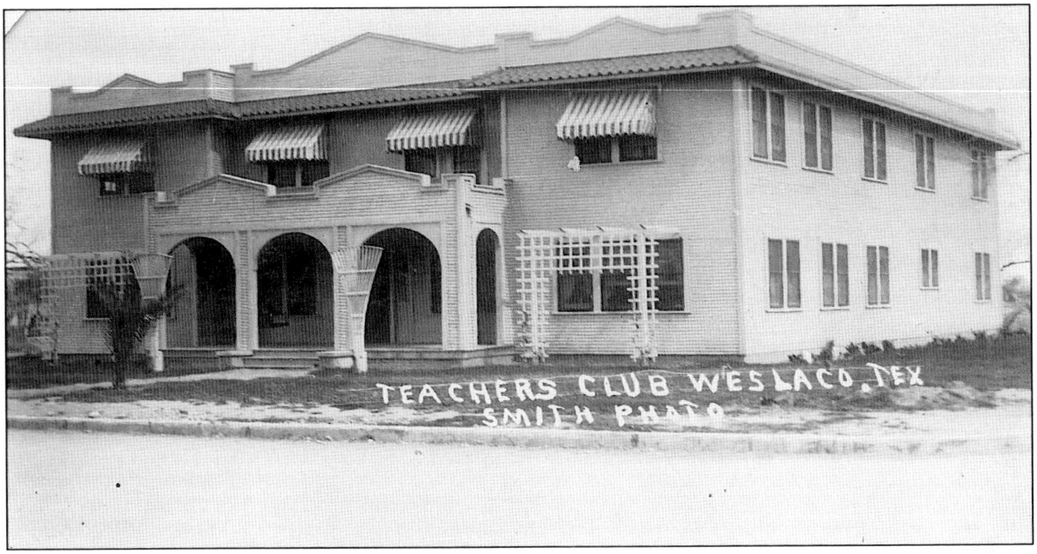


The Teachers Clubhouse, a boarding house for teachers that was built in 1920, was later renamed the Delta House. The building was razed in the 1980s. (Smith Photo.)

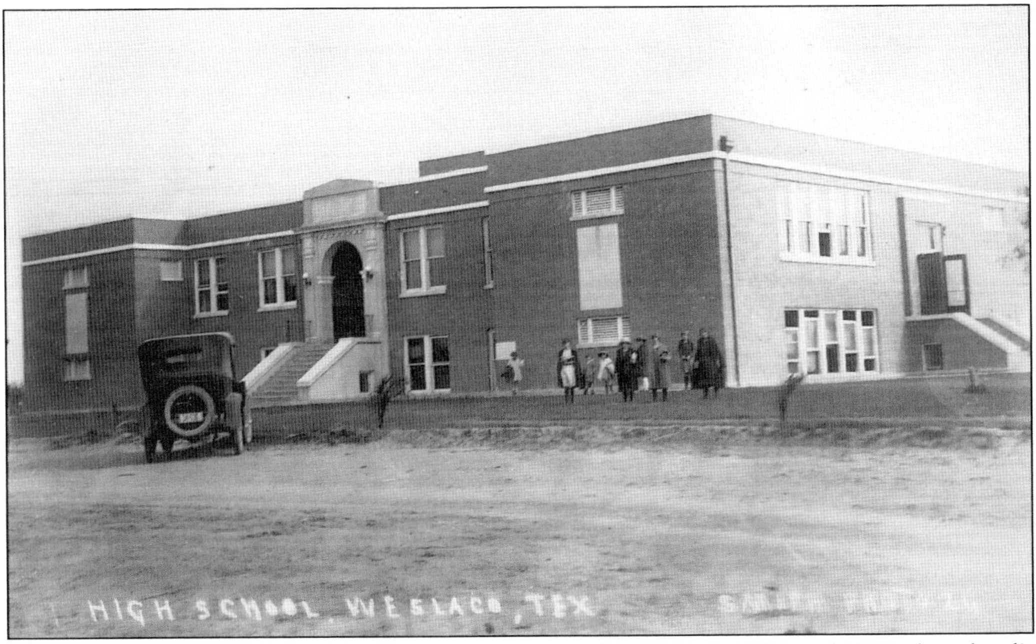


The first Weslaco High School building was constructed in 1920. In 1921 and 1922, the school's class colors were red and black. The faculty of four included the principal and superintendent. (Smith Photo.)

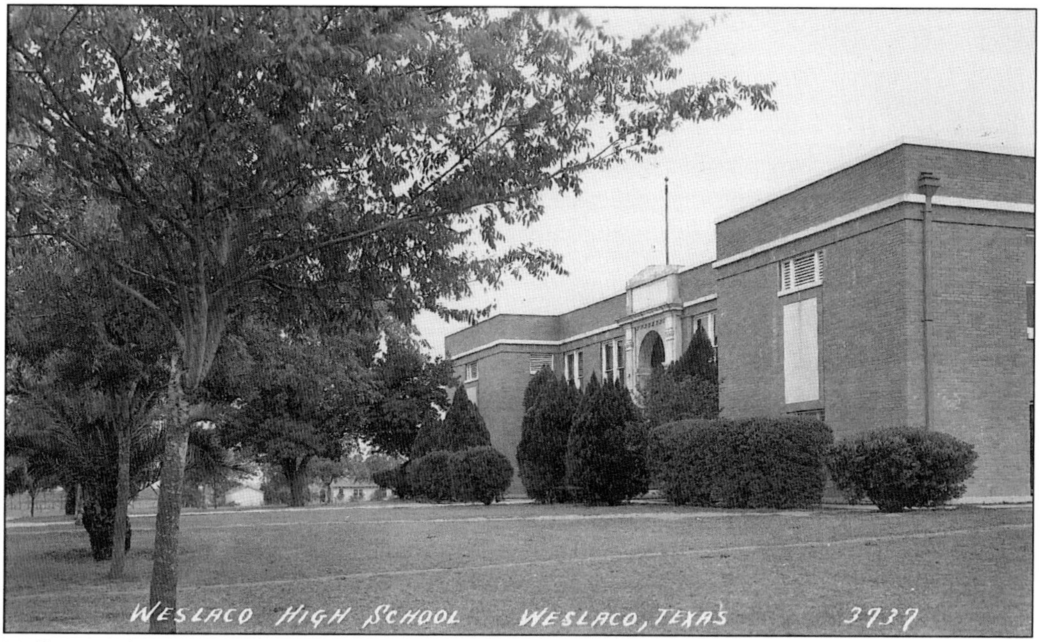

Valley residents considered Weslaco High School to be one of the most attractive campuses in the region because of the wide variety of greenery bordering the cement walk between the buildings. The late W.T. Barbee, Weslaco Independent School District superintendent in 1933, planted some of the trees.

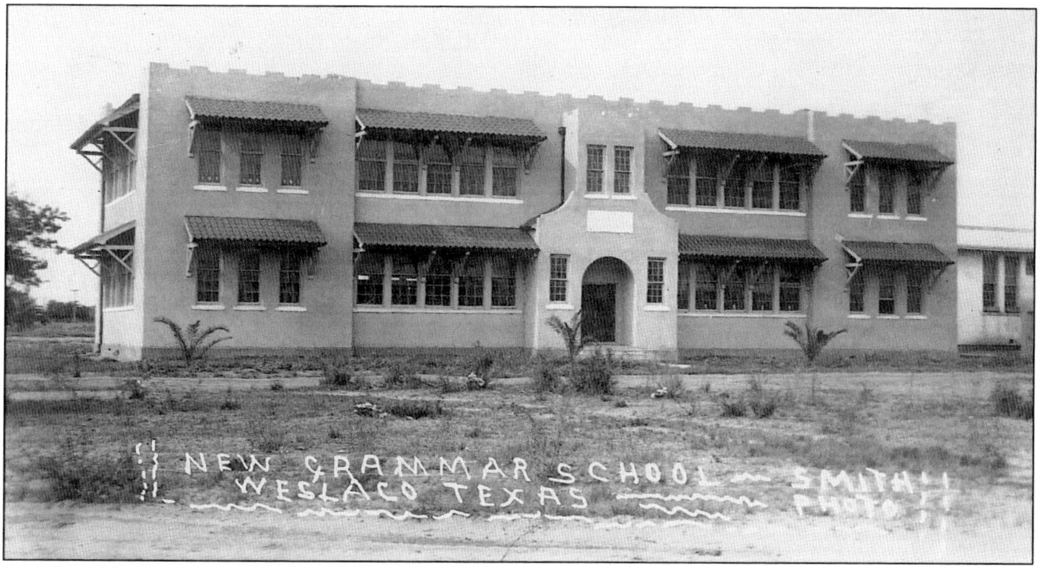

Stephen F. Austin was one of Weslaco's early grammar schools. In 1929, the school suffered a fire that caused $25,000 in damages. (Smith Photo.)

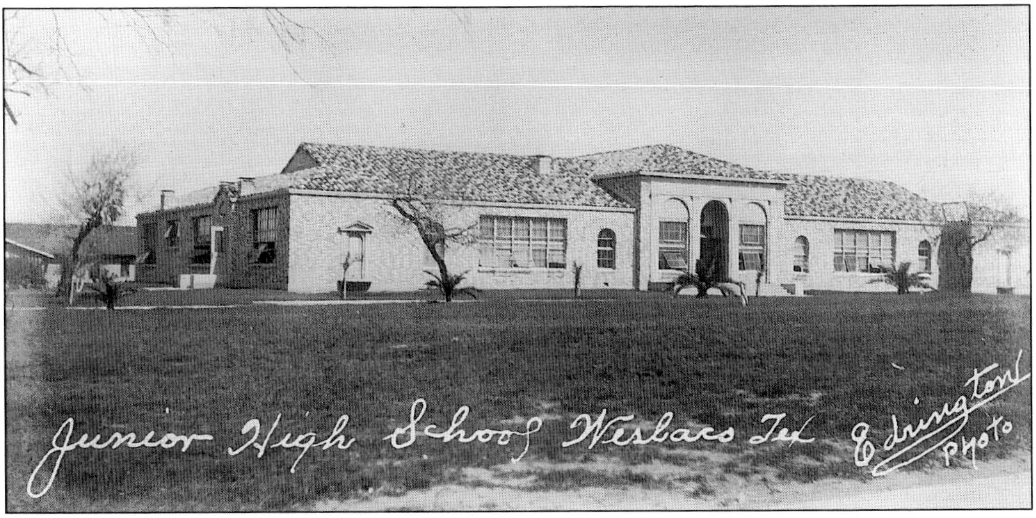


The Weslaco Junior High School faced the front of the Weslaco High School, with a sidewalk between them. The building housed 19 instructors in the 1930s. Both the former Weslaco High School and Junior High School buildings remain in existence but are no longer used for classrooms. (Edrington Studio.)

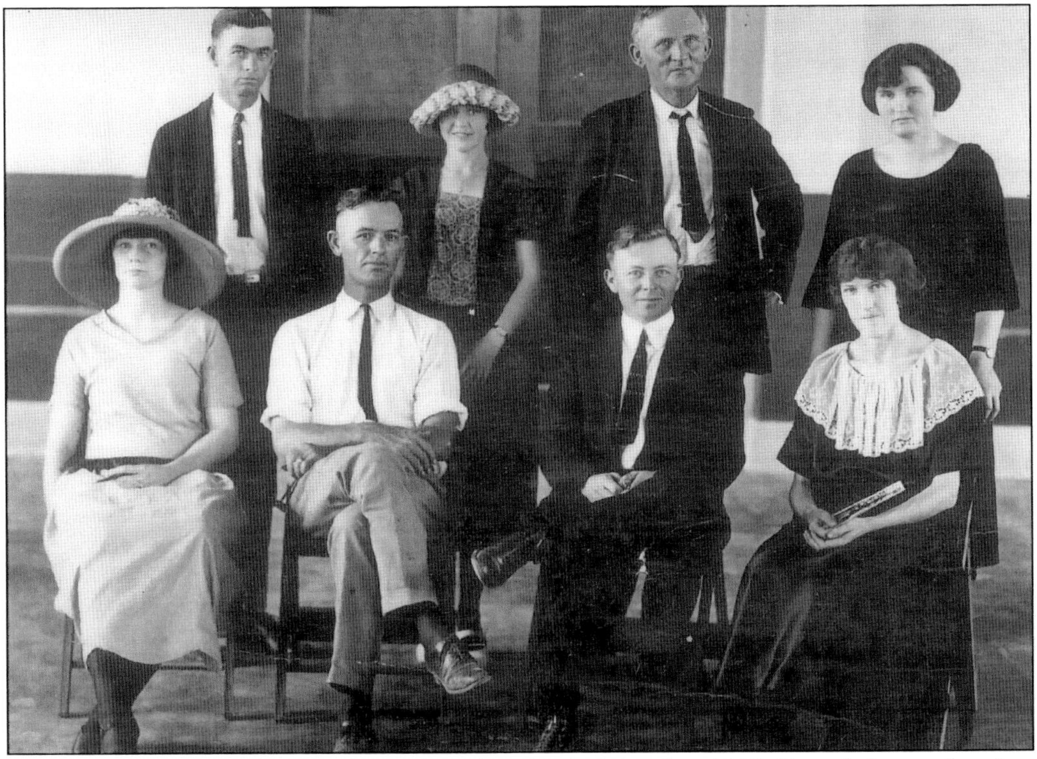

These are the first faculty members of Weslaco High School in 1923. From left to right, they are as follows: (seated) Mrs. Lily (W.T.) Barbee, home economics; W.T. Barbee, vocational agriculture; Milton Mathews, history; and Miss Louise Black, English; (standing) C.E. Kelley, principal; Miss Olga Arnold (Baxter), English and science; Harburd Tarpley, superintendent; and Miss Glee Dodson, Spanish.

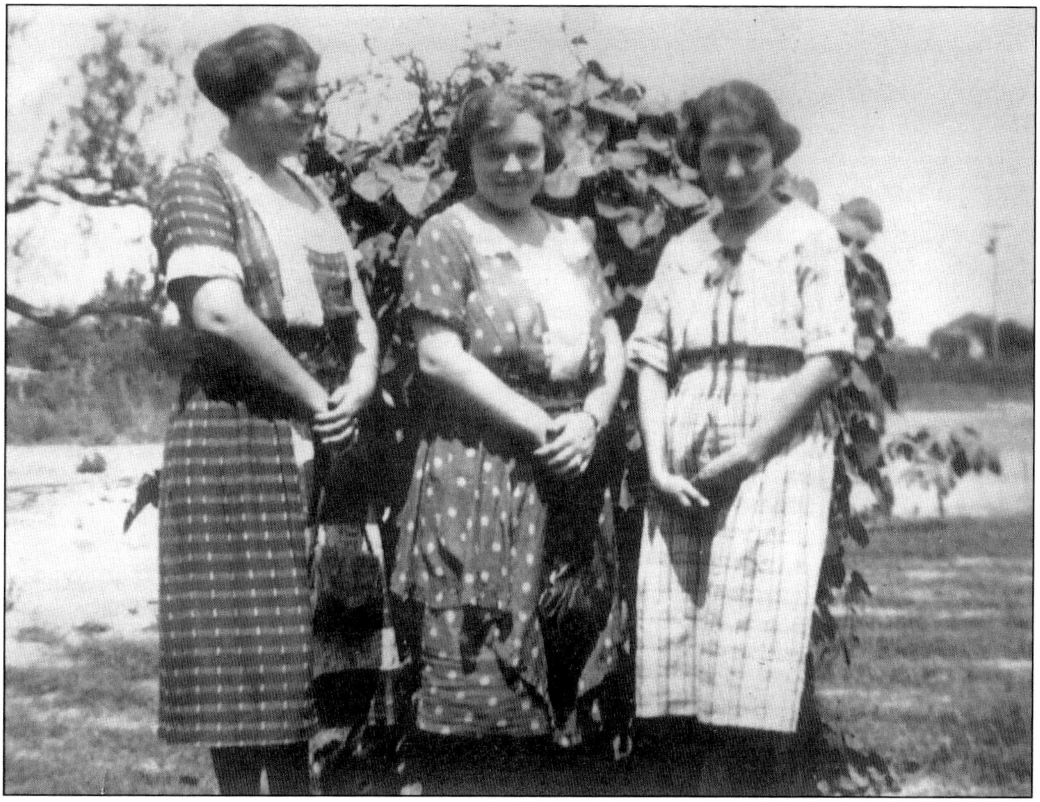

These ladies were early teachers in the Weslaco Independent School District. They are, from left to right, Ruby Warren, Blanche Couch, and Florence Richcreek.

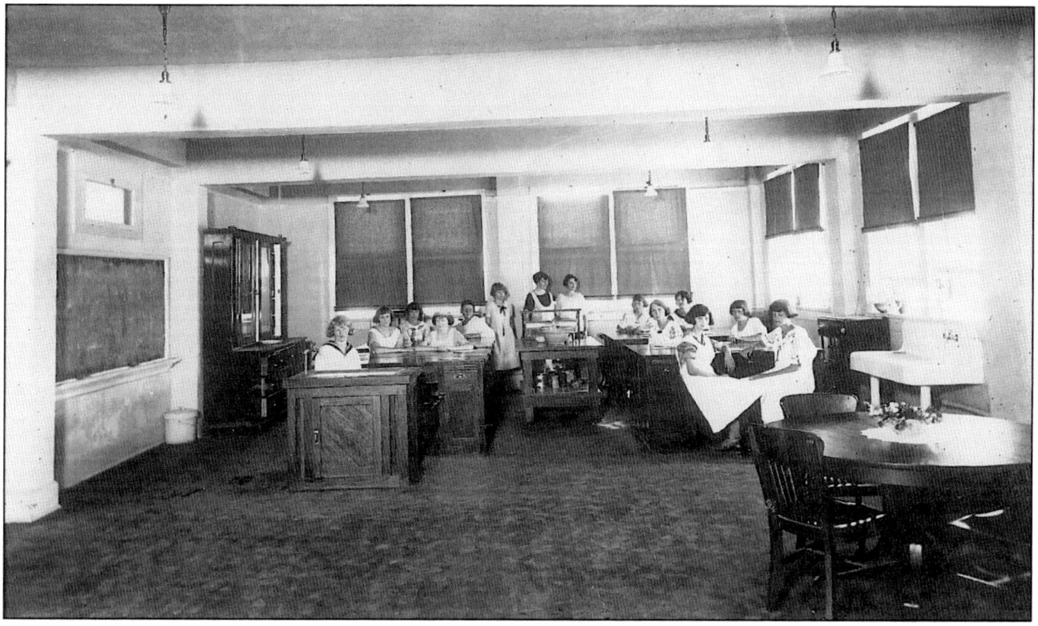

Mrs. Lily Barbee (standing, wearing apron) taught home economics in this laboratory. This 1923 photograph shows the all-female class.

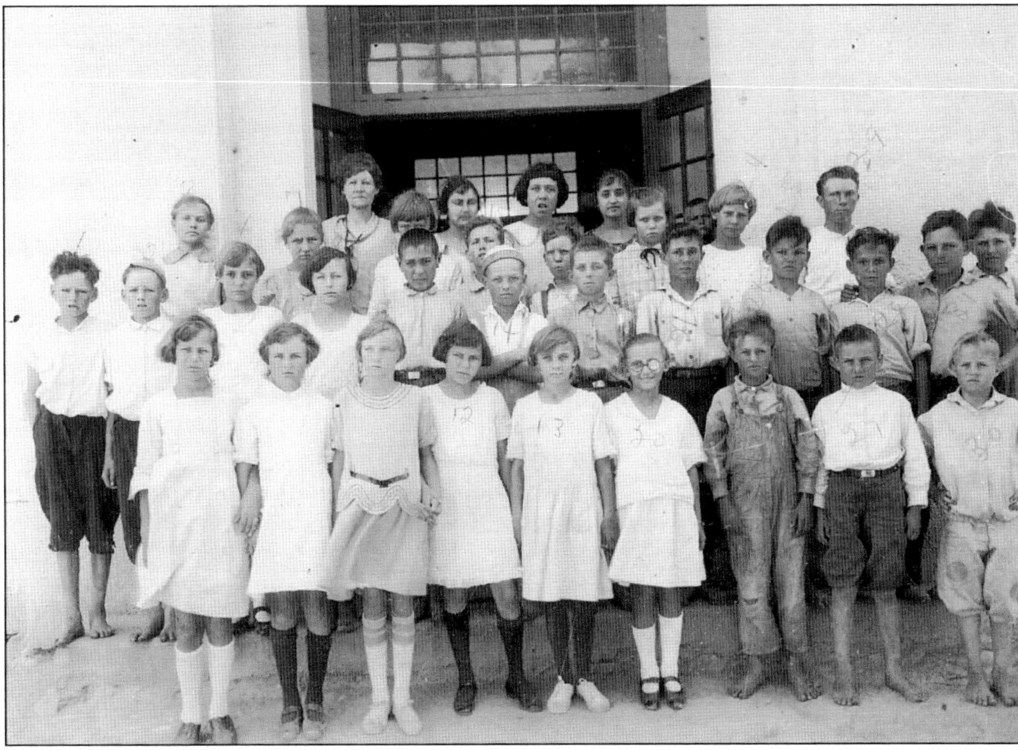

Mrs. C.D. Odom taught this fifth grade class in 1923.

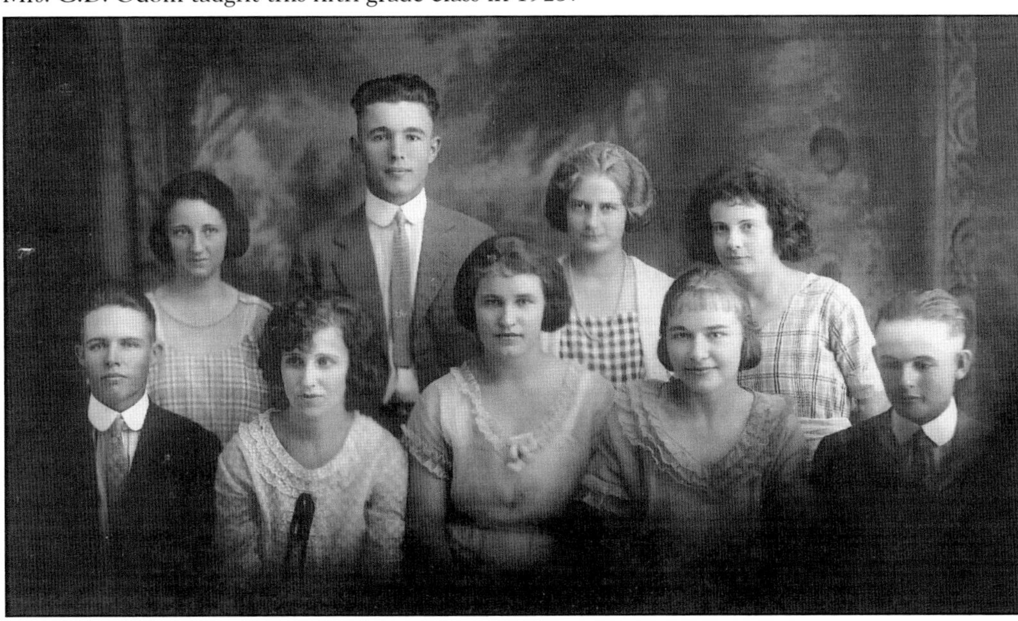

This is the Senior Class of 1922, the first class to graduate from the Weslaco High School building. Before a high school was constructed in Weslaco, these students attended classes in Donna. Pictured here, from left to right, are as follows: (seated) Howard Wright, Tressie Gore, Elizabeth Couch, Maurine Wright, and Hugh Tracy; (standing) Edith Whitson, Clifford Gibson, Wilma Gound, and Nina Whitson.

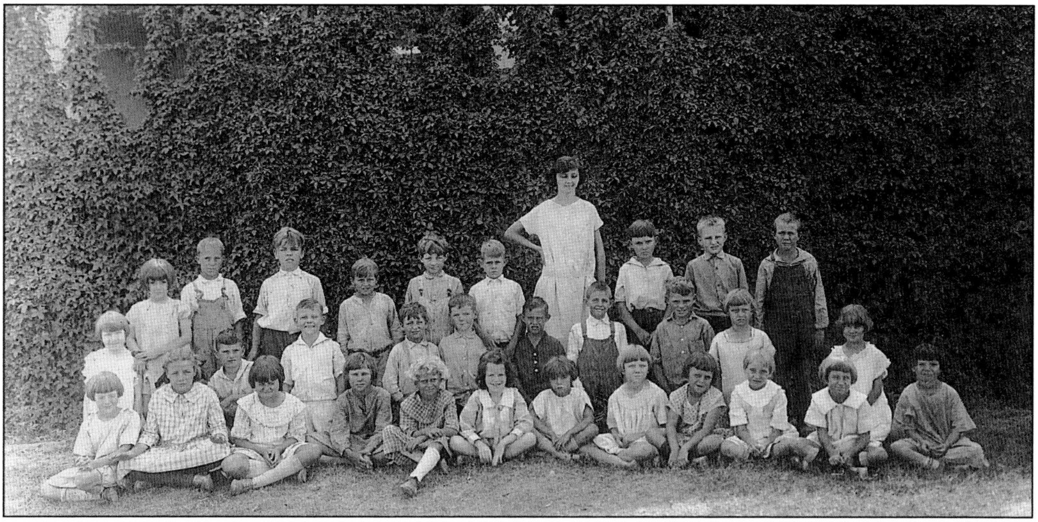

Miss Delia Winston taught this Weslaco grammar school class. Pictured, from left to right, are as follows: (seated) Josephine Harpst, Bertha Mae Wilson, Lenore Funk, Floy ?, Allie Waldron, Dorothy Belle King, Beth Wagner, Bessie Marshal, Golda LaDuke, and Catherine Donaldson; (kneeling) Mattie Myrl Cook, James ?, Ross Beamer, A.S. Pike Jr., Leonard Shives, Jimmy Ebeling, Roscoe Young, Willard Harrison, Verna Lee Nail, and Marjorie Kidder; (standing) Dorothy Haven, Carthel Foster, Woodrow Jackson, Lynn ?, Harold ?, William Barber, Miss Winston, David Clements, Neal Smith, and David Arnett.

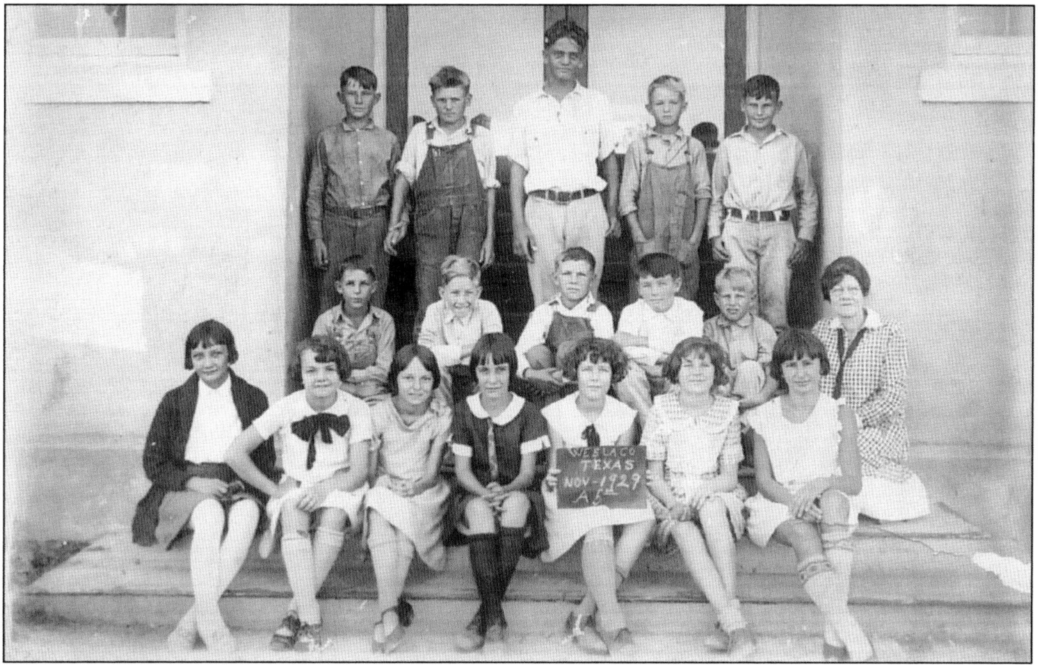


Mrs. C.D. Odom taught this fifth grade class in 1929. Pictured, from left to right, are as follows: (front row) unidentified, unidentified, Julia Andersen, Easter Fal Sheppard, unidentified, unidentified, and Hazel Clark; (second row) Fred Swinnea, Orville Alexander, Billy Clark, Coyle Carr, unidentified, and Mrs. Odom; (back row) unidentified, unidentified, Woodrow Baker, Carl Nobles, and Pat Martin.

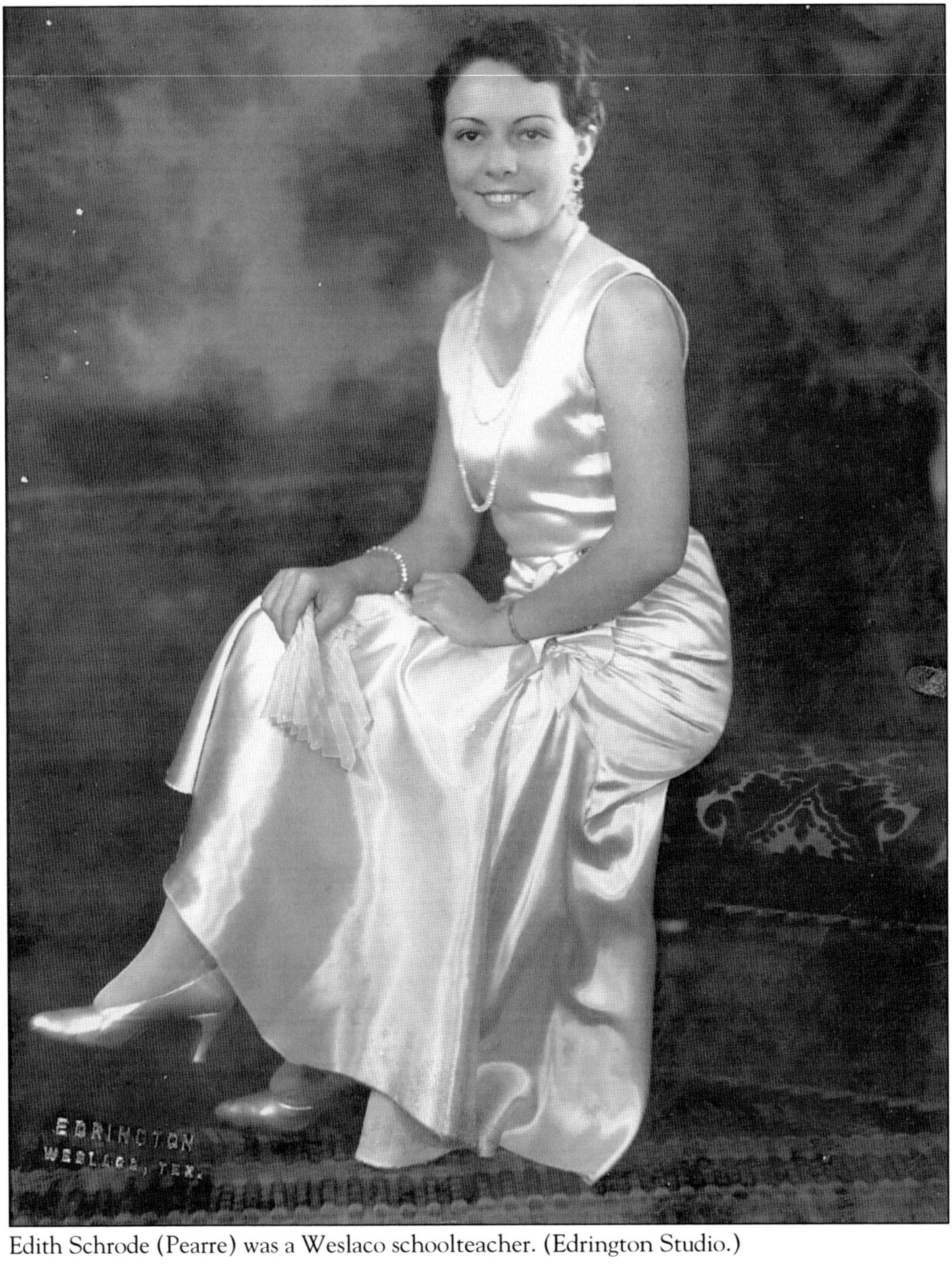


Edith Schrode (Pearre) was a Weslaco schoolteacher. (Edrington Studio.)

The Fine Arts Club sponsored the Burr Tuberculosis Cottage. The cottage could be moved to a home so that a patient could be isolated to prevent the spread of the disease and yet be near his or her family. This 1939 image shows nurse Connie Hankal in front of the cottage. (Hall Studio.)

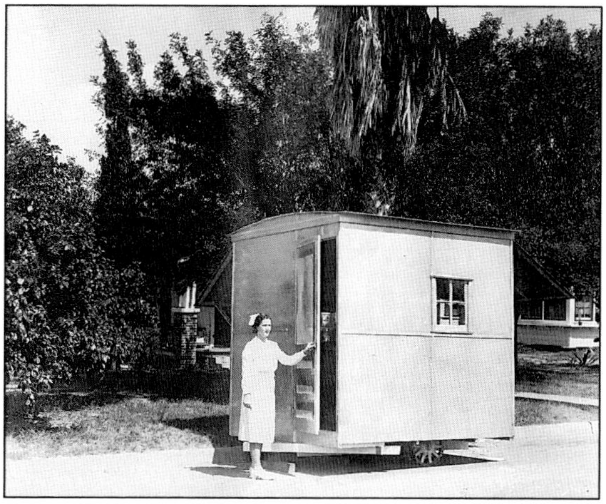

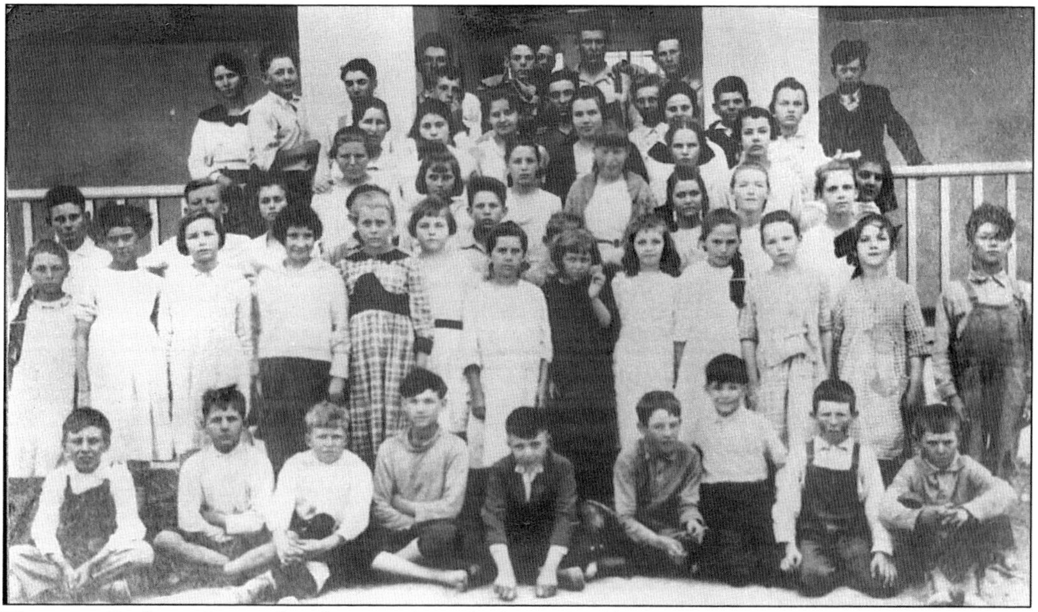

Florence Richcreek taught this combined class of fifth and sixth grades. This is the class picture for the 1920–1921 school year. The students are, in no particular order, Byron Gilmore, Dale Richcreek, Freeman Ford, Milton Weaver, Glenn Shepperd, J.D. Garnett, Marvin Williams, Ross Countryman, Verl Cole, Cornell Tilley, Hiram Wikoff, Hazel Stone, Andrea Chapa, Veda Ashford, Pearl Ashford, Maurine Cook, Erma Andersen, Nadine Weaver, Opal Evetts, Ruth Shepperd, Catherine Schaffer, Norma Van Vliet, Mavis Ford, La Verne Cook, Helen Winters, William Winters, Dixie Duncan, Joe Summers, Frank Summers, Oleta Bell Bishop, Earl Pike, Fretwell Gilmore, Noel Tilley, Howard Ham, Harley Deihl, John Lake Couch, Orville Tilley, Herbert Elliott, Omer Elliott, Edward Schaffer, Roland Blackwell, Opal Pike, Lois Clark, Miriam Linn, Ollie Wommack, Edith Barter, Ethel Barter, Ruby Warren, Wauneta Martin, Ruth Stewart, Letha Robison, Margaret Kesinger, Homa Moreland, Paul Duncan, Earnest Bishop, Inetta Roland, and Cecil Weinzierl. Not pictured are Truman Making, J.P. Triplett, Lowell Moore, Odell Countryman, Frank Allen, Jovita Garcia, Marie Felker, Martha Torres, Josefa Balderana, Bert Richmond, Ben Penick, A.L. Frizzell, James Gonseth, Lloyd Byrd, Otto Rosenthal, Walter McDaniel, Victoria Chapa, Frieda Rosenthal, Truman Gililland, and Audrey Tracey.

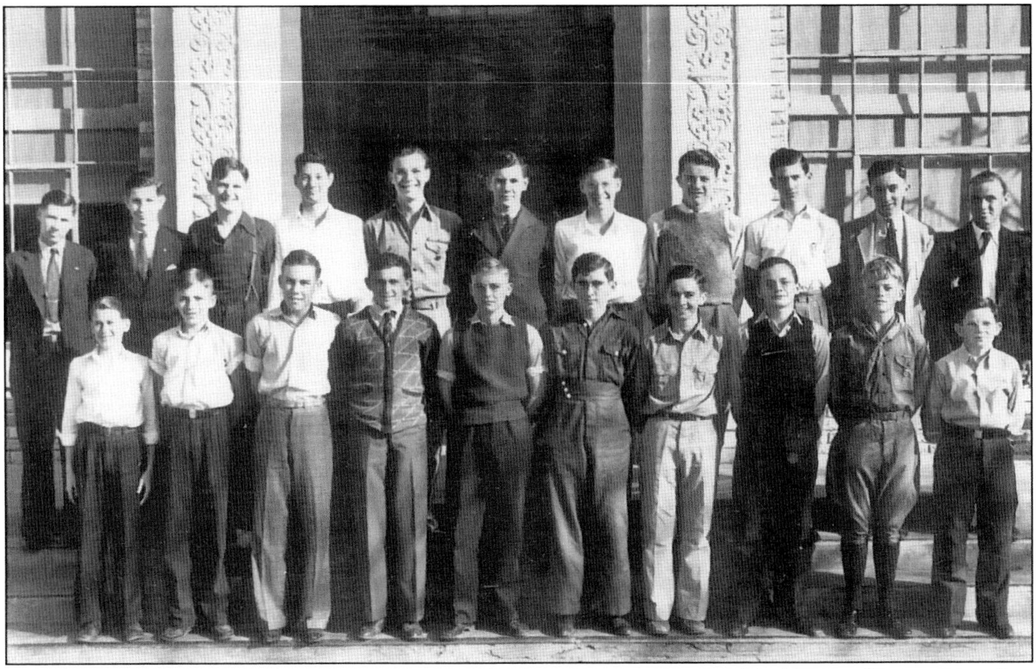

The Roliki Club, pictured *c.* 1940, was a youth organization sponsored by Rotary International.

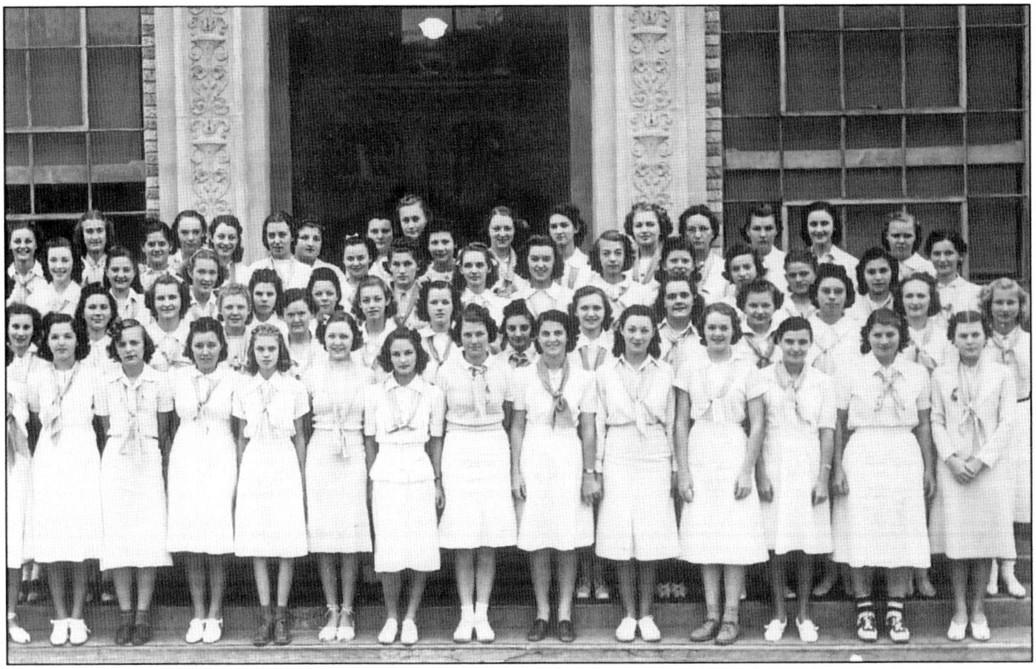

The Girl Reserves, pictured *c.* 1940, was a youth organization for the Weslaco Independent School District.

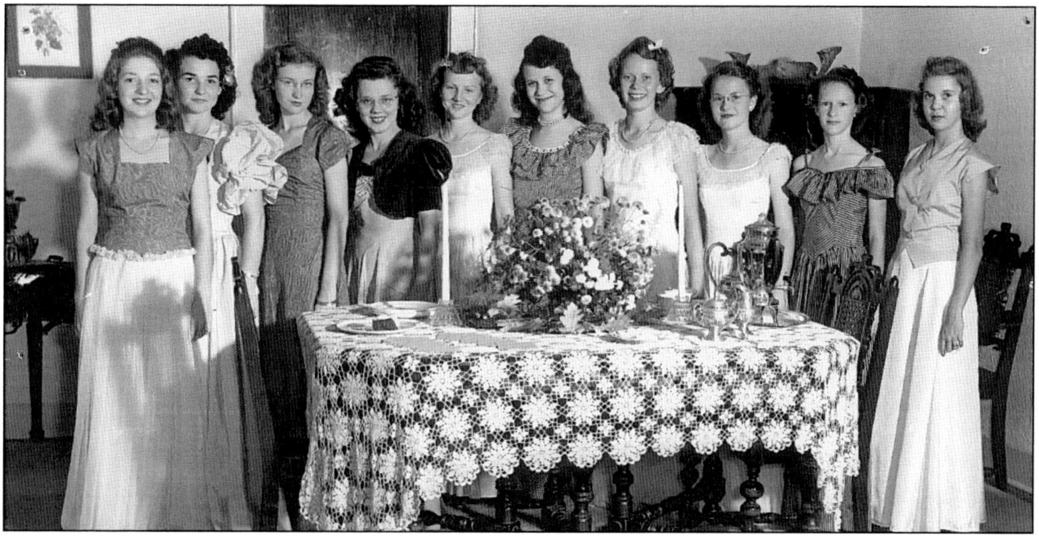

These young ladies were attending the annual party for "The Mid Valley Junior Club of the National Federation of Music Clubs," *c.* 1943. Pictured here, from left to right, are Patty Shellhamer, Clara Fay Garnett, Doreen Yoder, Marjorie Rogers, Jean Barber, Margaret Kopecky, Betty Jean Robertson, Dean Barber, Dolores Triplett, and Peggy Kirgan.

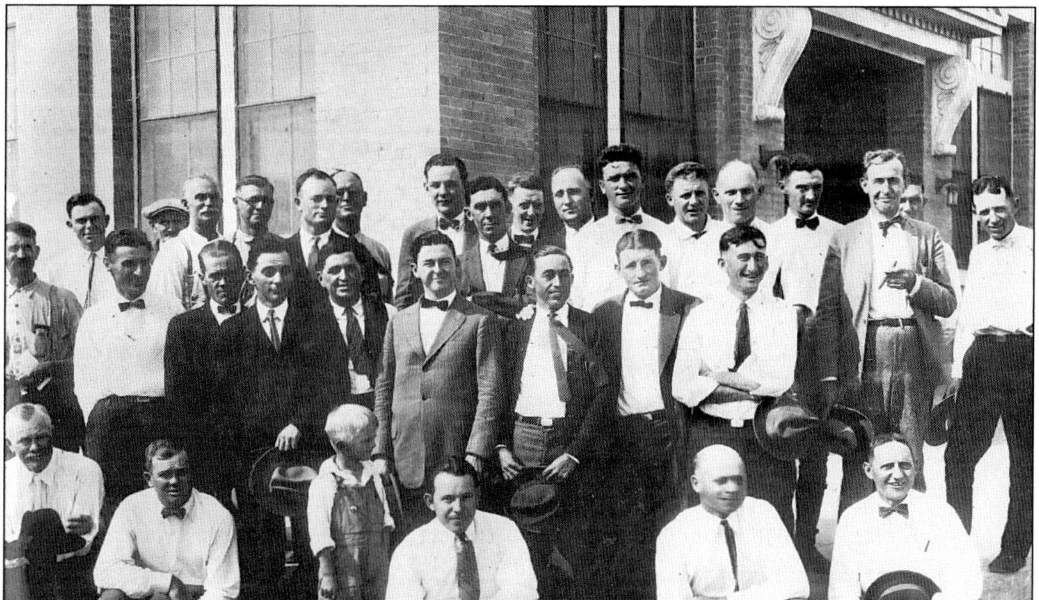

The Live Right Club was a men's athletic and service club founded in 1922. From left to right are as follows: (front row) Joe Metzger, Clell Solether, unidentified, Norris Stewart, Harry Solether, and Bob Sparks; (middle row) ? Scott, L.M. Holland, Bob Dixon, John Arant, John Davis, Miller Armstrong Jr., ? Bracken, Luther Hughes, and Jimmy Betts; (back row) Earl Stone, unidentified, C.C. Voigt, John Herald, Monk Wilson, Jack Line, Ed Williams, Dr. E.L. McCalip, J.H. McLeese (founder of the *Weslaco News*), Dr. T.W. Glass, Lester Skaggs, Harry Stebbins, Luther Garrett, H. Raymond Mills, Judge R.E. Erwin, W.H. "Bill" Friend, and Judson Friday.

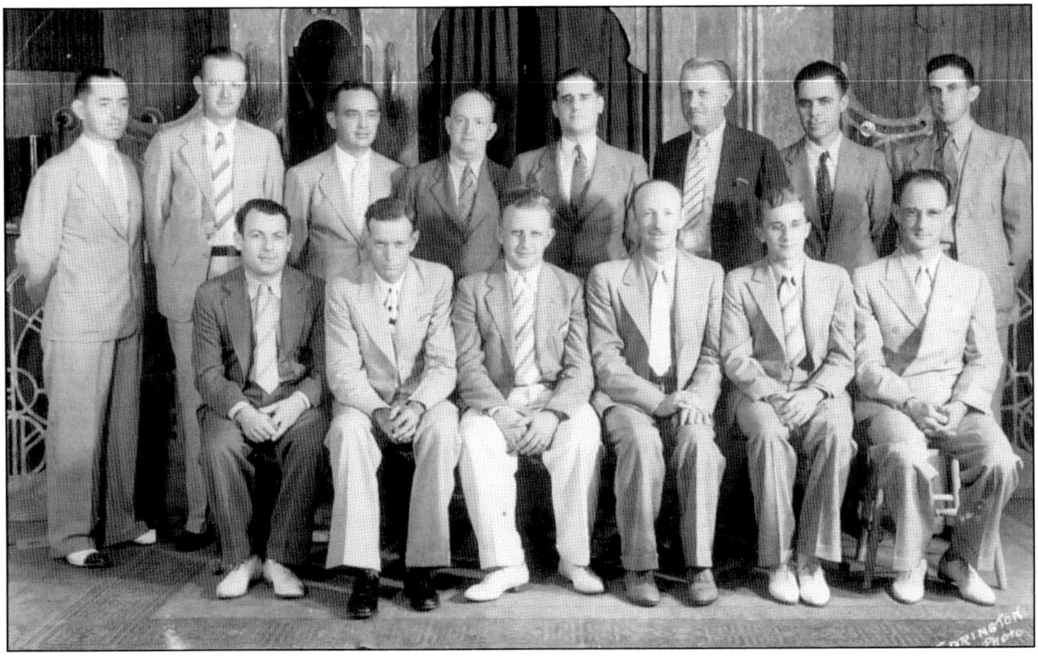

The Weslaco Lions Club was another service organization. Pictured, from left to right, are the following: (front row) Mike Falk, E.B. Ballard, Jack Drake, A.B. Wren, Buddy Burton, and Martin Strobel; (back row) Gerry Tesar, Raymond Clifford, B.L. Harrington, Dick Henderson, Louis Zeiser, R.D. McIntosh, H.D. Haas, and Monte Richards. (Edrington Studio.)

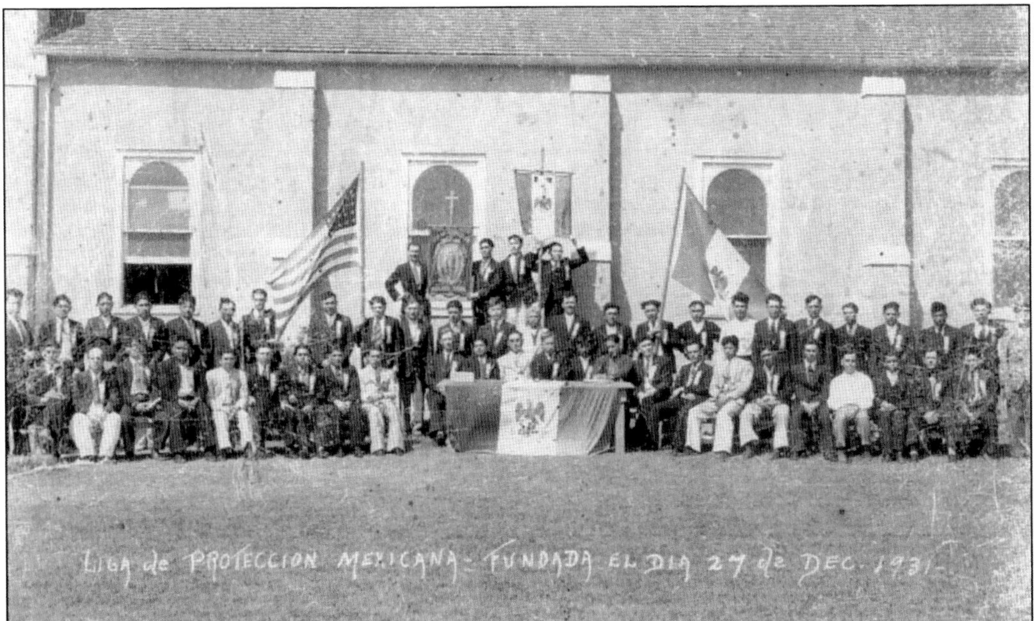


Members of the St. Joan of Arc Catholic Church, which was dedicated on December 11, 1921, founded the Liga de Protección Mexicana (Mexican Protection League) on December 27, 1931, to help Mexican Americans in need. This picture is dated April 1934. (Edrington Studio.)

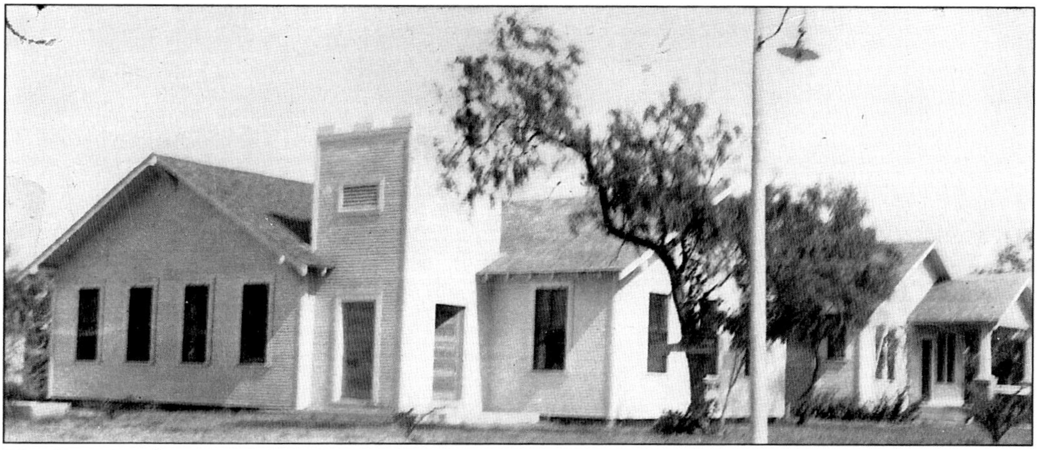

The First Presbyterian Church in Weslaco was initially located at the corner of Sixth Street and Texas Boulevard but was later moved to the north side of Weslaco to serve as a mission church. This is how the church looked in 1921.

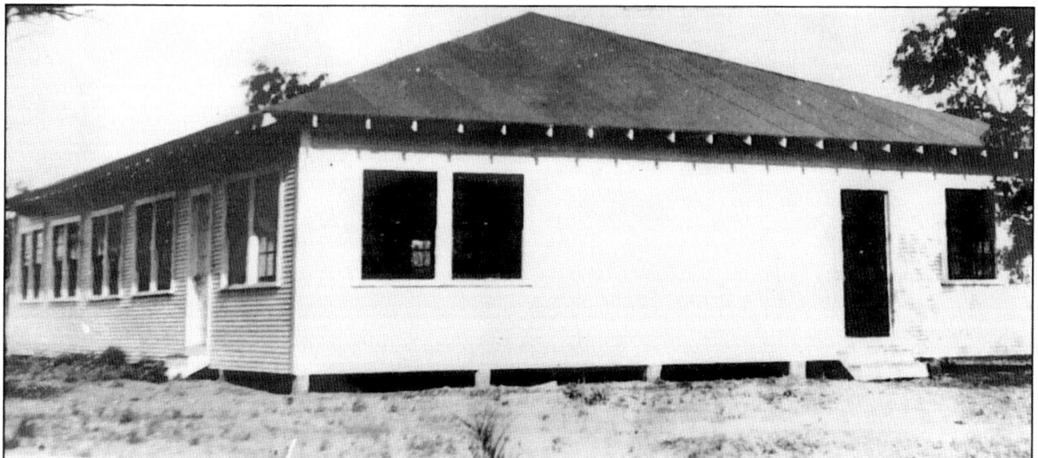

This is the First Baptist Church in 1921.

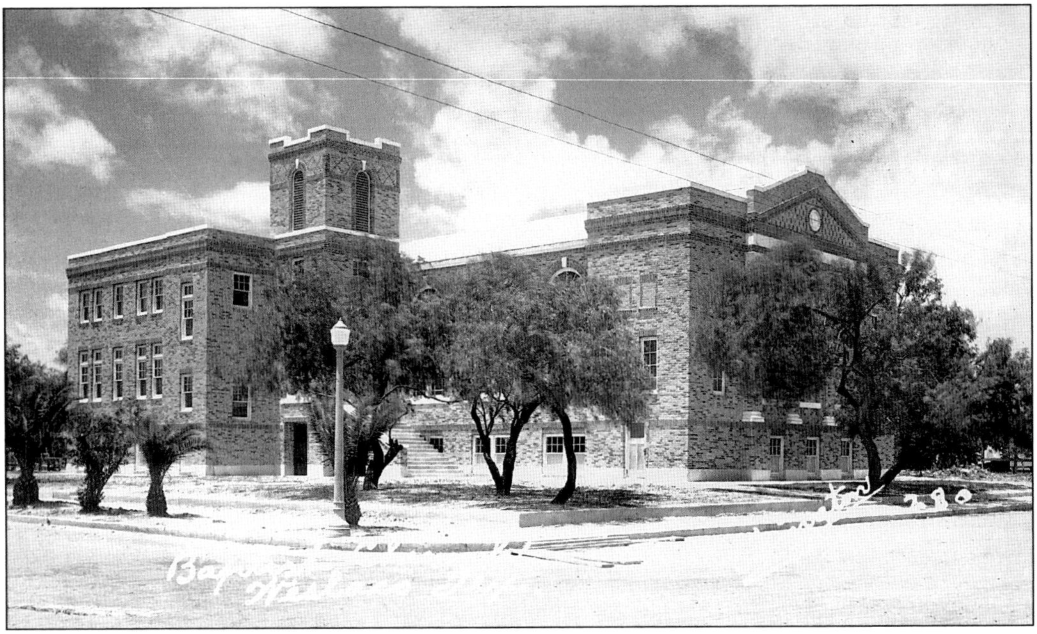

During 1926 and 1927, a large modern brick building was constructed as the new Baptist Church and is still in use by the Baptist community of Weslaco. When Weslaco was less than two years old, three evangelists came to the city: Rev. R.L. Cole and Mr. and Mrs. J.L. Blankenship, who were gospel singers. Three days after their series of meetings began, a group of Baptists decided they were in sufficient numbers to call a conference for the purpose of organizing a church. This followed, by only a few months, the organization of two other churches in Weslaco, prior to which time all of the Christian congregations had been worshiping in the community building. (Edrington Studio.)

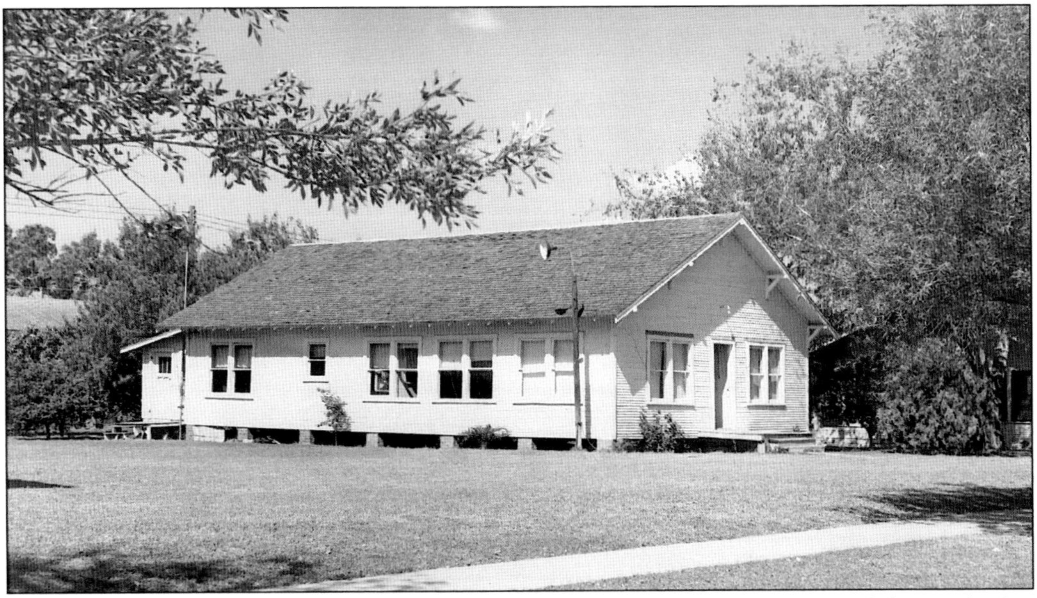

This frame building was Weslaco's first Methodist church, built in 1922. It served the Methodist community from 1922 through 1925.

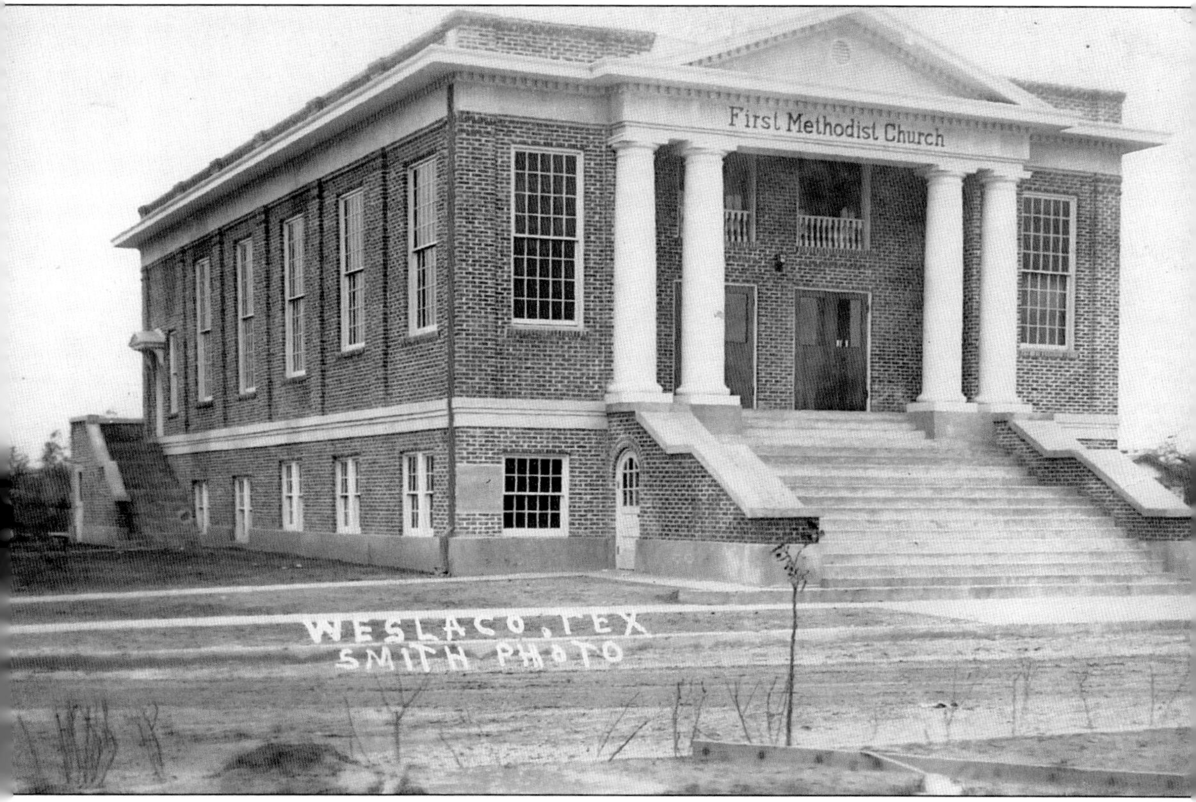


Weslaco's first brick Methodist church, built in 1925, was located at Illinois and Sixth Streets. The church remained in use through 1958 and was later razed. (Smith Photo.)

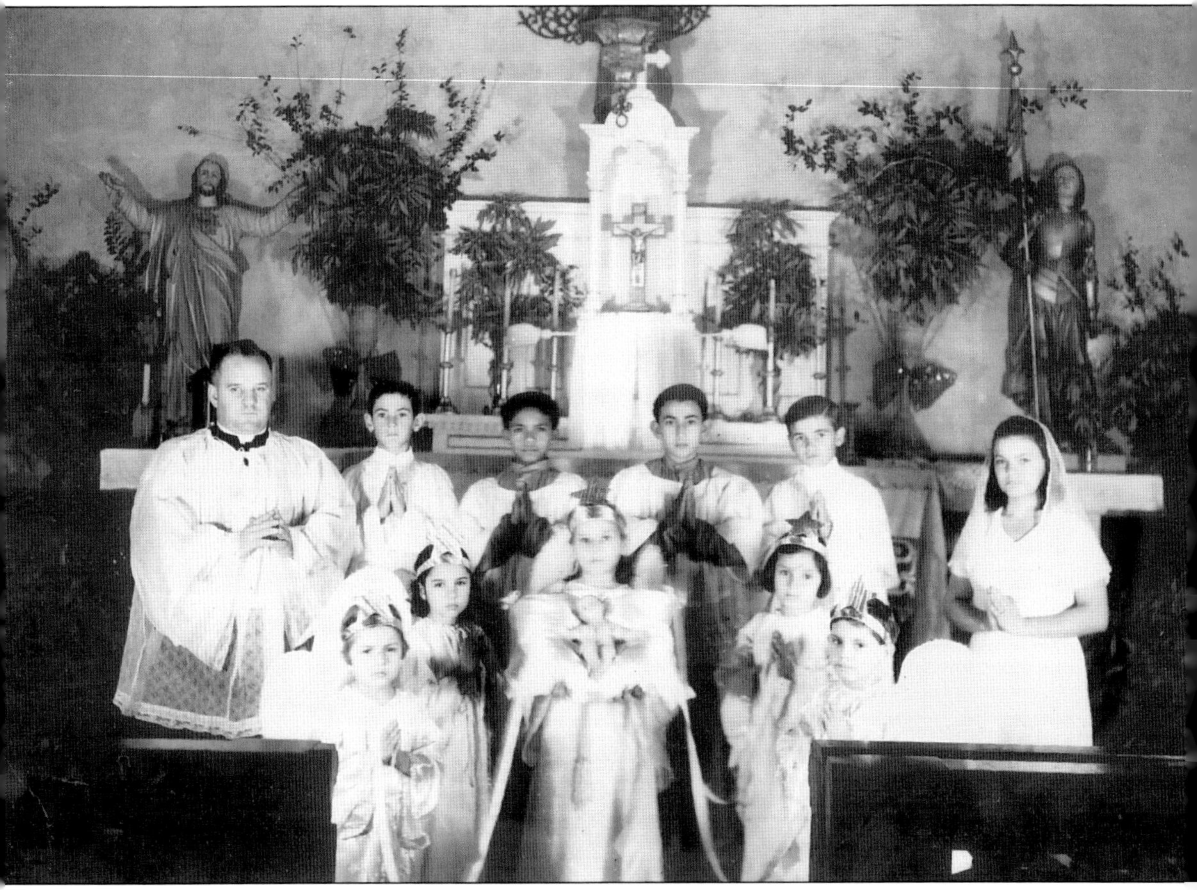

This was the interior of St. Joan of Arc Catholic Church during the 1930s. From left to right are Fr. James R. Cassidy, Ruben Cuellar, Tomas Ayala, Hilario Guerra, and Renato Cuellar. Two of the girls are Nora Garza and Isabela Tijerina; the others are unknown. Father Cassidy served as parish priest for 14 years (1938–1952) and later transferred to Raymondville.

# *Four*

# GOOD TIMES

Weslaco staged its first birthday party on December 10, 1929, in defiance of the stock market crash and the beginning of the Great Depression. The party was a great success and continued to be held for many years thereafter. With business grinding to a halt during the winter of 1931–1932, S.M. Patterson conceived the idea of expanding Weslaco's Trades Day into a larger event. To stimulate business, merchants sponsored "Carrot Days" on April 7th and 8th, 1932, and the first style show took place downtown on April 8th. Models stepped out of business establishments and onto a ramp that extended several blocks. The popular event became known as "The Fruit, Vegetable, and Flower Show" and was later incorporated into the city's annual birthday party celebration. The style shows stopped after the 1941 production but were revived in 1947. During the 1960s, the style shows and birthday parties came to an end, but the Citrus Fiesta held in Mission each January continues the celebration and the tradition of colorful costumes.

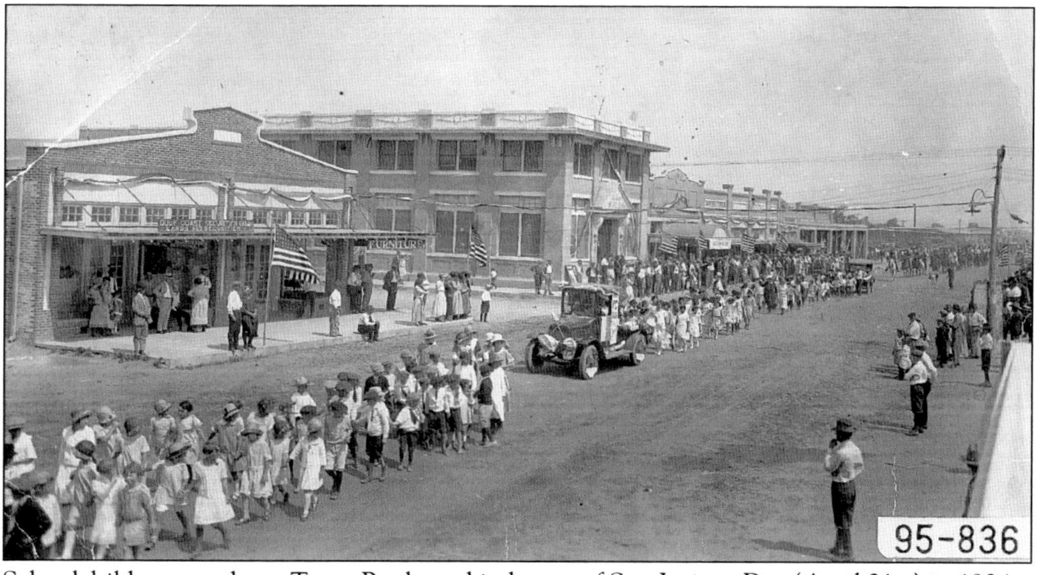


Schoolchildren parade on Texas Boulevard in honor of San Jacinto Day (April 21st) in 1924.

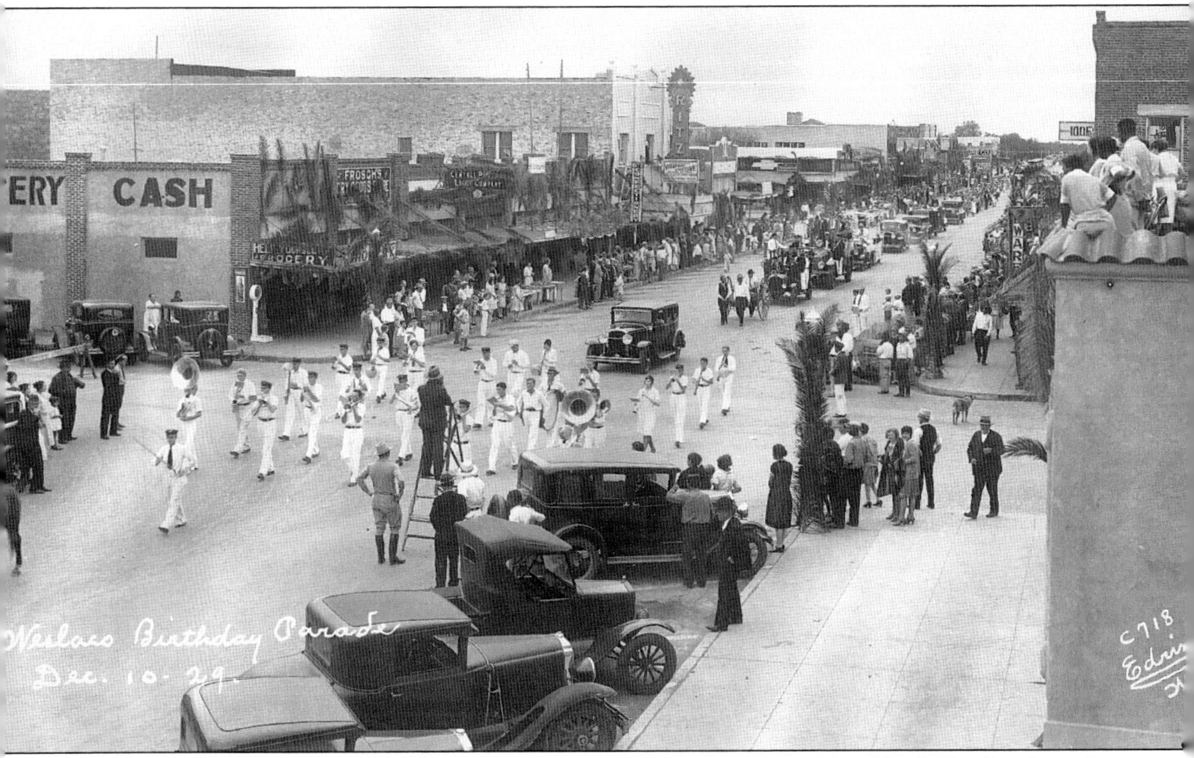


Weslaco staged its first birthday party on December 10, 1929. Sandford Hardy, the editor of the *Weslaco News*, suggested a tenth birthday party in a front page story in the *News* on October 24, 1929. The festivities included a high school band concert, turtle races, a rolling pin throwing contest, a football game, burro polo, chariot races, and toe dances. In this image, photographer S.L. Edrington is standing on the ladder. Fred Turner, a local businessman, is standing at the base of the ladder. The gentleman on the far right, standing on the sidewalk, is W.G. Wren. The two young women to his right are his daughter Aline Wren and granddaughter Mozelle Elliott. Hotel workers are watching the parade from the roof of the Cortez Hotel. (Edrington Studio.)

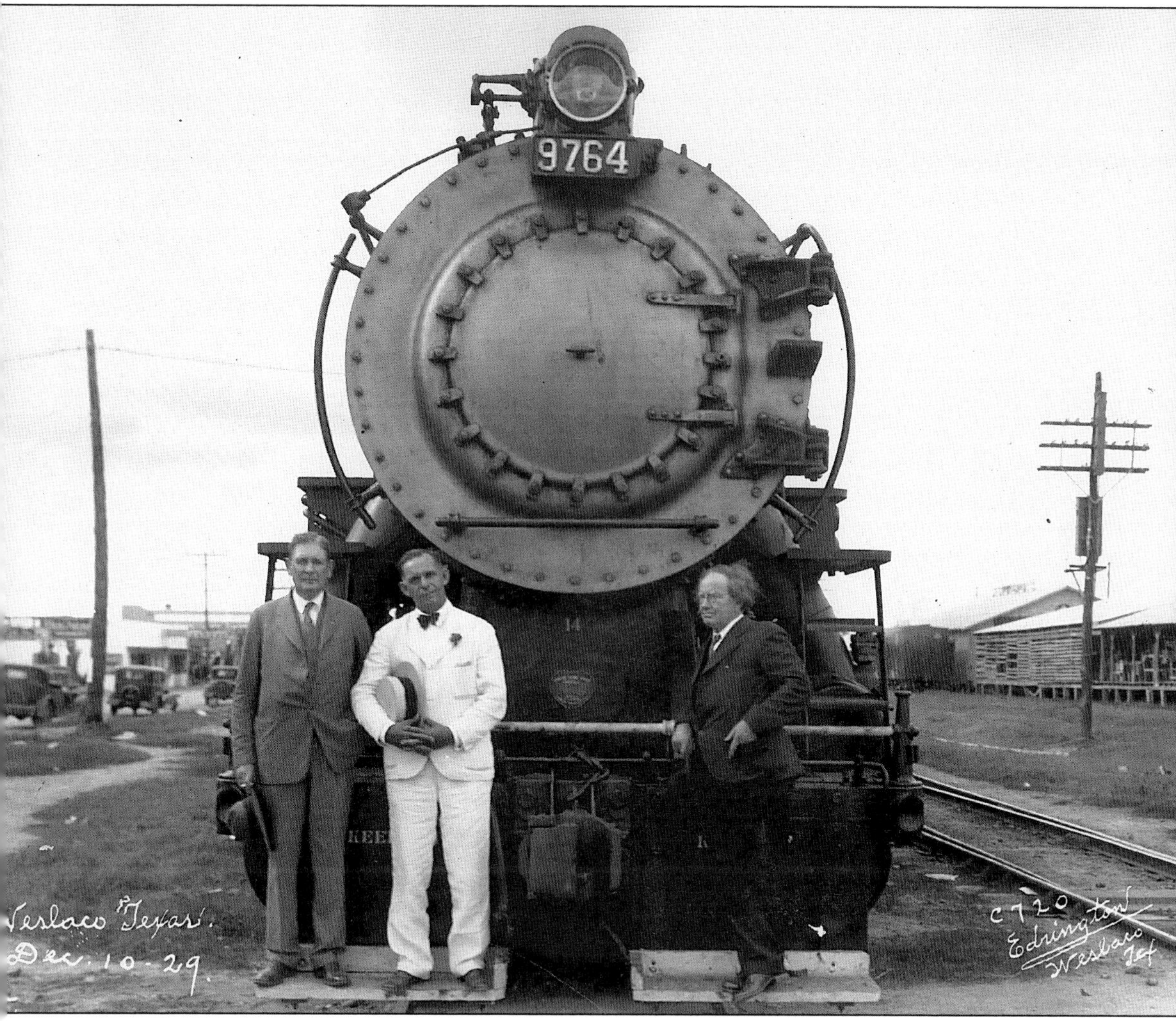


Pictured, from left to right, are B.C. Holland, chamber of commerce manager; Dave Kirgan, Weslaco mayor; and Lon C. Hill of Harlingen. Photographer Edrington took the picture during Weslaco's first birthday celebration on December 10, 1929. (Edrington Studio.)

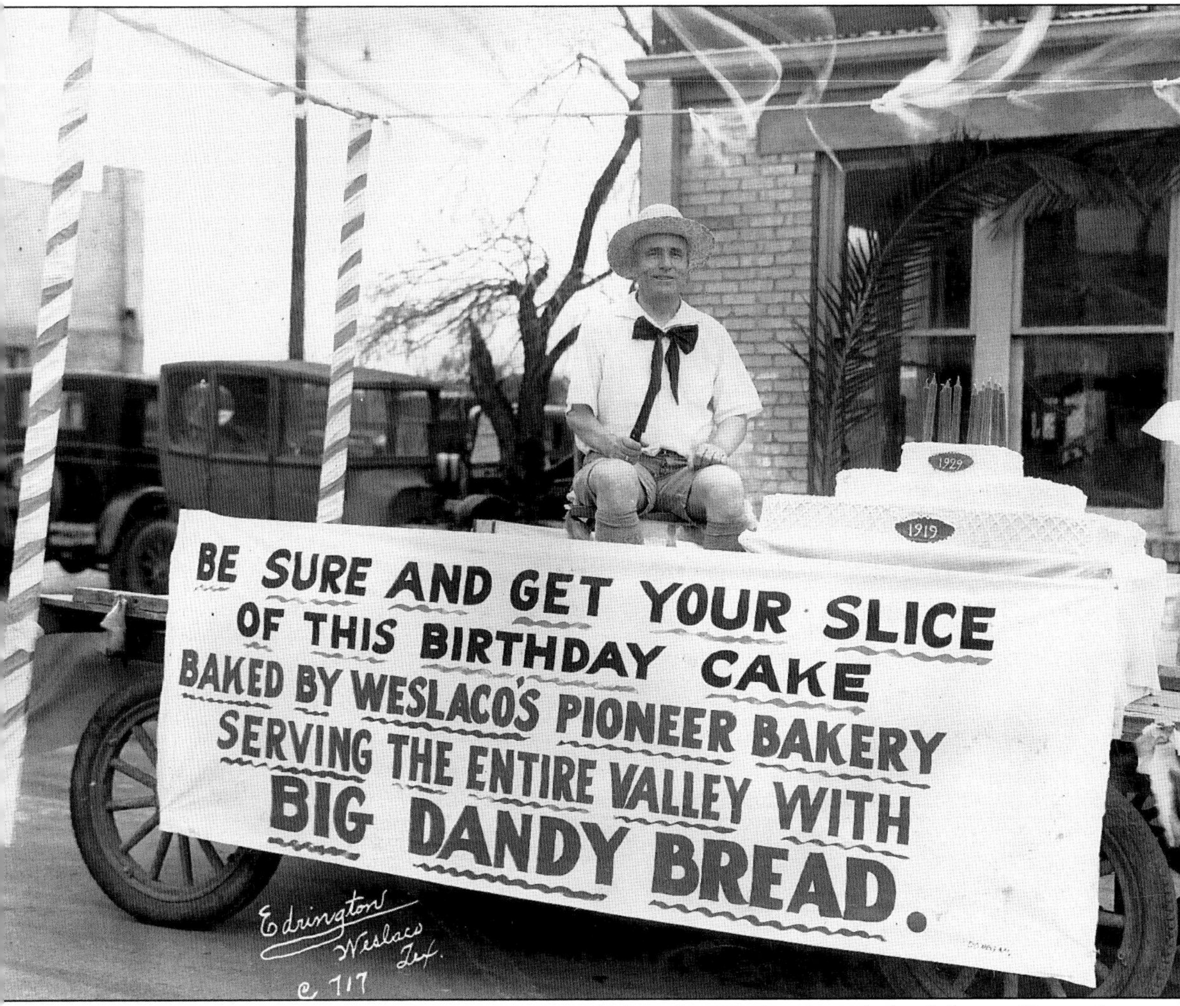


Banker Ed C. Couch dressed as a ten-year-old boy for Weslaco's 11th birthday in December 1930. He rode on the float alongside the cake because he was one of the founders of Weslaco. He cut the cake and served it to the crowd. (Edrington Studio.)

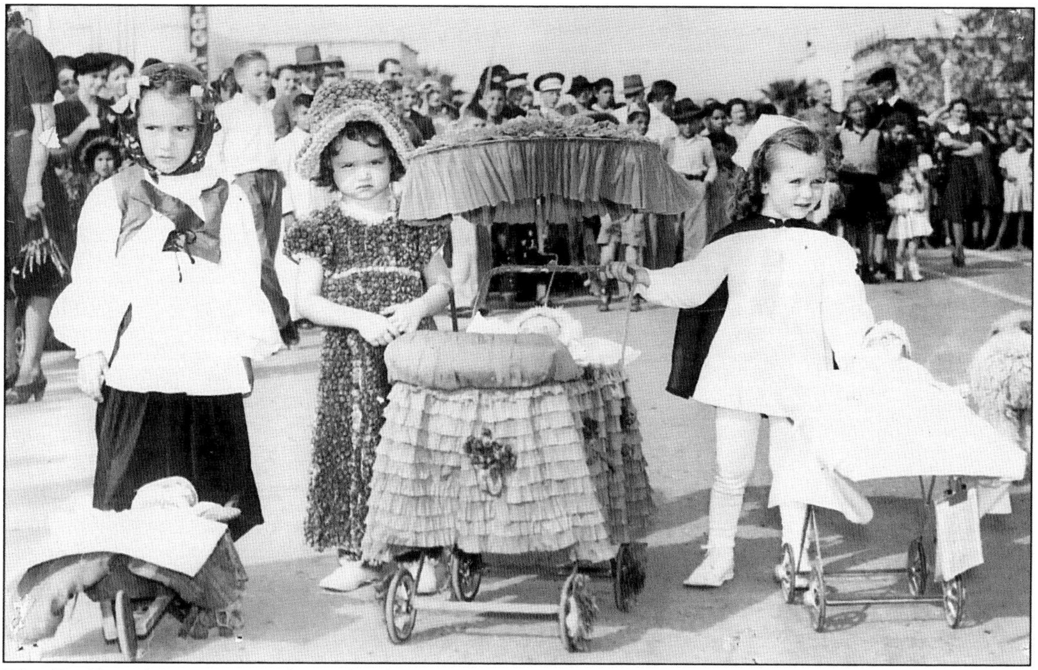

The Doll and Buggy Parade took place on Texas Boulevard and offered a grand prize of $2 for the best decorated buggy. This parade took place on Wednesday, December 13, 1933, at 2 p.m. The little girl in the center is Sonya Ann Bullard.

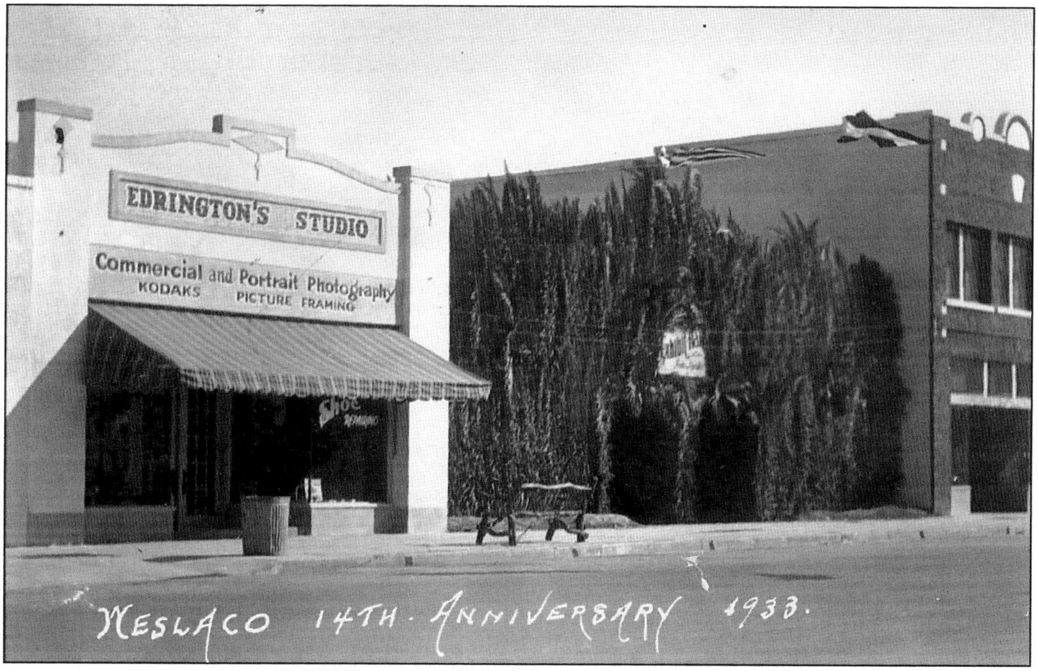


S.L. Edrington specialized in commercial and portrait photography. This view shows the studio in 1933, during Weslaco's 14th anniversary celebration.

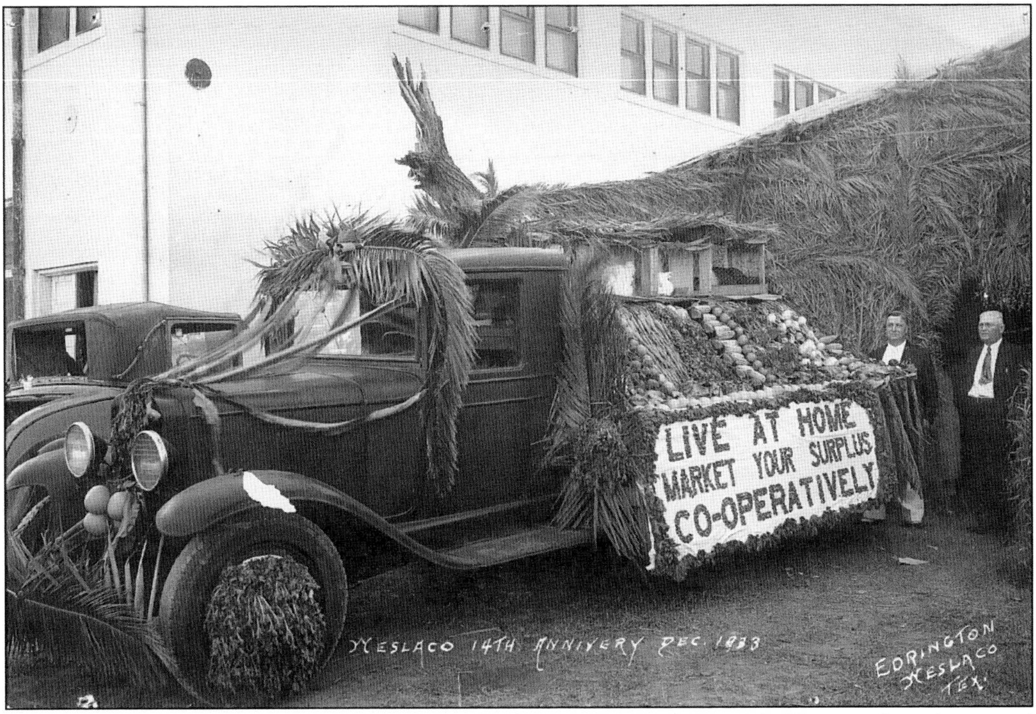


Weslaco's 14th anniversary celebration took place in December 1933. The truck is decorated with palm fronds and displays of fruit and vegetables. (Edrington Studio.)

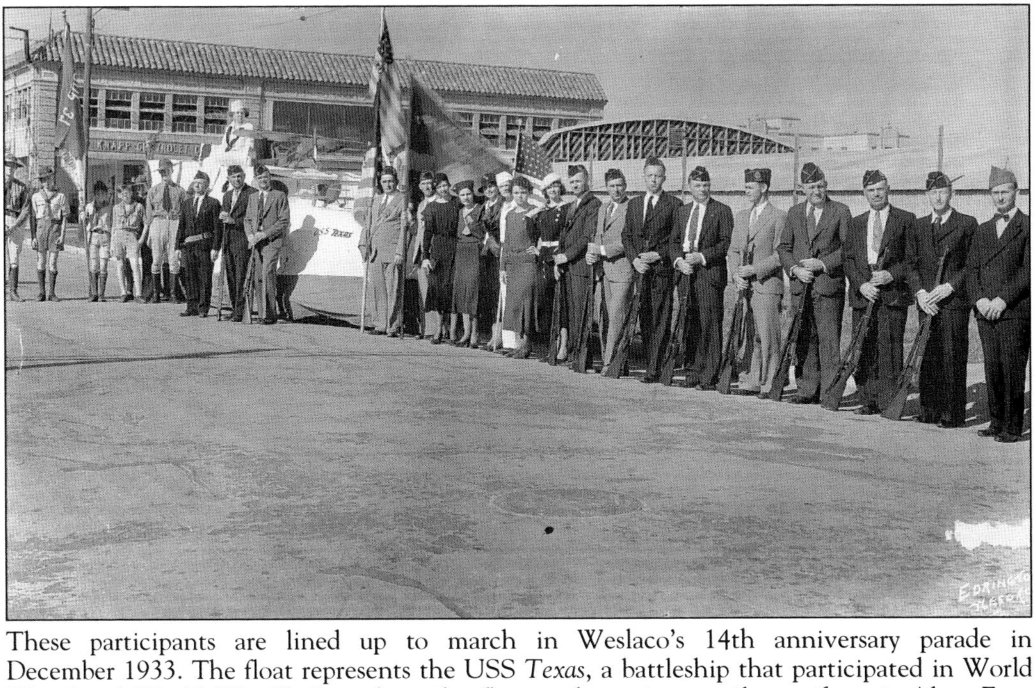

These participants are lined up to march in Weslaco's 14th anniversary parade in December 1933. The float represents the USS *Texas*, a battleship that participated in World War I and World War II. Seated on the float and wearing a sailor uniform is Alma Fort. (Edrington Studio.)

Bette Jean Voelkel won first prize as Little Bo Peep in Weslaco's 1934 pet parade. Pet parades were incorporated into all major events and celebrations. (Courtesy of Mr. and Mrs. Otto McFarland.)

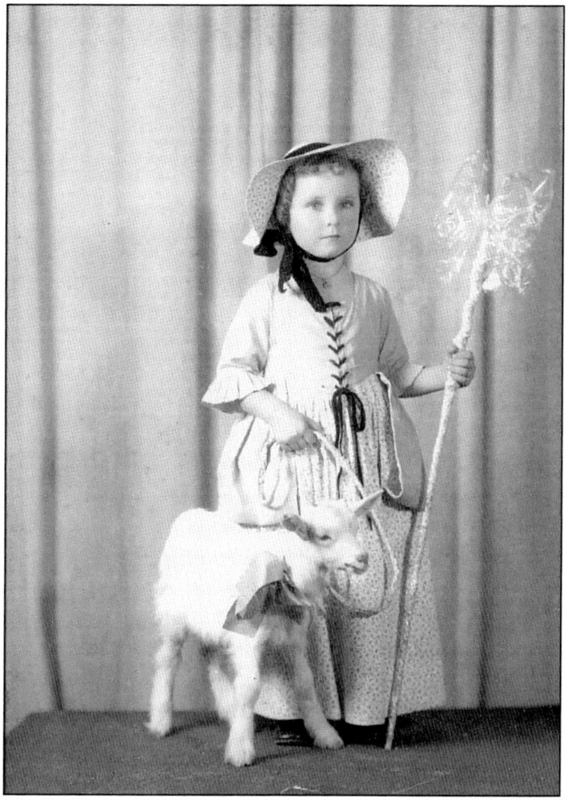

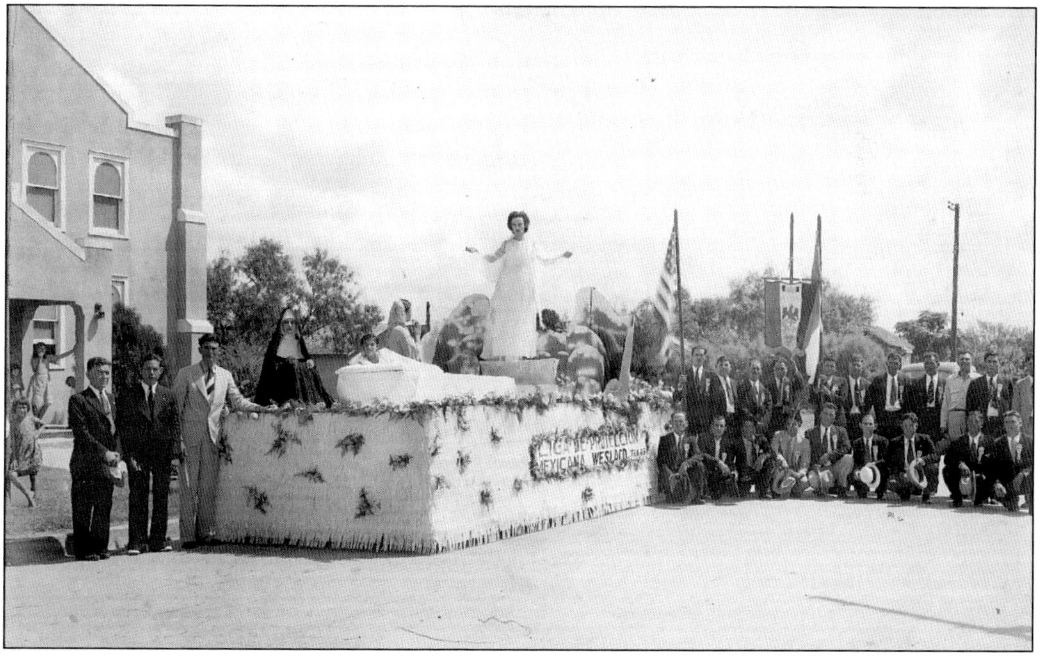


The fraternal organization Liga Protección Mexicana (Mexican Protection League) took part in celebrating Mexican national holidays. This 1936 image depicts a float for a parade held in honor of Mexico's Independence Day, September 16th. (Edrington Studio.)

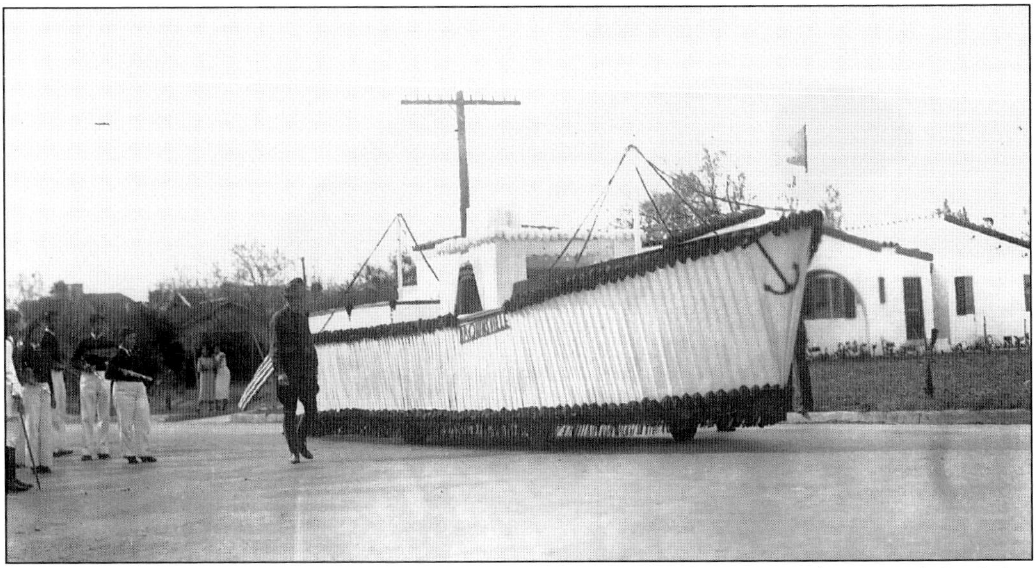

In 1936, the Brownsville Chamber of Commerce entered this float in Weslaco's 17th birthday party and won first prize in the municipal division of the parade. Ten thousand people attended the celebration. The first citrus style show took place on a platform constructed between the Masonic building and B.K. Traylor Man's Store on Texas Boulevard. Many Weslaco citizens consider this the most successful of the birthday parties.

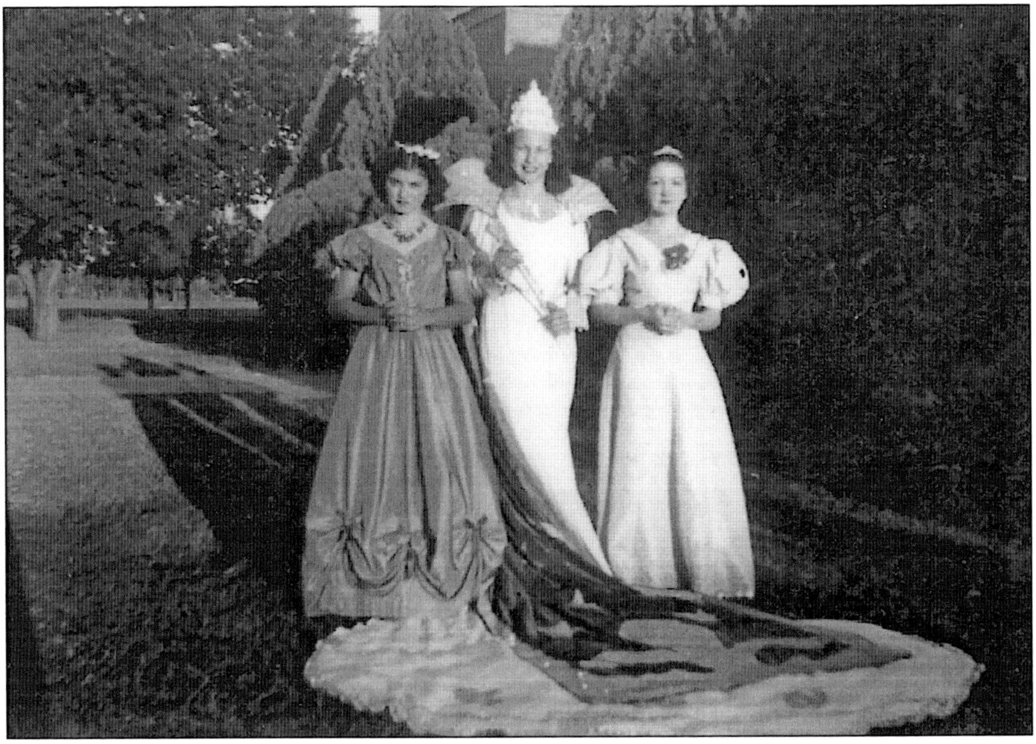

Miss Concepción Leyva (center) was the queen of the September 16, 1339 Mexican Independence Day celebration. Her court consisted of Miss Dominga Villarreal (left) and Miss Trinidad Molina (right). (Courtesy of Connie Lincoln.)

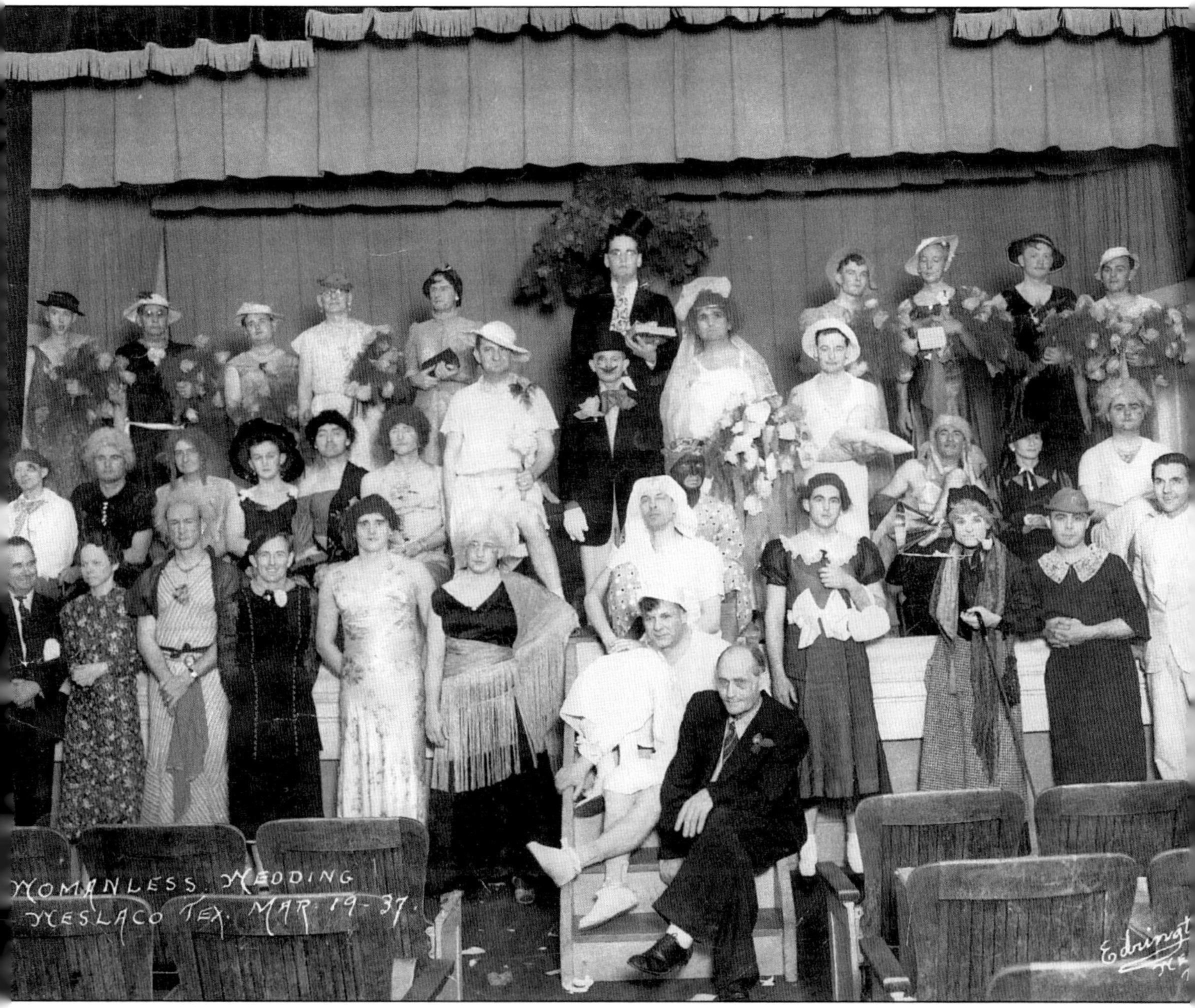


One of the men's clubs staged a "womanless wedding" on March 19, 1937. (Edrington Studio.)

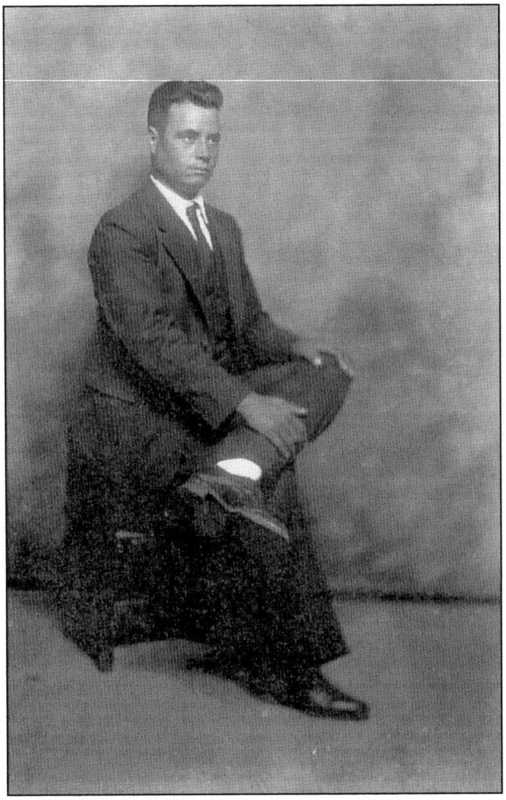

Don Alberto Leyva, a prominent businessman and the father of Concepción Leyva, was a native of Spain. Between 1930 and 1939, he owned a gasoline station and grocery store. Leyva was also a field foreman and citrus buyer for packing sheds. (Courtesy of Connie Lincoln.)

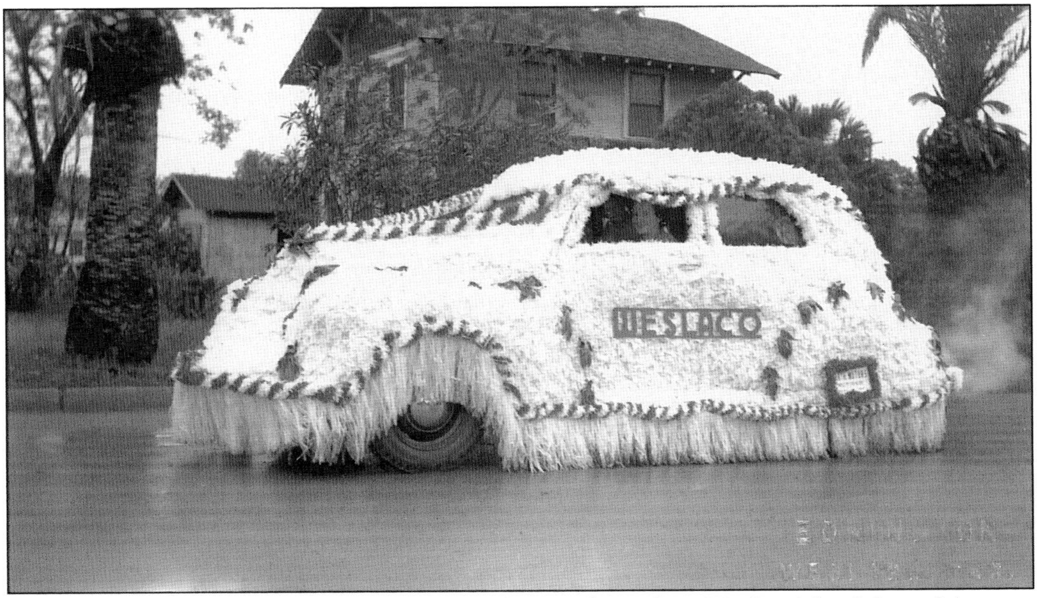


This decorated early model car was entered in the grand parade at Weslaco's birthday celebration on December 11, 1937. (Edrington Studio.)

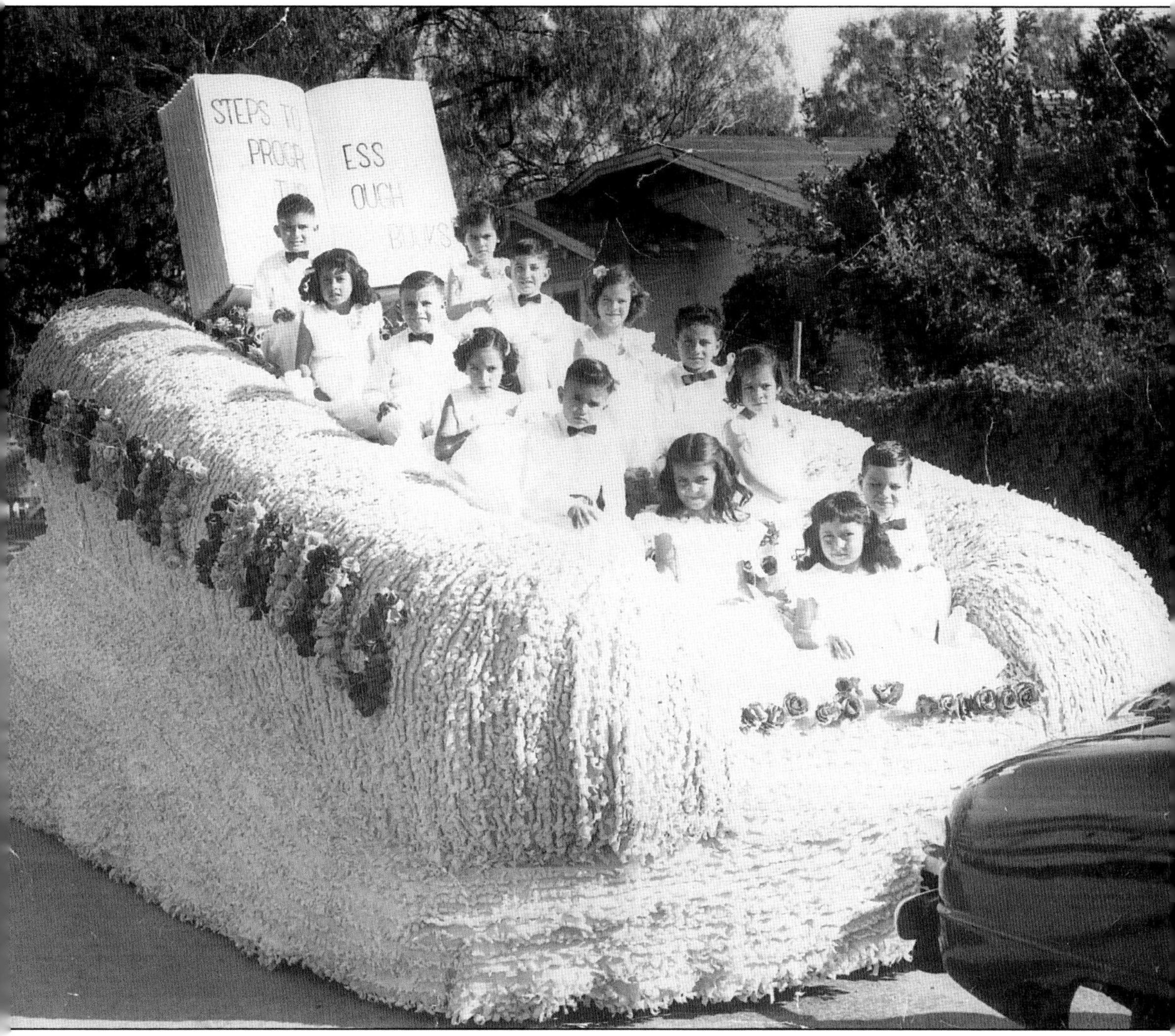


Over the years, floats entered in Weslaco parades and birthday celebrations became more elaborate. This is a float entered in Weslaco's 29th anniversary parade on December 9, 1948.

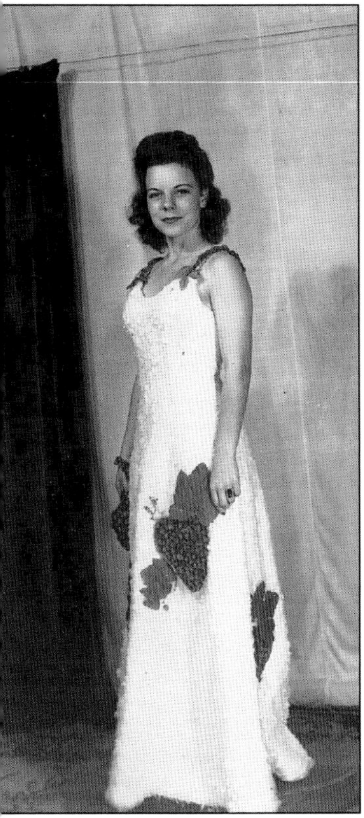
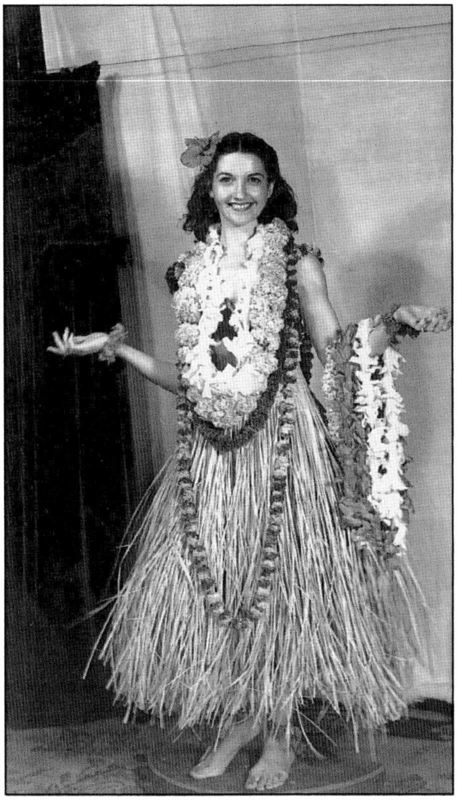
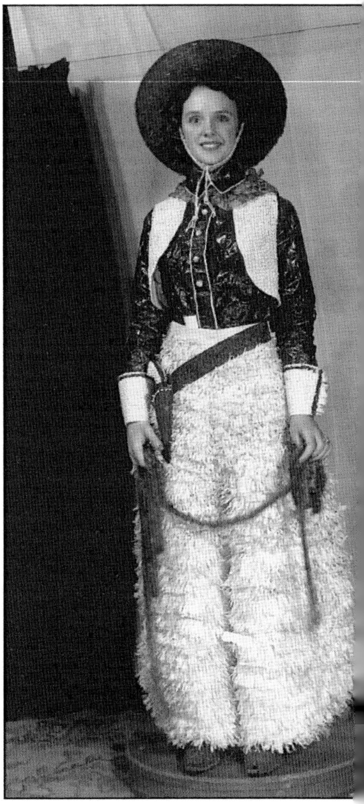

Costumes for "The Fruit, Vegetable, and Flower Show" required creativity, hard work, and secrecy. Each costume was planned over several months and with one model in mind. The basic garment was made of unbleached muslin, often dyed to match the fruit, vegetable, or flower being used to cover it. Dressmakers used cellophane to wrap fresh fruit or vegetable parts to keep them from drying out. Dried citrus membrane proved to be the most versatile raw material. Every article worn by the model had to be covered with parts of a fruit, vegetable, or flower, including shoes and jewelry. The finished costumes were stored in an icehouse and taken out at the last possible moment to be worn by a shivering model.

*Left:* Miss Shirley McCasland, representing the Junior Literary Review Club of Weslaco, wore an evening gown made of hand-carded and quilted cotton. The grape cluster trim of bachelor button blooms was adorned with real grape tendrils and leaves. (Edrington Studio.)

*Center:* Mrs. Ann Farley of Mercedes, Texas, represented the Weslaco Fine Arts Club. The skirt of her Hawaiian hula costume was made of pampas grass and Valley-grown chrysanthemums, roses, marigolds, bougainvillea, and red honeysuckle. Hibiscus formed the leis. (Edrington Studio.)

*Right:* Marjorie Schwartz represented Brown-Williams Produce Company of Mercedes. The chaps of her cowboy outfit were made with corn husks, and the shirt and pants were grapefruit leaves. The hat, belt, gun, and boots were made of ground grapefruit leaves. (Edrington Studio.)

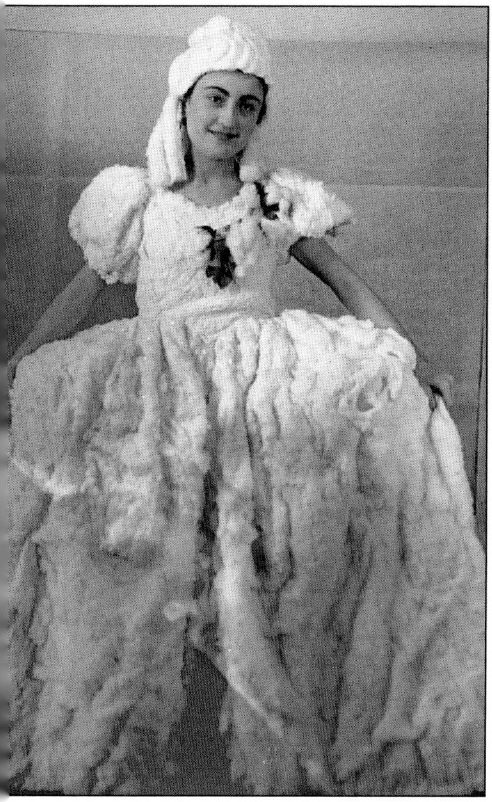

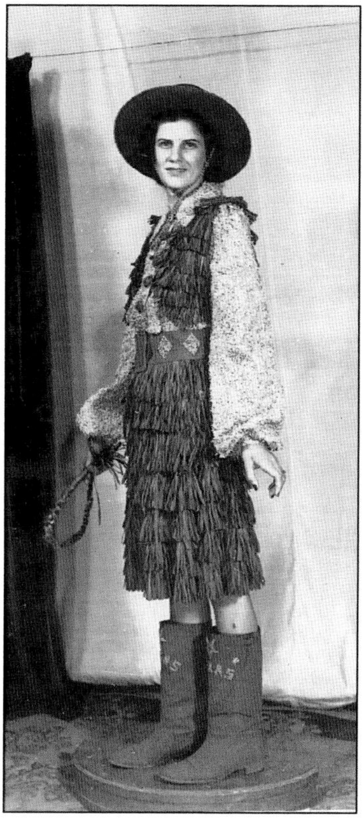

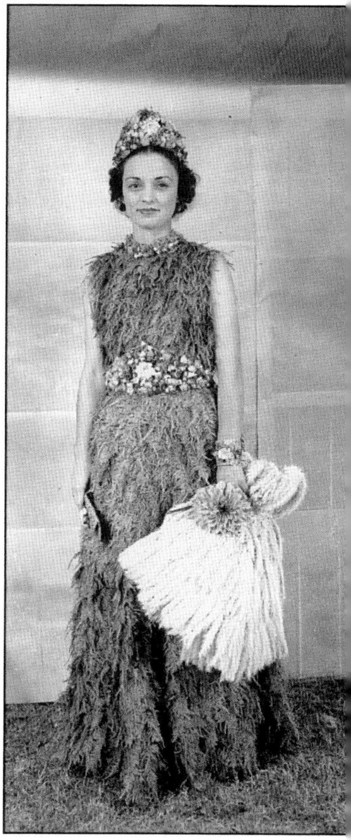

*Left:* Miss Amparo Rodriguez of Reynosa wore a costume and wig made of carded cotton from the Rio Grande Valley.

*Center:* Mrs. Phillip O'Connell, representing Evergreen Farms Co. of Elsa, wore a costume covered with dehydrated cereal grass. Her blouse was of barley seeds, and the skirt and jacket were made of oats.

*Right:* Mrs. Noah Fry of Elsa, representing F.H. Vahlsing, wore an evening dress made of 325 bushels of parched parsley.

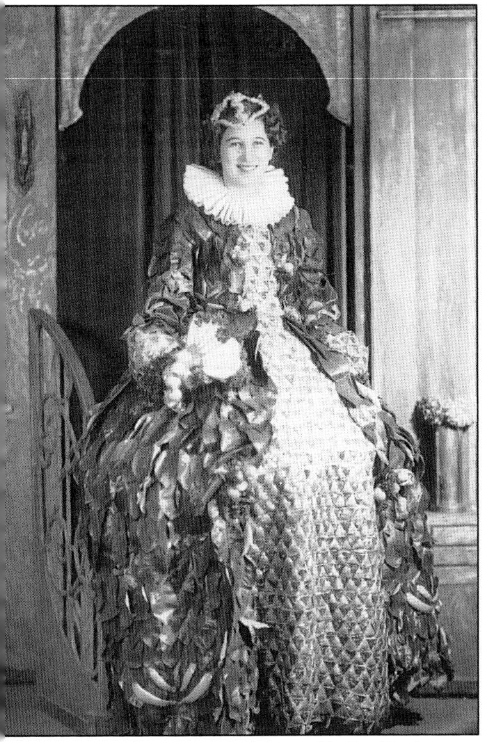

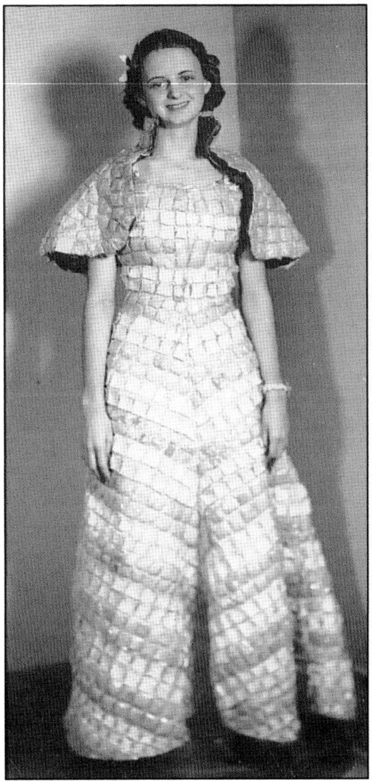

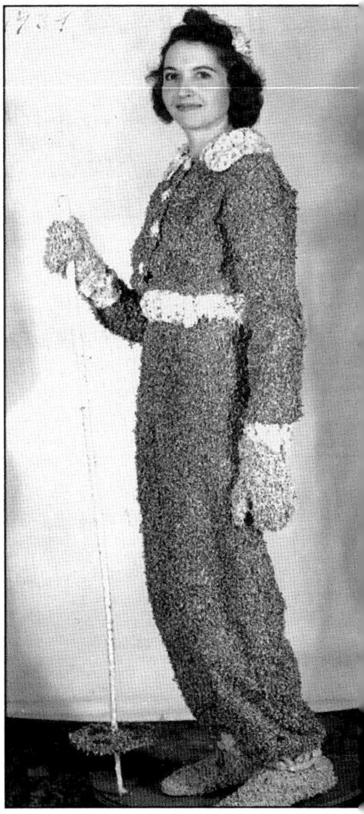

*Left:* Mrs. Golda LaDuke Roberts wore this Elizabethan costume in 1936. The headpiece was constructed of wire covered in citrus seeds. The ruff was made of the inside of citrus peel, while the dress was covered in citrus leaves and trimmed with grapefruit, orange, and tangerine peel. The puffed sleeves, decorative front panel, and her fan (with parched parsley trim) were also made of citrus peel. (Edrington Studio.)

*Center:* Miss Mardelle Kendall won first prize in the evening wear division in 1937. She represented Weslaco Business and Professional Women's Club. The evening dress was made in strips of orange peel and the reverse of grapefruit peel, making orange and white stripes. The cape was reversible, with grapefruit leaves on one side. The costume required six bushels of grapefruit and 2,400 pieces of grapefruit of 1.5 inches square and wrapped in cellophane, plus 425 hours to complete. (Edrington Studio.)

*Right:* Miss Ann Farley represented Weslaco Business and Professional Women's Club in 1939. This third-prize ski costume was made of petals of bachelor button flowers and trimmed with white baby chrysanthemums. The alpenstock was made of citrus wood covered with the inside portion of citrus. (Edrington Studio.)

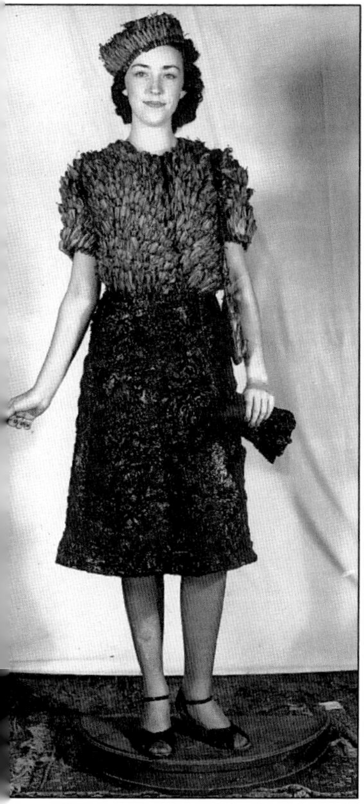

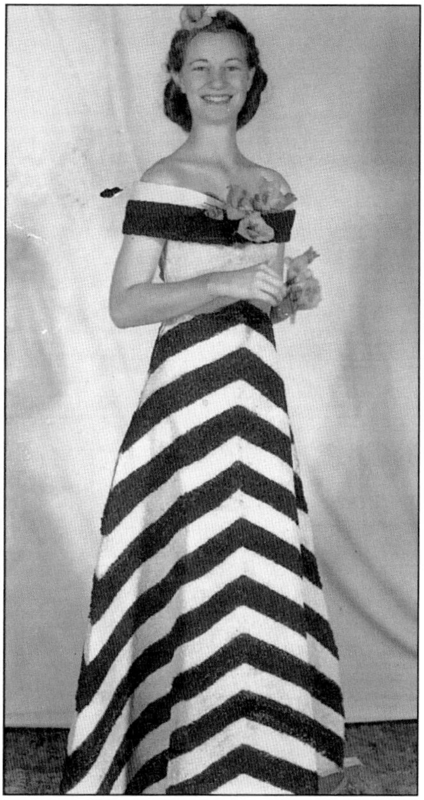

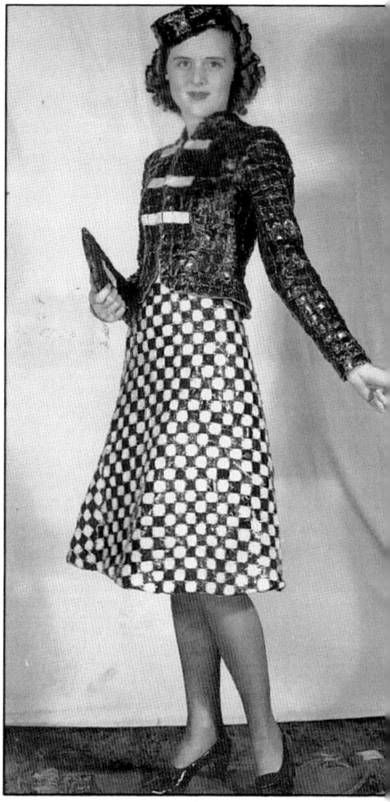

*Left:* Millicent Yoder represented Brown-Williams of Mercedes in 1939. Her skirt and gloves were made of 200 peppers. The bodice, hat, and shoulder bag required 1,200 turk's cap blossoms.

*Center:* Betty Compere represented Weslaco Kiwanis Club in 1939. This lovely evening gown was fashioned of stripes formed by black onion seed and white ground corn. The accents of the corsage and headdress were made of red gladiola petals.

*Right:* Alice Edrington took first place in the street costume division in 1939. Her suit was constructed of eggplant with checks of eggplant and citrus membrane. These were cut in one-inch squares and also covered her pillbox hat and envelope purse. Miss Edrington represented the Weslaco Parent-Teachers Association.

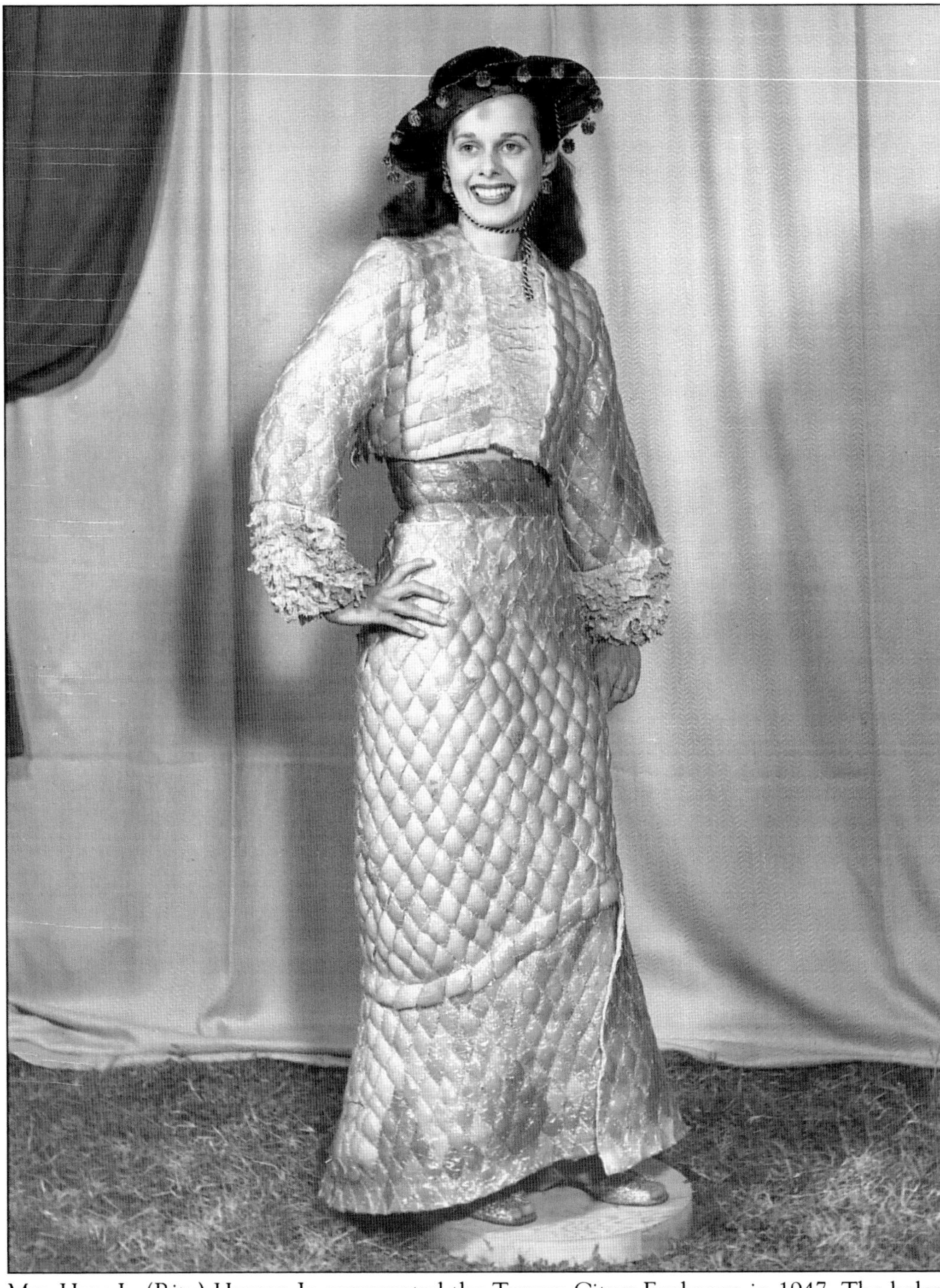

Mrs. Hans L. (Rita) Hansen Jr. represented the Texsun Citrus Exchange in 1947. The bolero jacket and skirt were made of orange peel wrapped in cellophane. The cummerbund, trim, and flounce on the skirt were made of lemon peel, while the blouse and sleeve ruffles were dried grapefruit membrane. The hat was eggplant peel with balls of bachelor buttons. The costume cost only $5.

Grace Dixon, who took first prize in 1939, represented Weslaco High School Band parents. Like the green and gold band uniform of Weslaco High School, the trousers were made of green peppers with braid trim of stems of date palm blossoms. The coat was made of the inside of grapefruit peel. The plume of the hat was yellow cockscomb, and the baton was bamboo with golden fruit on the end. (Edrington Studio.)

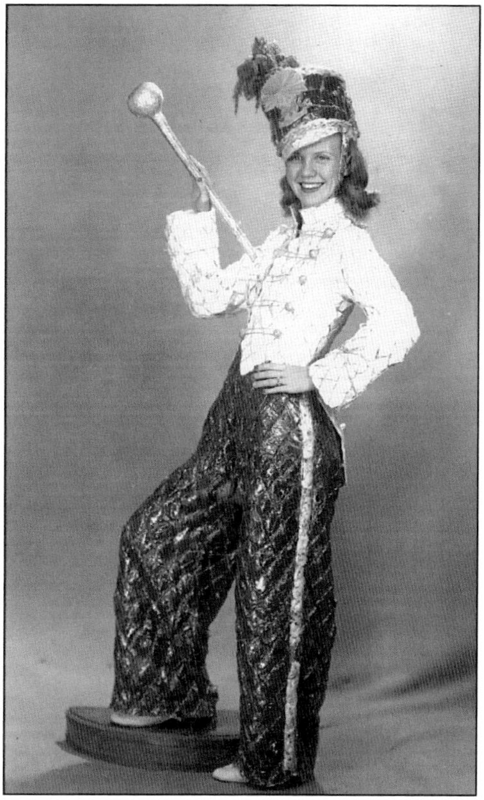

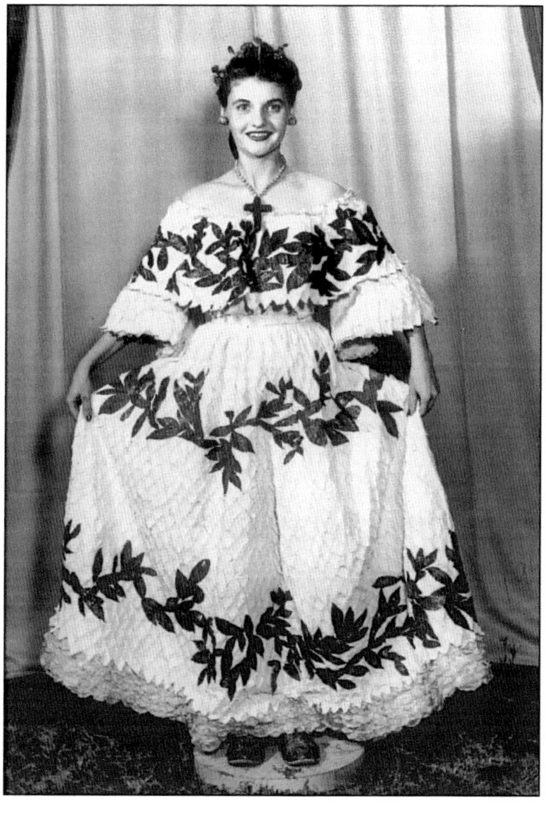

Mrs. Loretta Barbee was sponsored by the Weslaco Garden Club in 1948. She wore a gypsy dancer costume made mostly of the white, soft part of grapefruit peel. Grapefruit membrane was used for the lace, petticoat, and lining in the sleeves, and red poinsettias for the garland trim and slippers.

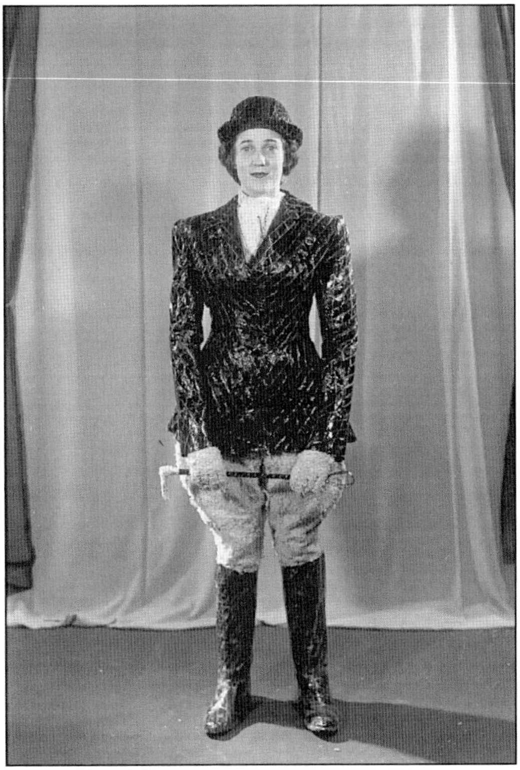

First place in the 1950 costume division went to Mrs. Henry Griffin Jr., for her riding costume. The coat, boots, and derby were all made of eggplant peel.

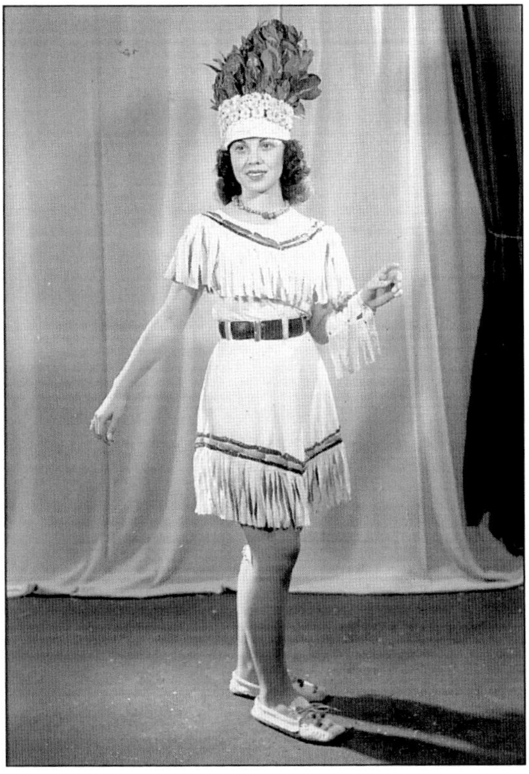

Miss Pat Arrington was an American Indian maid in the 1950 show. Her dress was made of finely ground cornmeal with trimming of radish, green pepper, and popcorn.

# *Five*

# Gambling on Mother Nature

The soil of the river delta was rich, but insect pests were healthy, water had to be supplied by pumps and canals, and produce had to travel a long way to market. Disasters, whether natural or man-made, often meant ruin for farmers and city folks alike. In 1923, Texas A&M University built an agricultural experiment station in Weslaco to study crops, soil, and water conservation, fertilizer use, insects, plant diseases, and the effects of climate. In 1938, the U.S. Department of Agriculture established a research facility in Weslaco as well. Texas College of Arts and Industries (now Texas A&M University-Kingsville) opened its citrus and vegetable training center for citrus research in 1947. The work of scientists at the research stations has led to better-tasting fruit, improved marketing techniques, and the control of plant diseases.

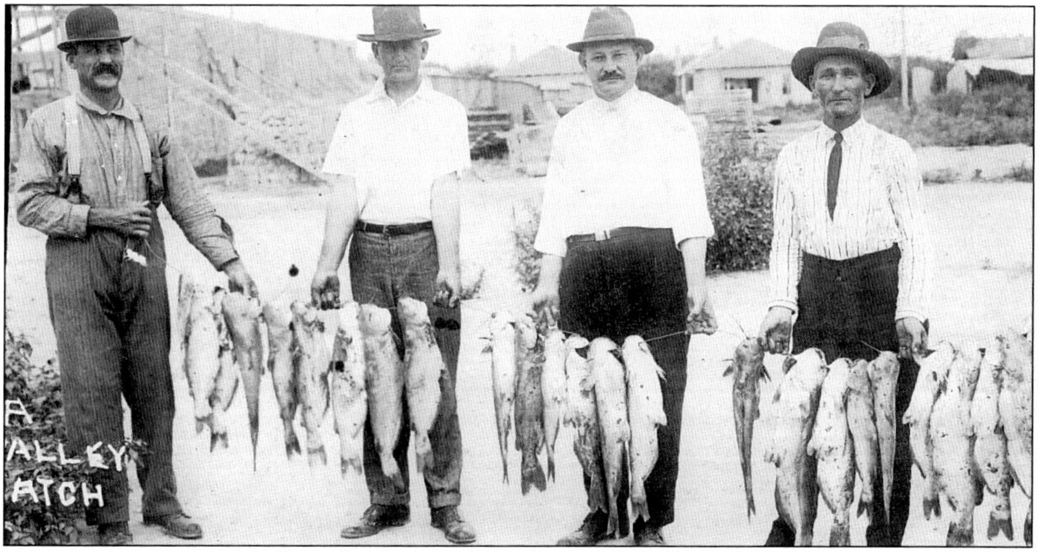

Fishing was a popular and usually successful pastime for Valley residents and visitors.

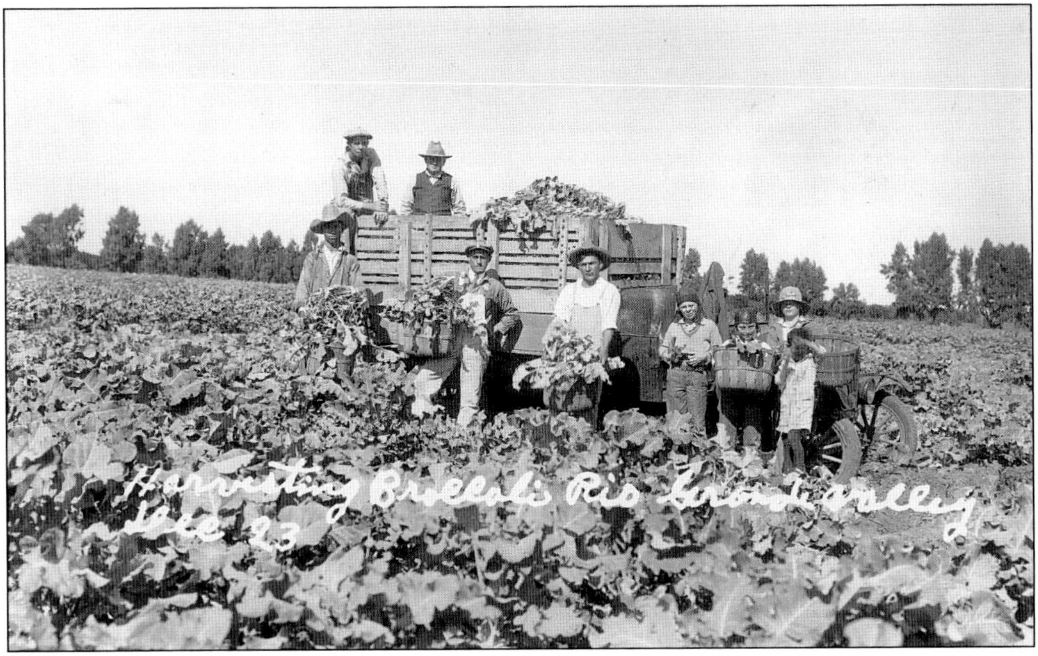


Broccoli had to be harvested by hand.

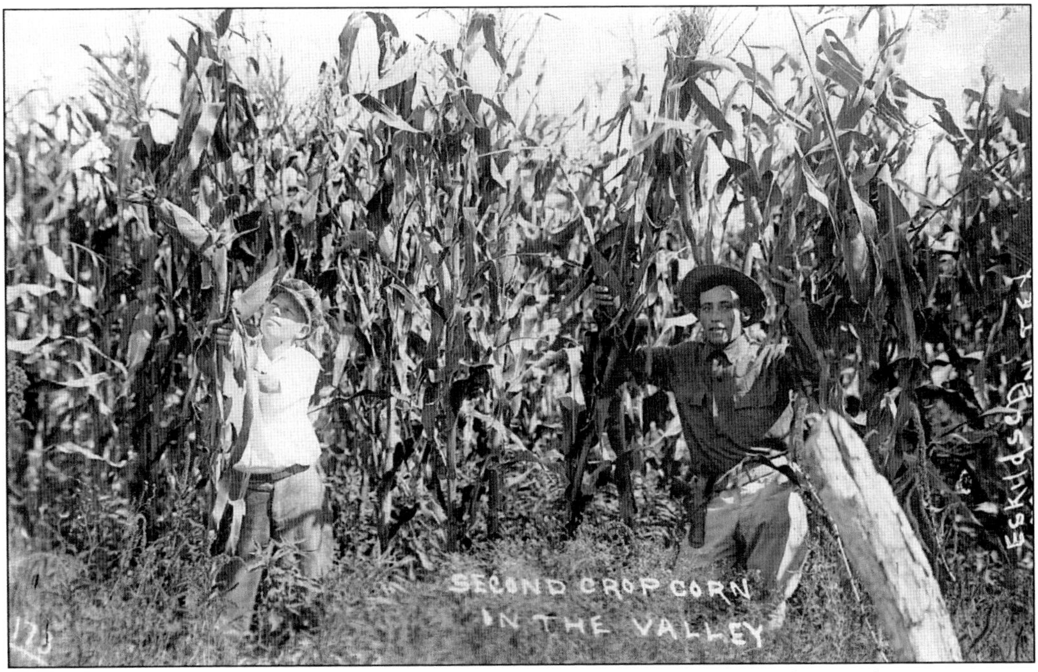


Agriculture in the Rio Grande Valley was heavy in corn. This is a second crop of corn grown in one season. Note the gun and holster worn by the man on the right. (Eskildsen Studio.)

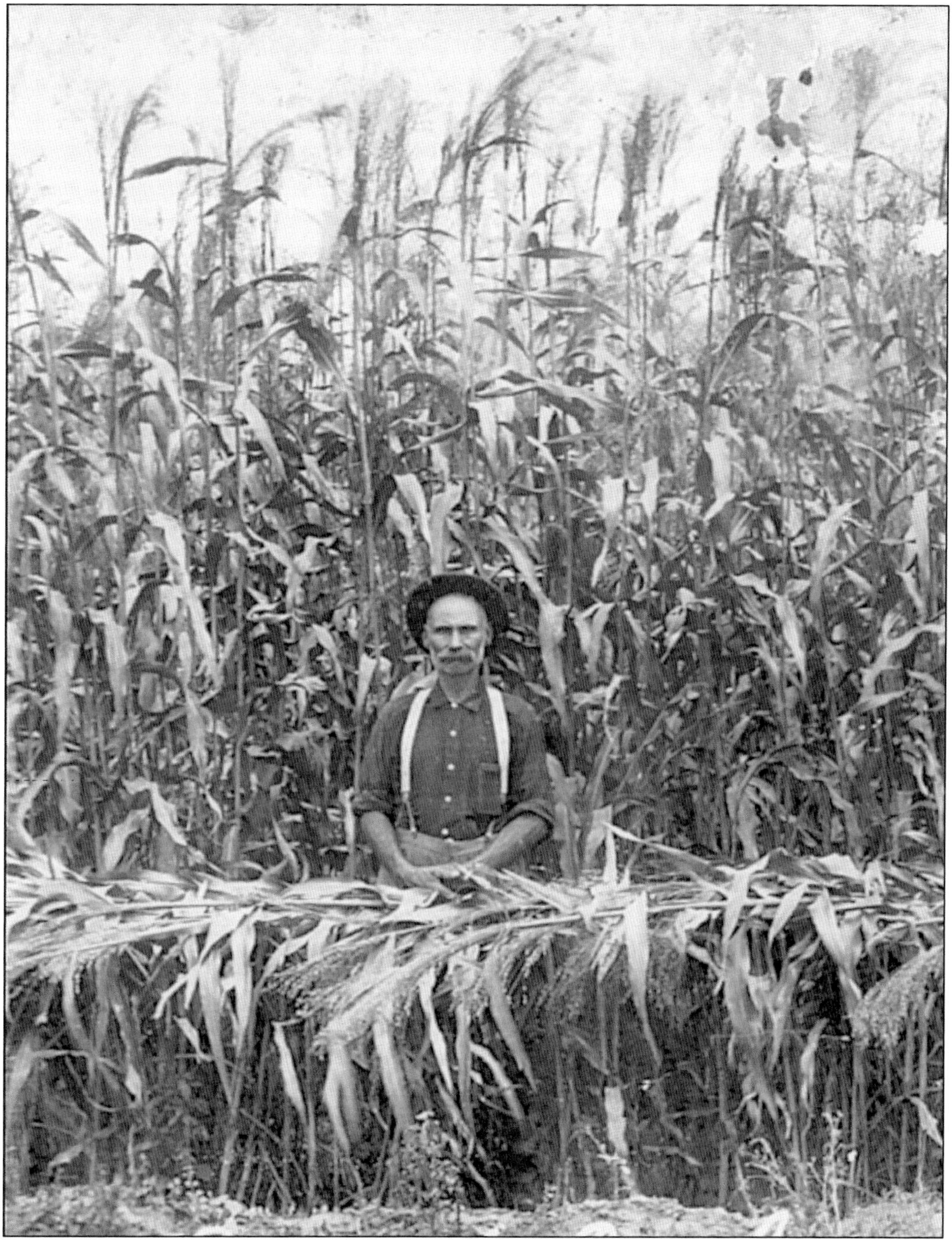

A Valley farmer grew this crop of broom corn. The corn was threshed in a wooden box with two spiked drums rotating in opposition to each other. Stems were recovered and sold to broom manufacturers.

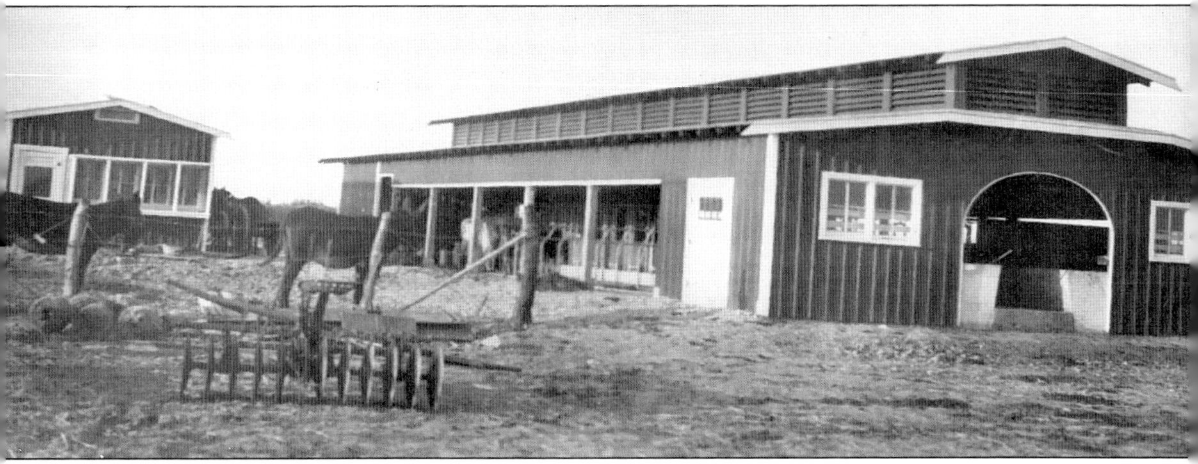

Lassiter's Jersey Dairy Barn, a showcase in 1922, was located at 616 East Sixth Street in Weslaco. (Yoder.)

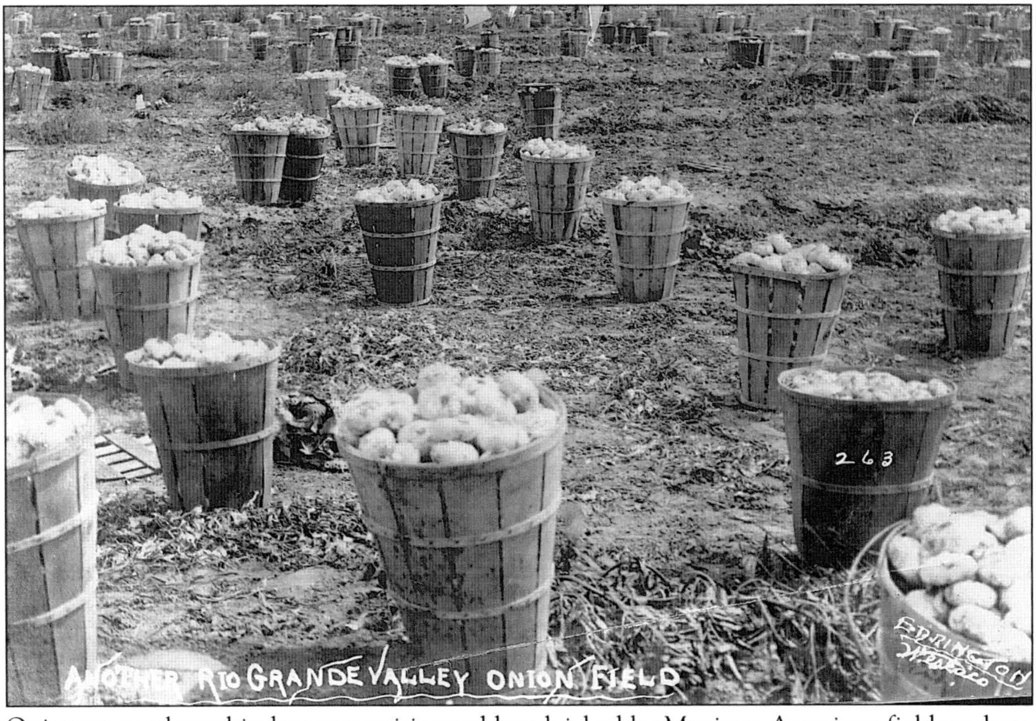


Onions were planted in large quantities and handpicked by Mexican-American field workers. (Edrington Studio.)

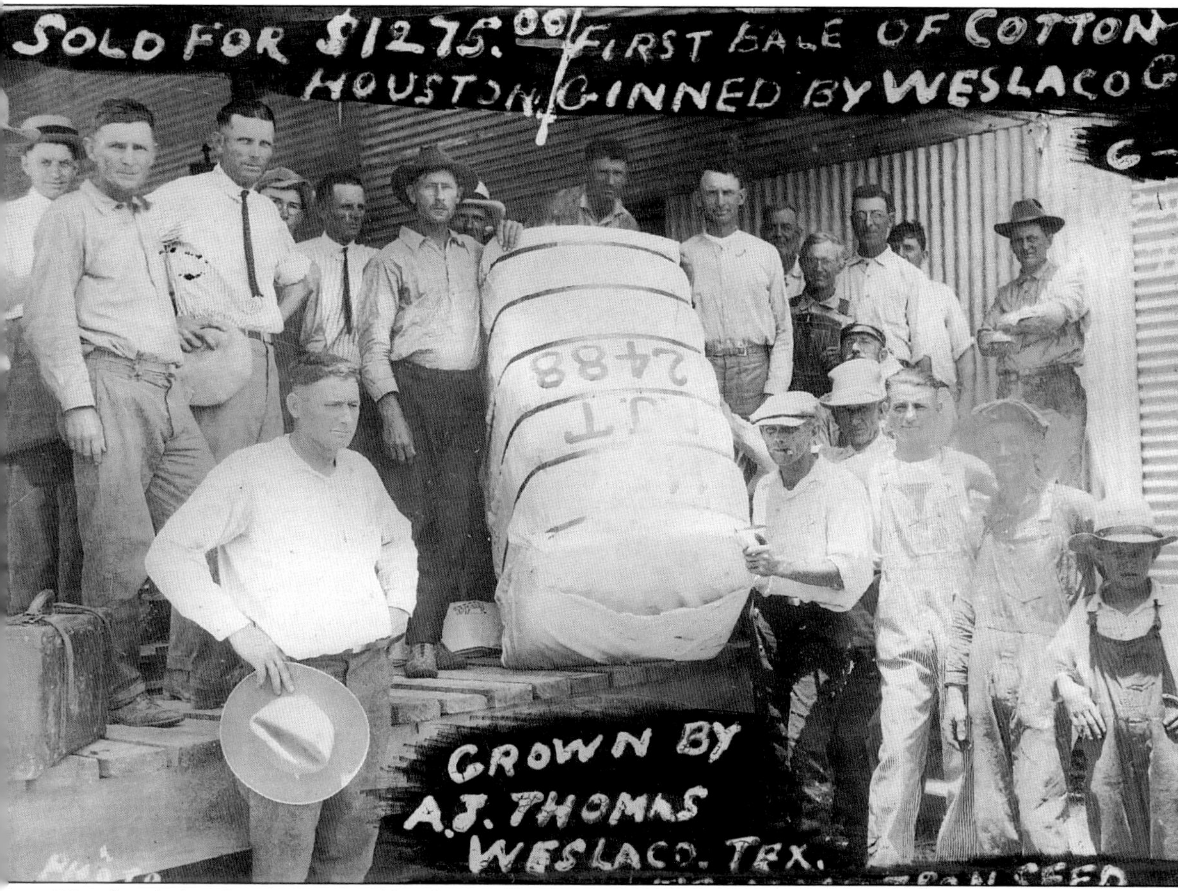


The first bale of cotton ginned by the Weslaco Gin Company on June 15, 1922, sold for $1,275 in Houston. The cotton was grown by A.J. Thomas of Weslaco using Watson Seed. Valley cotton is often the first cotton ginned in Texas each fall season. (Moore.)

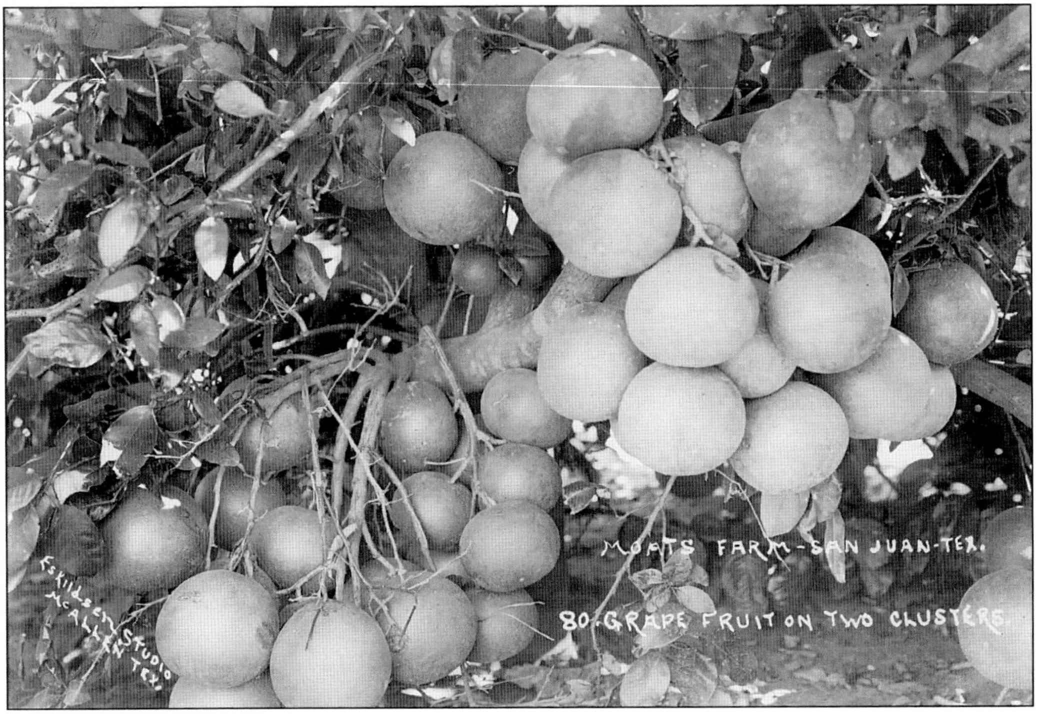


The Rio Grande Valley is widely known for its citrus production. Even in the early days, citrus was not only a main attraction but also an impressive cash crop. Moat's farm in San Juan, Texas, grew this citrus tree with 80 grapefruit on two clusters. (Eskildsen Studio.)

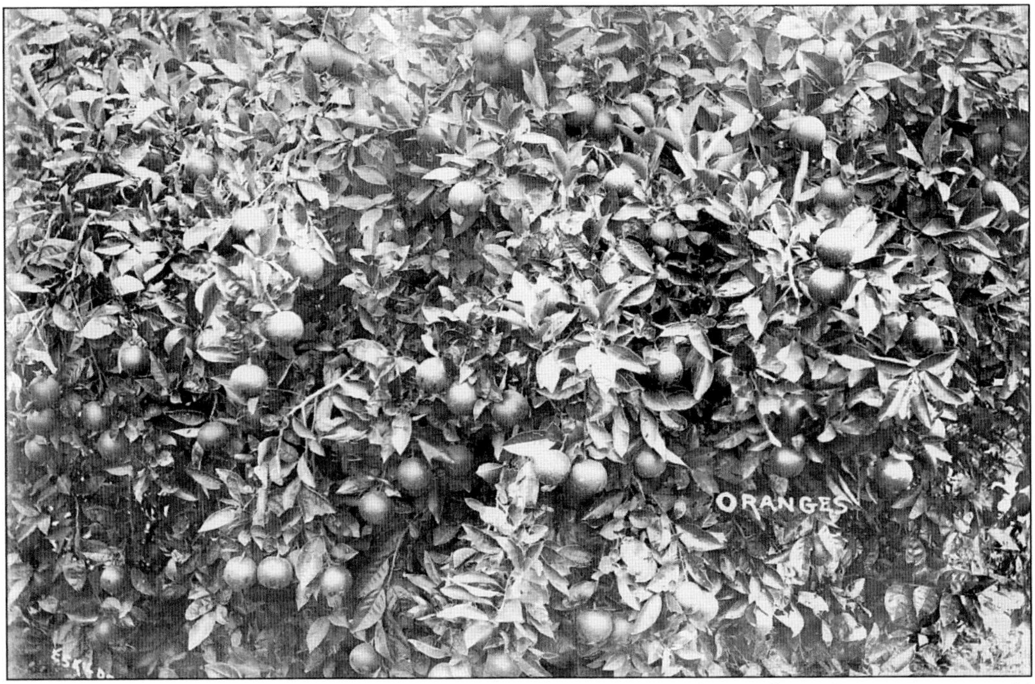


In addition to grapefruit trees, orange trees were grown in the Valley. Oranges were sold throughout Texas and the nation as fresh fruit and as juice. (Eskildsen Studio.)

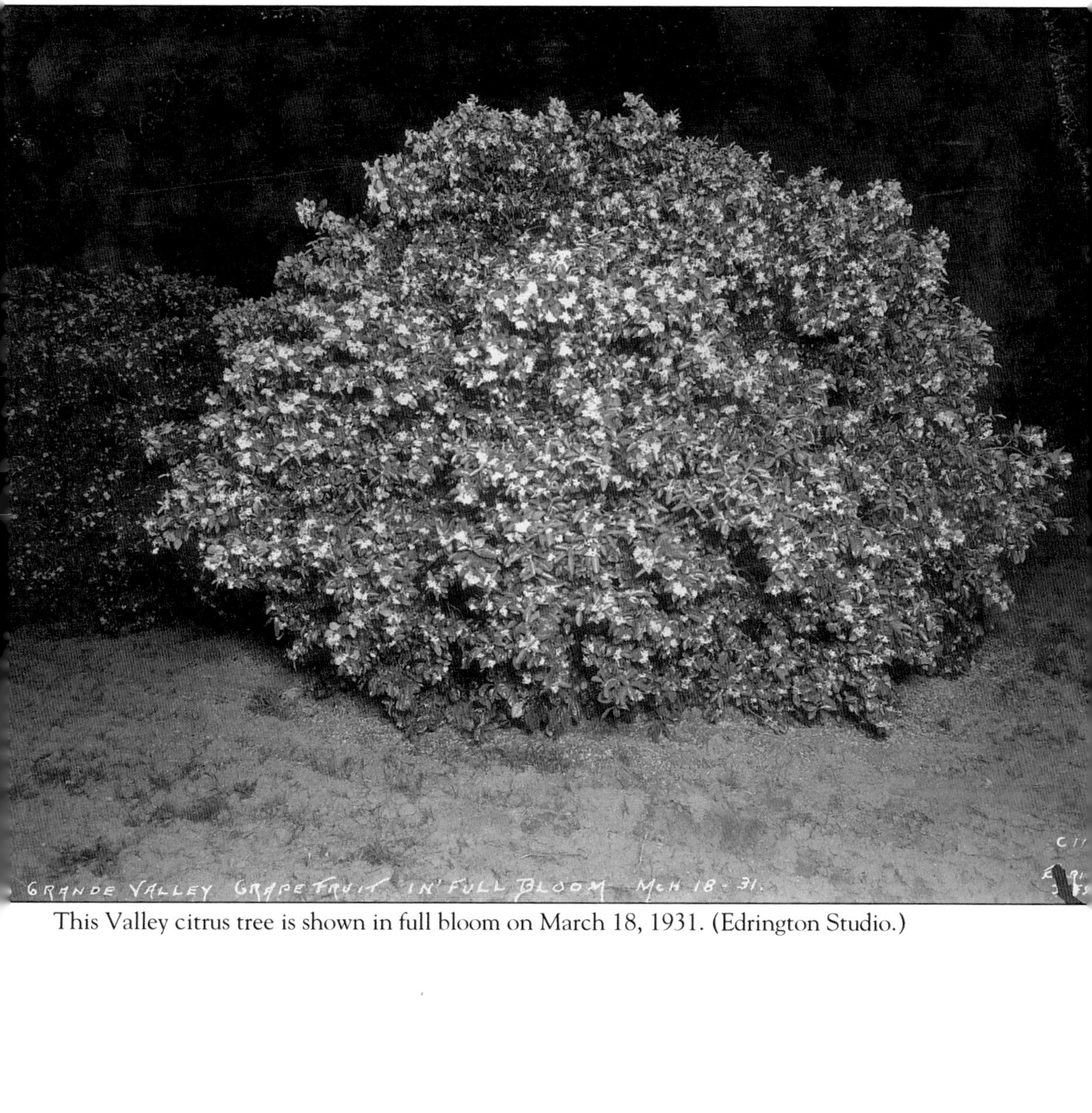


This Valley citrus tree is shown in full bloom on March 18, 1931. (Edrington Studio.)

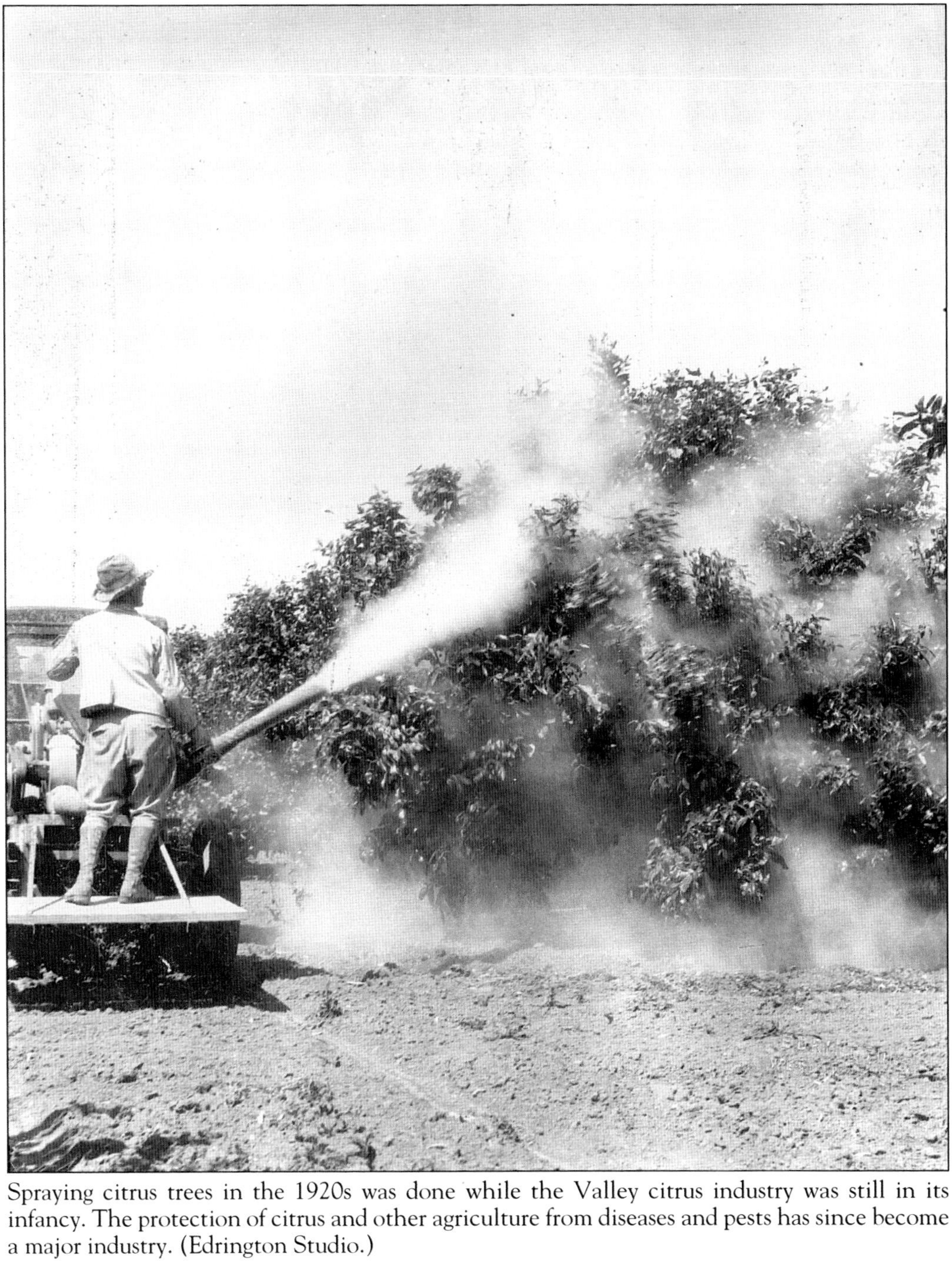

Spraying citrus trees in the 1920s was done while the Valley citrus industry was still in its infancy. The protection of citrus and other agriculture from diseases and pests has since become a major industry. (Edrington Studio.)

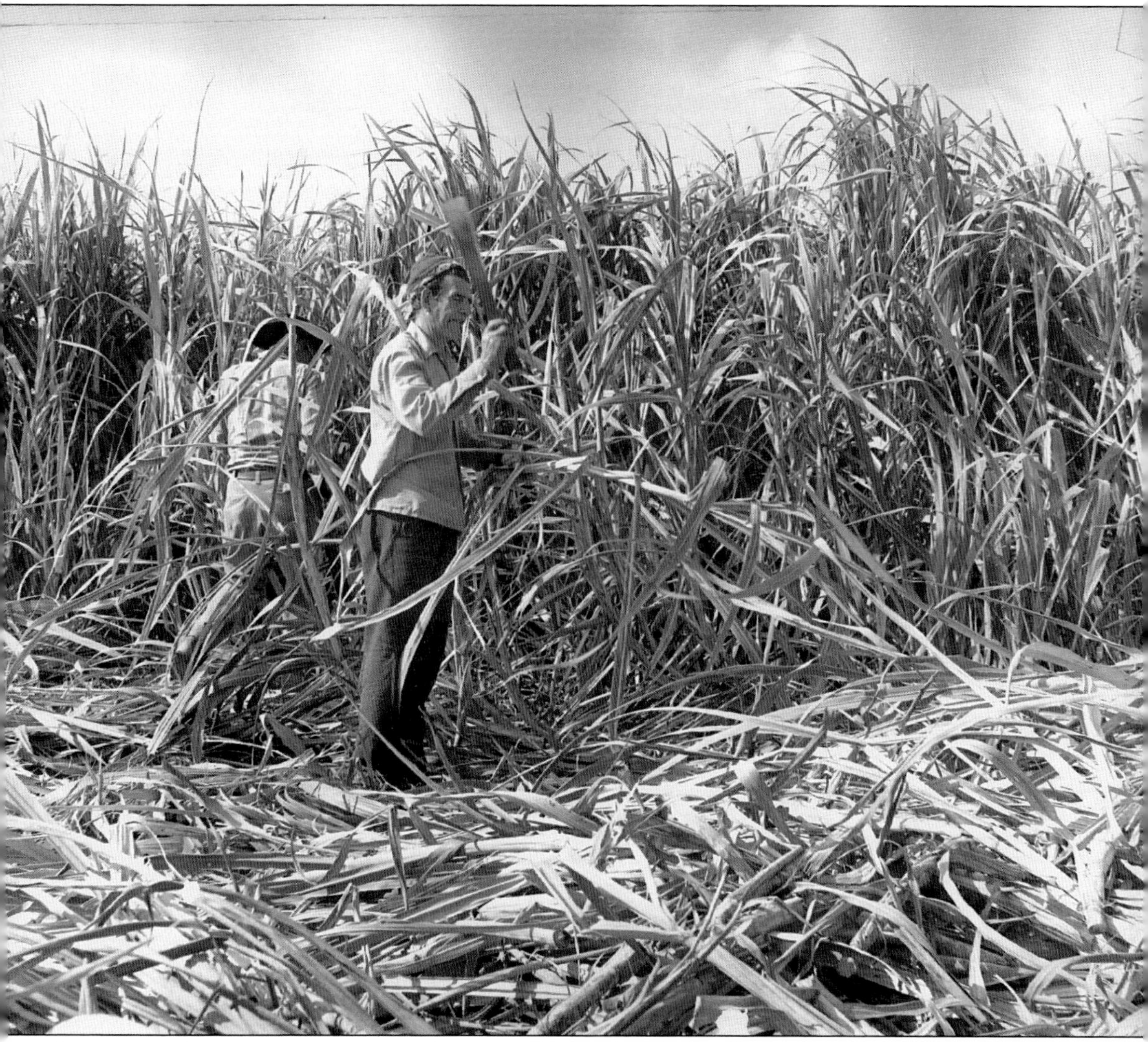

Growing and harvesting sugarcane began in the Valley during the early 1800s. By 1913, five large mills were in operation. Workers could harvest between 30 and 80 tons of raw product per acre, and the average was 40 tons per acre. Once sugarcane has been harvested, it does not need to be replanted but every eight to ten years. This image shows a field worker harvesting sugarcane by hand.

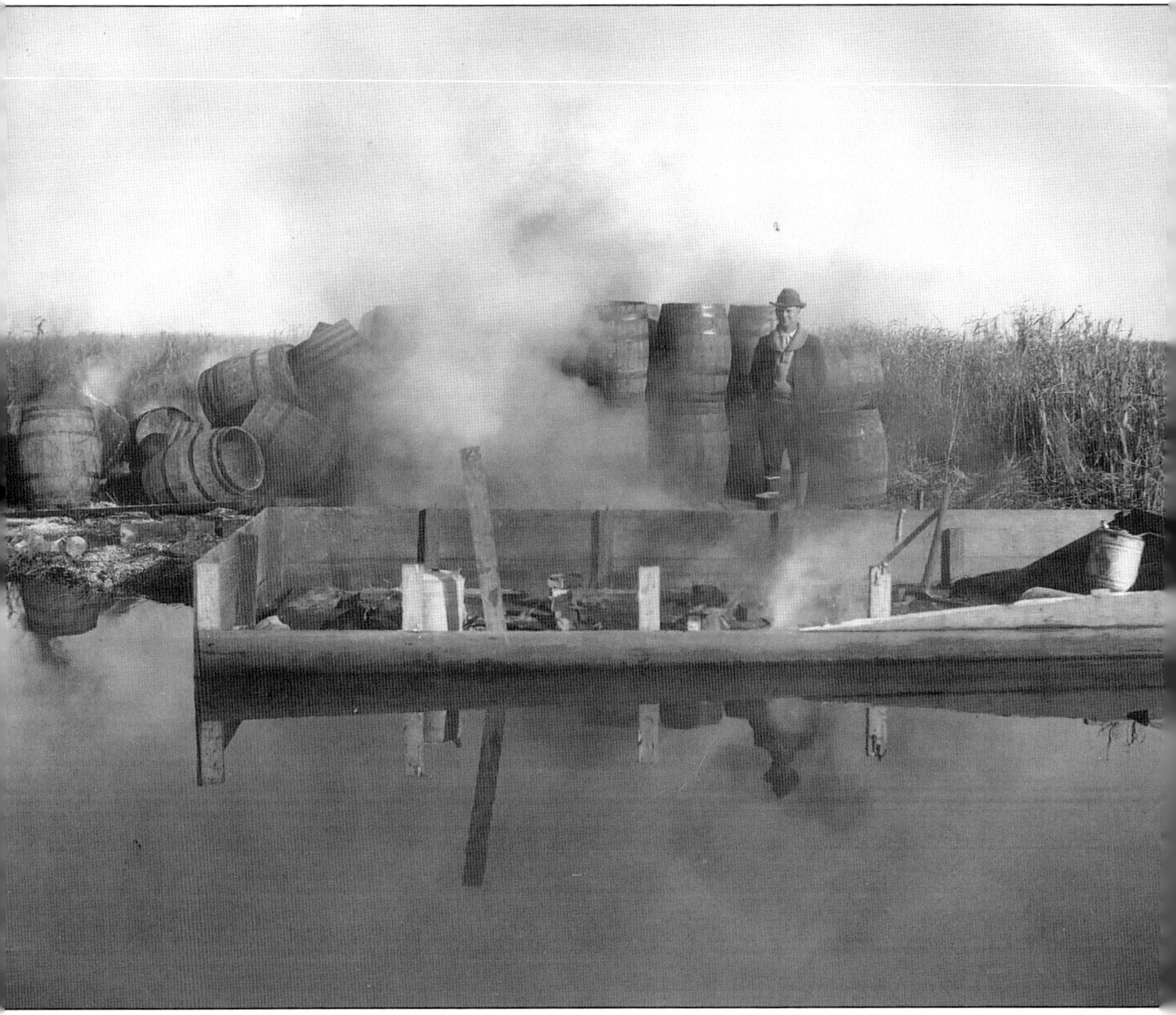

Pioneer Louis Brulay, a Matamoros merchant, opened a plantation in Brownsville in 1870 and later built a sugar mill. Even with poor transportation, there was money to be made with sugarcane, and it soon became a Valley cash crop. Another pioneer was John Closner, who planted sugar at his San Juan, Texas plantation. Other plantations sprang up in the Valley after World War I, but adverse economic conditions led to the demise of the sugar industry, and the last mill closed in 1921. This photograph shows the burning of sugarcane to begin the process of making syrup. The man supervising is unidentified. [Author's note: The sugarcane industry has since been revived.]

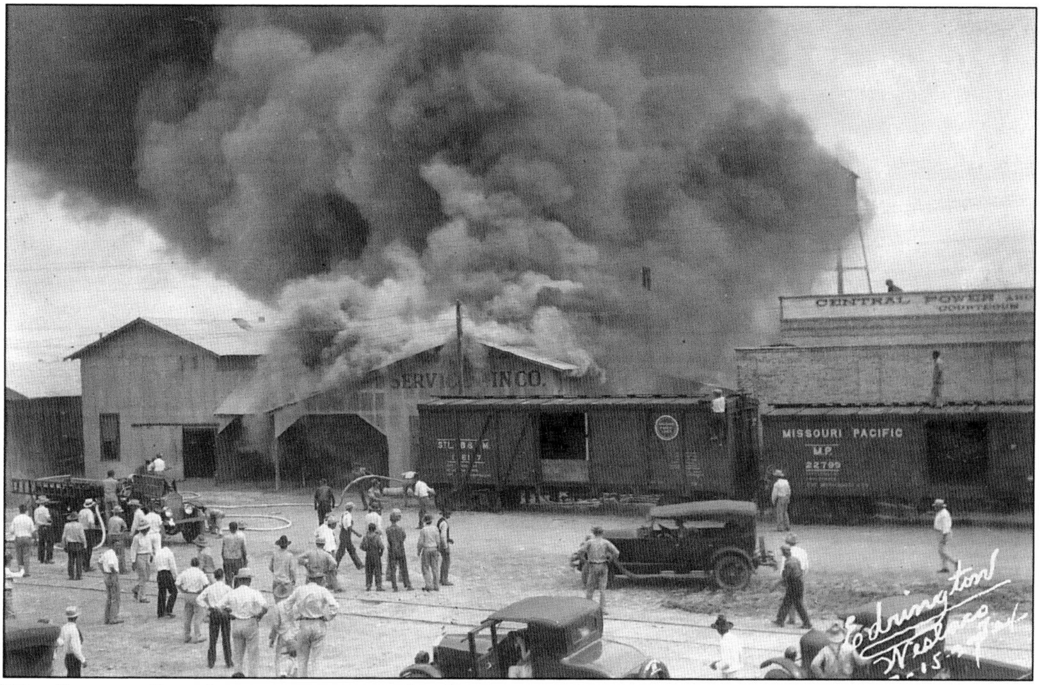


The Service Gin Company sustained a devastating fire on July 15, 1927. In 1926, there were three cotton gins operating in Weslaco, and together they ginned 10,000 bales of cotton. The Service Gin recovered after the fire and remained in business for many more years. (Edrington Studio.)

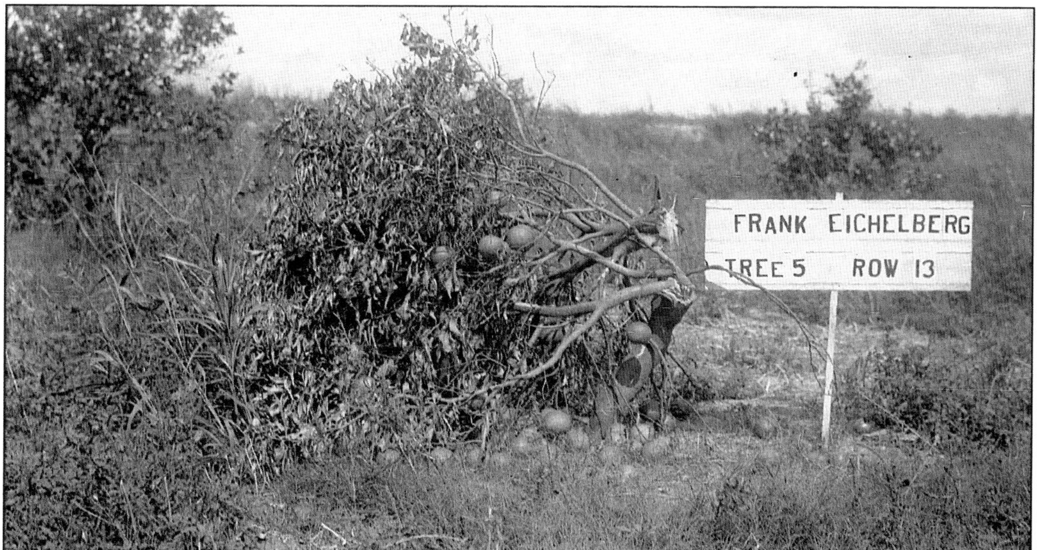


On Labor Day, September 4, 1933, a hurricane made landfall at Brownsville. Winds reached 130 miles per hour on the beaches and 106 miles per hour on land before winds blew away the anemometer. In the Rio Grande Valley, 40 people were killed, 500 were injured, and damages amounted to $16,903,100. Ninety percent of the entire citrus crop was destroyed. This photo shows a downed grapefruit tree at Engelman Gardens, an experimental farm north of Weslaco. (Edrington Studio.)

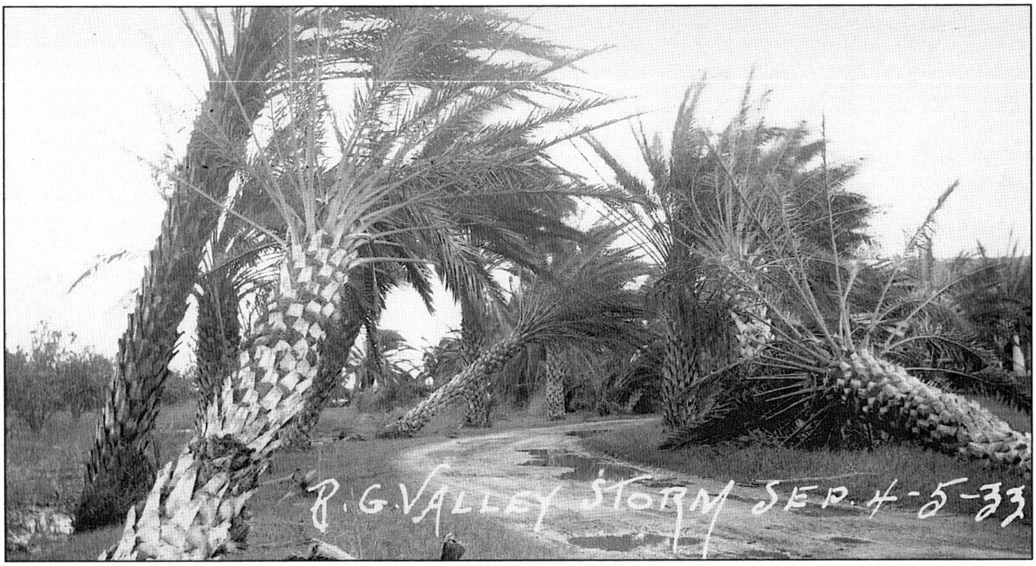


Palm trees were severely damaged all over the Valley.

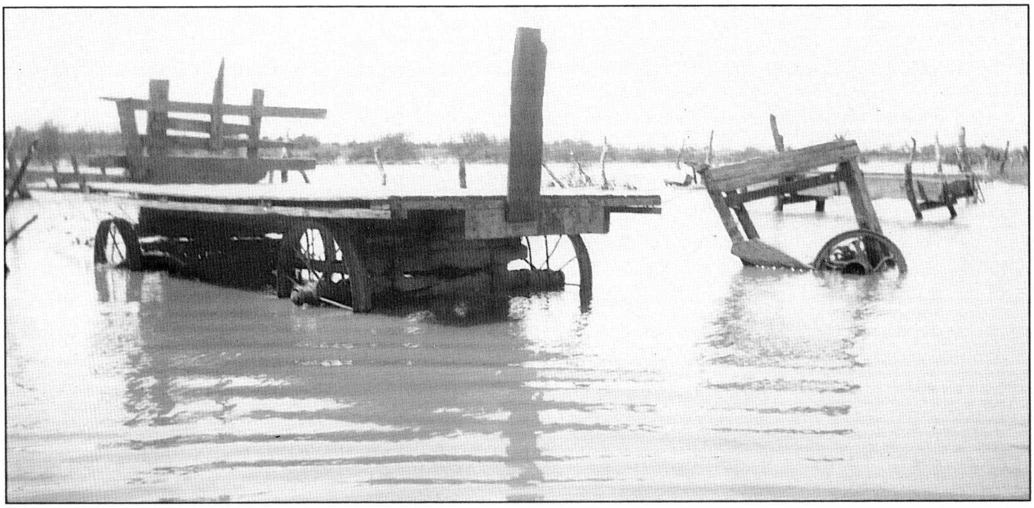

Farm equipment and a wagon are partially submerged in the flood waters resulting from the hurricane. (Edrington Studio.)

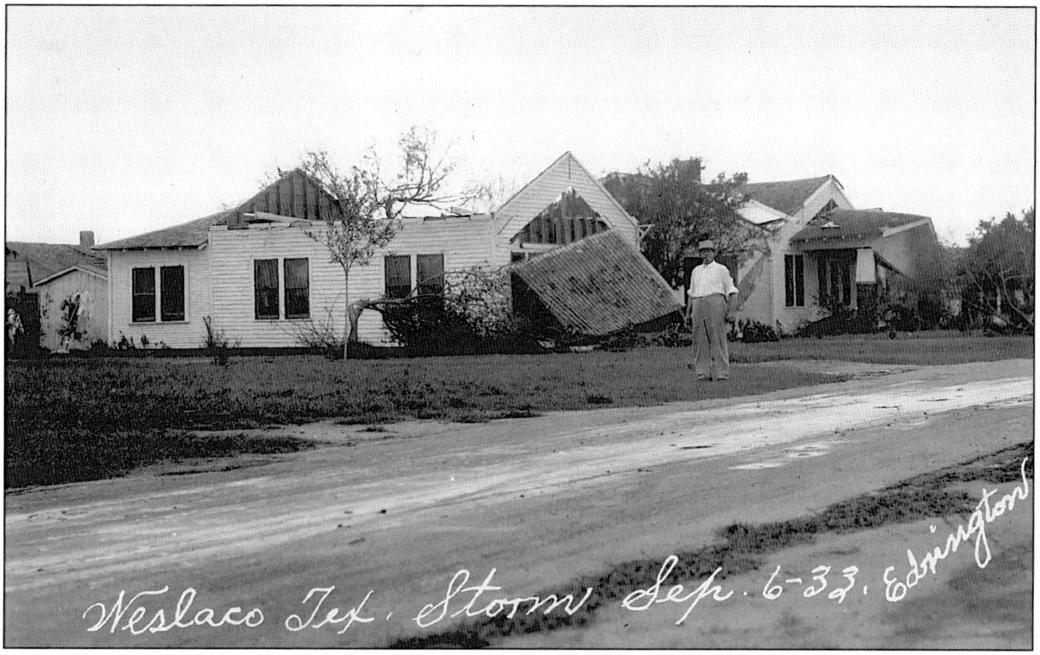


The hurricane damaged homes near the Lutheran Church in Weslaco. (Edrington Studio.)

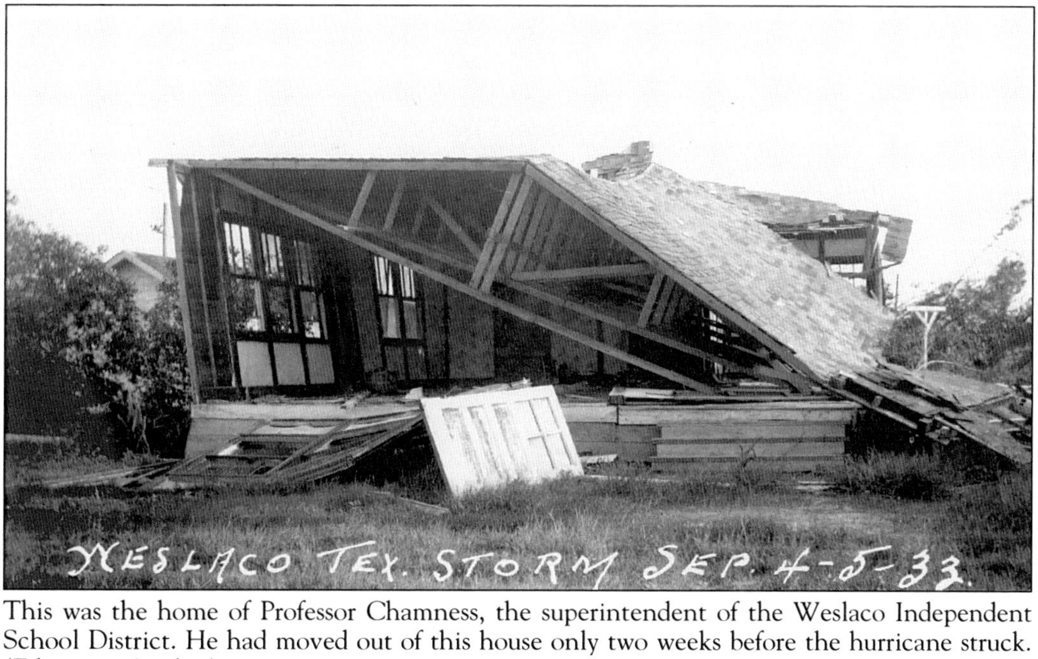


This was the home of Professor Chamness, the superintendent of the Weslaco Independent School District. He had moved out of this house only two weeks before the hurricane struck. (Edrington Studio.)

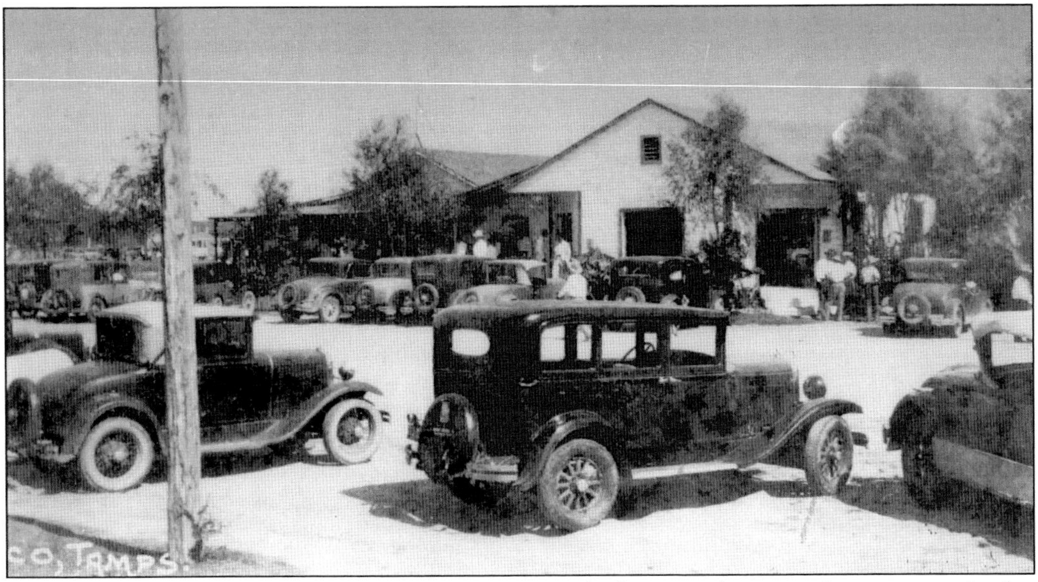

During 1928 and 1929, the B&P Bridge Company built a two-lane, steel suspension bridge across the Rio Grande. The U.S. toll station at Thayer, a short distance from the Mercedes pump station, had an 18-room stucco building for customs, health, and immigration. Across the bridge, a small town called Nueva Mercedes sprang up near the Mexican customs house. Woody Tullis was the toll collector at Thayer. (Woody Tullis photo—Courtesy of Hidalgo County Historical Museum for the Hidalgo County Historical Commission.)

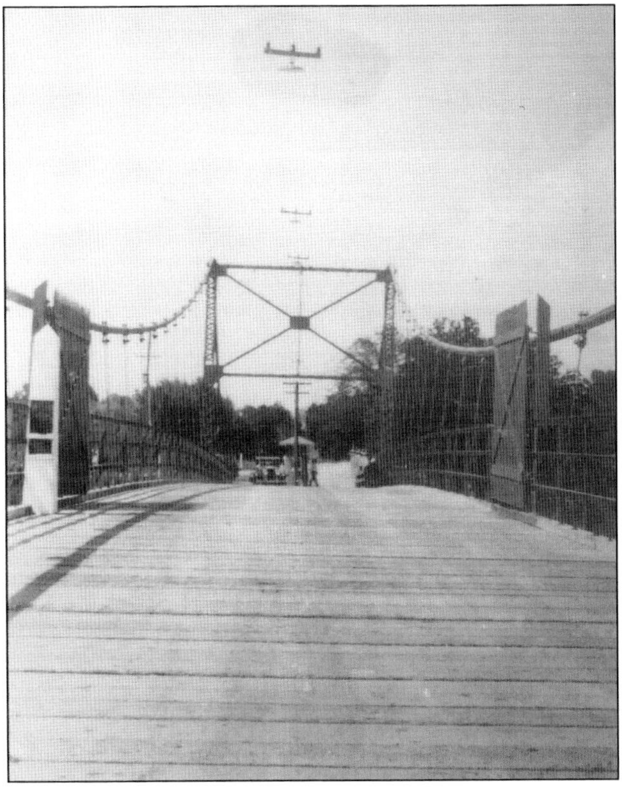

Nueva Mercedes became known as Rio Rico because of the Rio Rico Kennel Club, which owned a 20-acre greyhound racetrack there. A night club, saloons, and other businesses attracted U.S. visitors who came to enjoy the illegal activities during Prohibition. A Chicago syndicate bought the racetrack and most of the resort in 1928. Al "Scarface" Capone is thought to have visited Rio Rico between 1929 and 1931, when he also lived periodically in Weslaco. The Rio Rico bridge had an international boundary marker (seen on the left side of the bridge) halfway across. The gates were locked at midnight. (Woody Tullis photo—Courtesy of Hidalgo County Historical Museum for the Hidalgo County Historical Commission.)

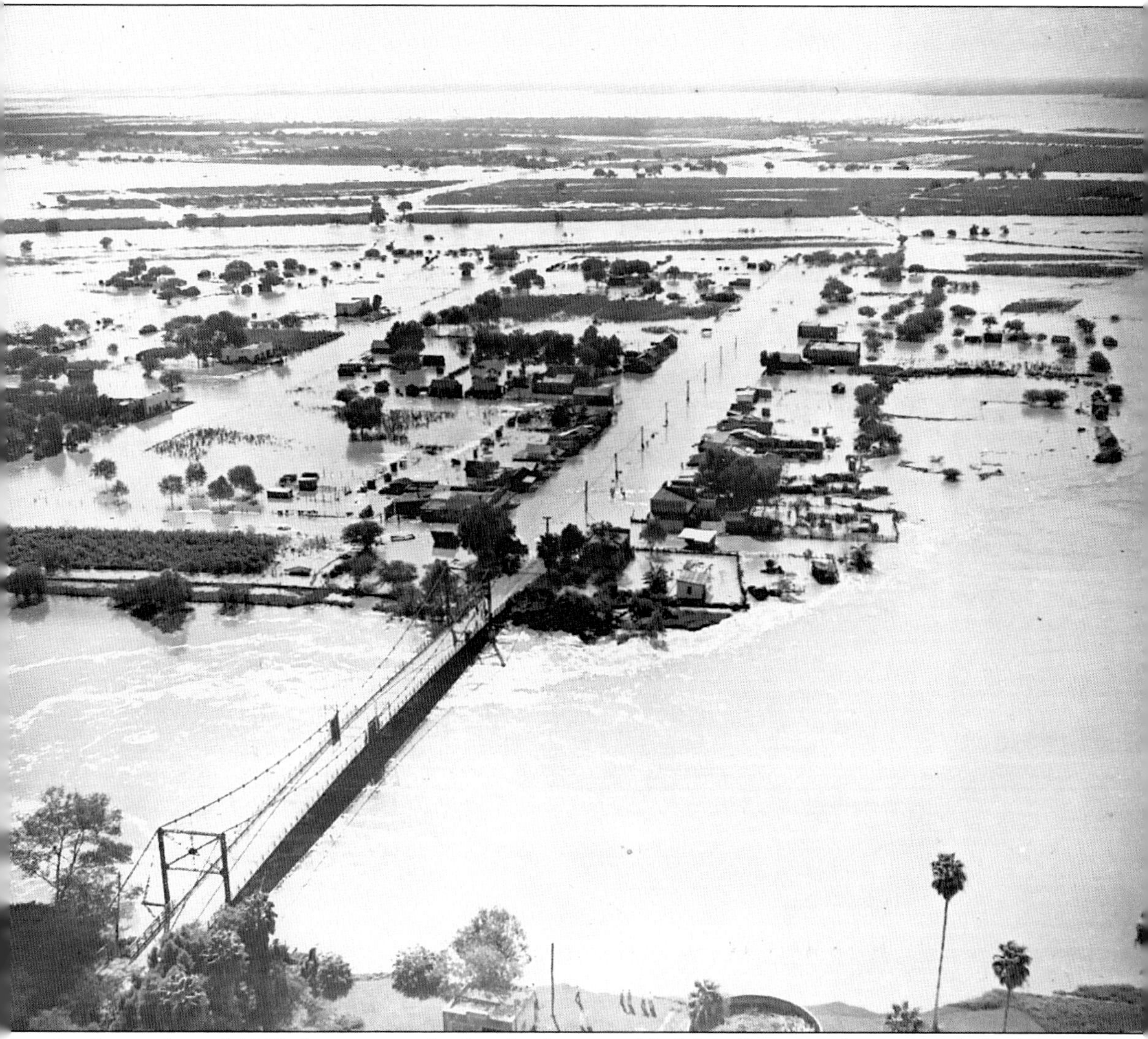

In September of 1941, heavy rains broke the levee and left Rio Rico residents stranded. The swollen river weakened piers and anchors and swept away much of the foundation. On October 27, 1941, the bridge failed and sank into the river, pulling the Mexican customs house into the Rio Grande. After several attempts to restore access to Rio Rico failed, a new bridge, which remains in service today, was built at Progreso near Weslaco. (Stouffer Graphic Arts.)

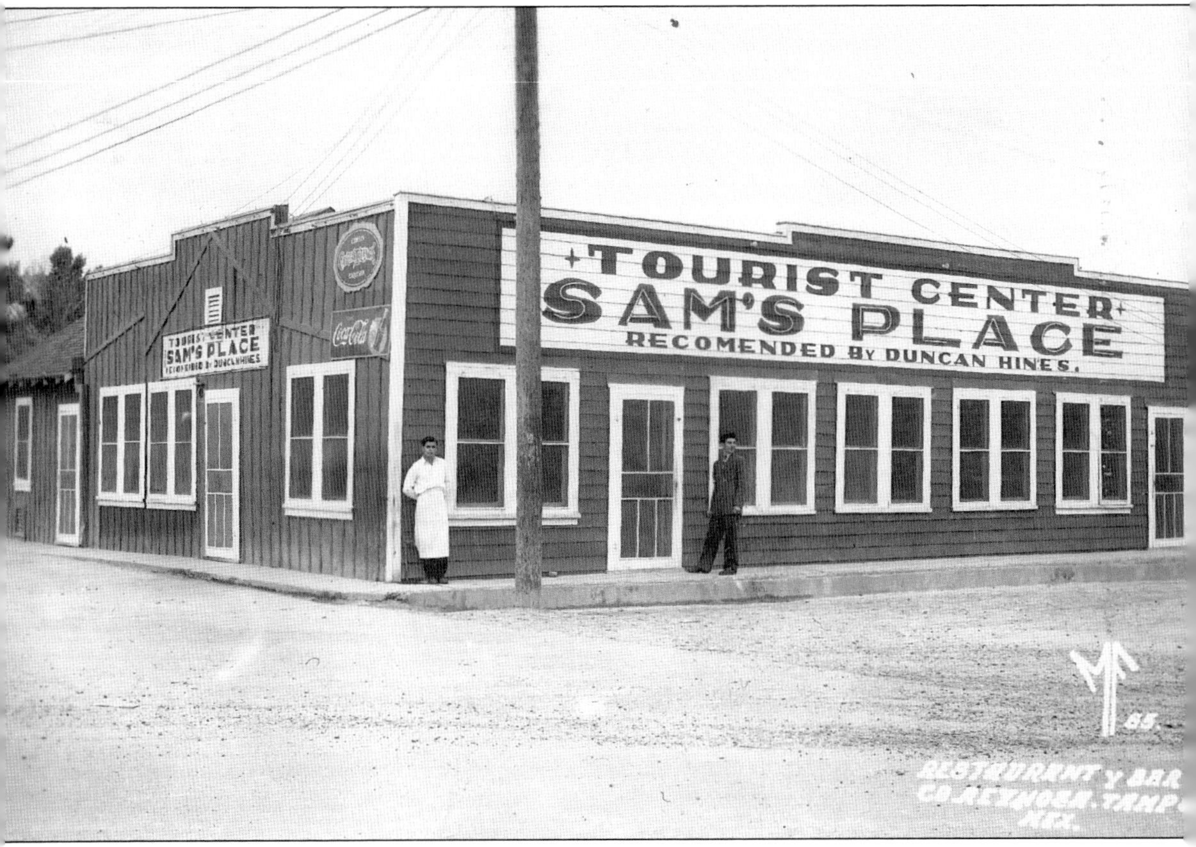


Sam's Place was a popular Rio Rico restaurant.

# *Six*

# TEXSUN:
## THE WORLD'S LARGEST JUICE CANNING PLANT

Citrus grove owners sold their fruit to local markets, to an ever-increasing number of visitors, and to merchants filling gift orders. Growers shipped fruit by rail to markets in Northern and Midwestern cities. However, shipping costs remained high; for example, packers charged fees as high as $1.25 per box. Valley growers, organizing themselves through local associations, searched for ways to lower and stabilize their costs. The Rio Grande Valley Citrus Exchange, comprised of 17 citrus associations, met for the first time (in Weslaco) and chose a board of directors on July 1, 1932.

Needing a master brand for its products, the exchange bought the brand names Texsun and Tex-Maid from the Brownsville Citrus Association for $2,500. Citrus production increased during the 1920s. In 1932, the exchange contracted with the National Fruit and Vegetable Exchange to sell Rio GrandeValley citrus fruit. During the 1935–1936 season, the exchange set up its own marketing department, which continued until the exchange ended the sale of fresh fruit in 1951.

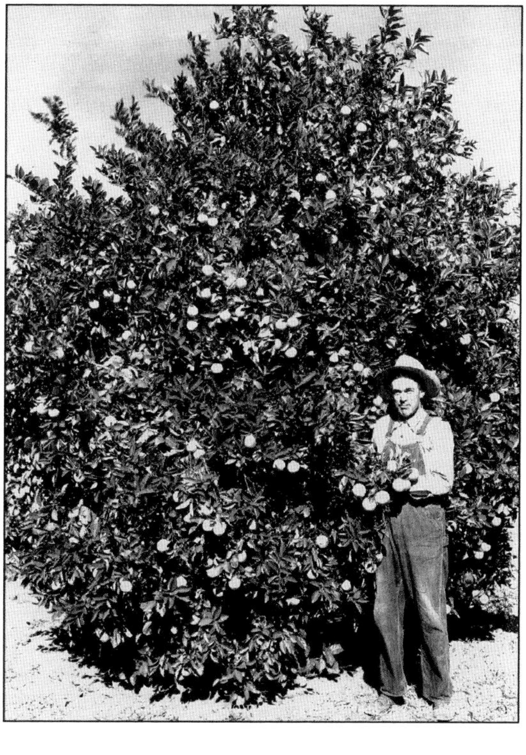

J.H. Williams owned this ten-year-old Parson Brown orange tree. Soon after the railroad reached Harlingen in 1904, citrus production expanded from a few experimental farms to large commercial groves.

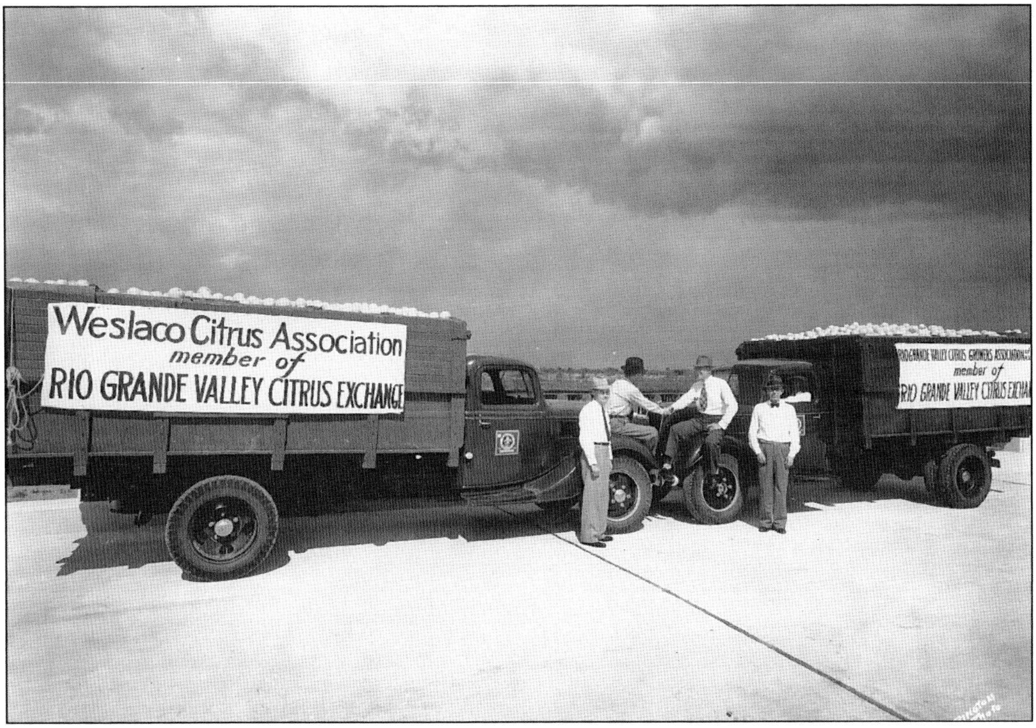


These trucks belonged to the Rio Grande Valley Citrus Exchange. The first rail car load of fruit, hand-polished and packed in onion crates, was shipped in 1920. (Edrington Studio.)

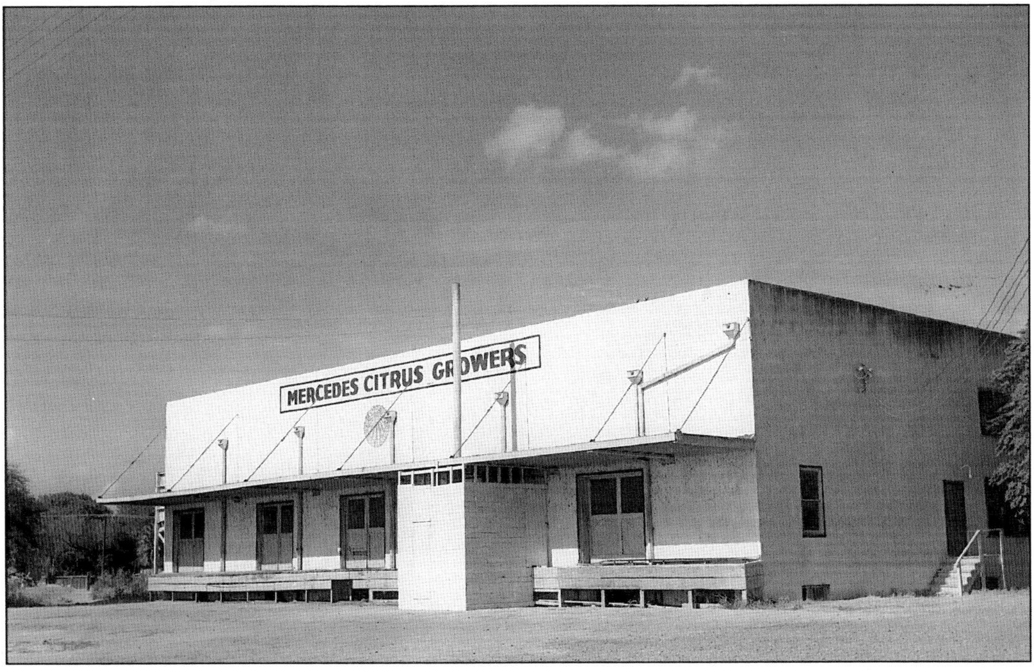


This is the citrus packing plant, often called a "packing shed," at Mercedes. Due to an abundance of fruit and high marketing costs during the Depression, Valley growers, through local associations, formed a cooperative to pack, handle, and market the crops of its members.

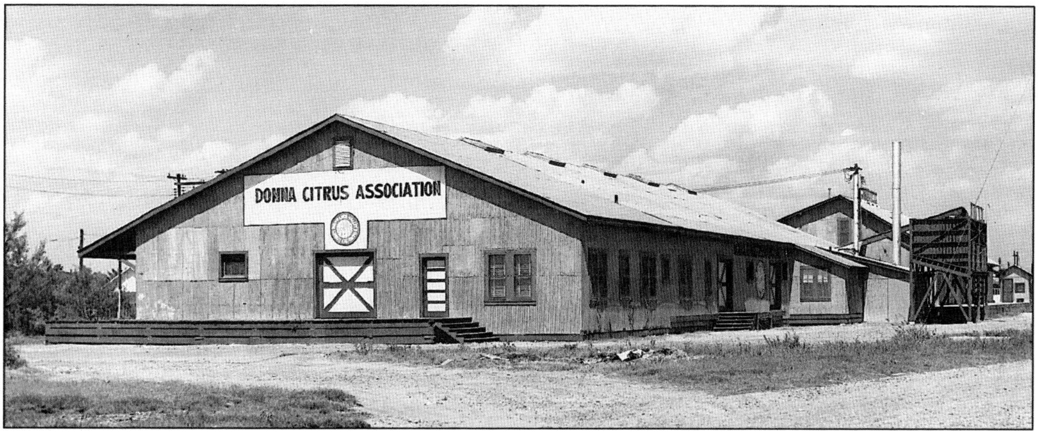


This is the Donna Citrus Association packing shed. A 1929 federal census indicated that over 5 million citrus trees were in production, and during the 1929–1930 season, almost 6,000 rail car loads of fruit left the Rio Grande Valley. During the 1935–1936 season, the exchange set up its own marketing department to sell Valley citrus fruit throughout the United States. The exchange ended the sale of fresh fruit in 1951. (Ken Snyder.)

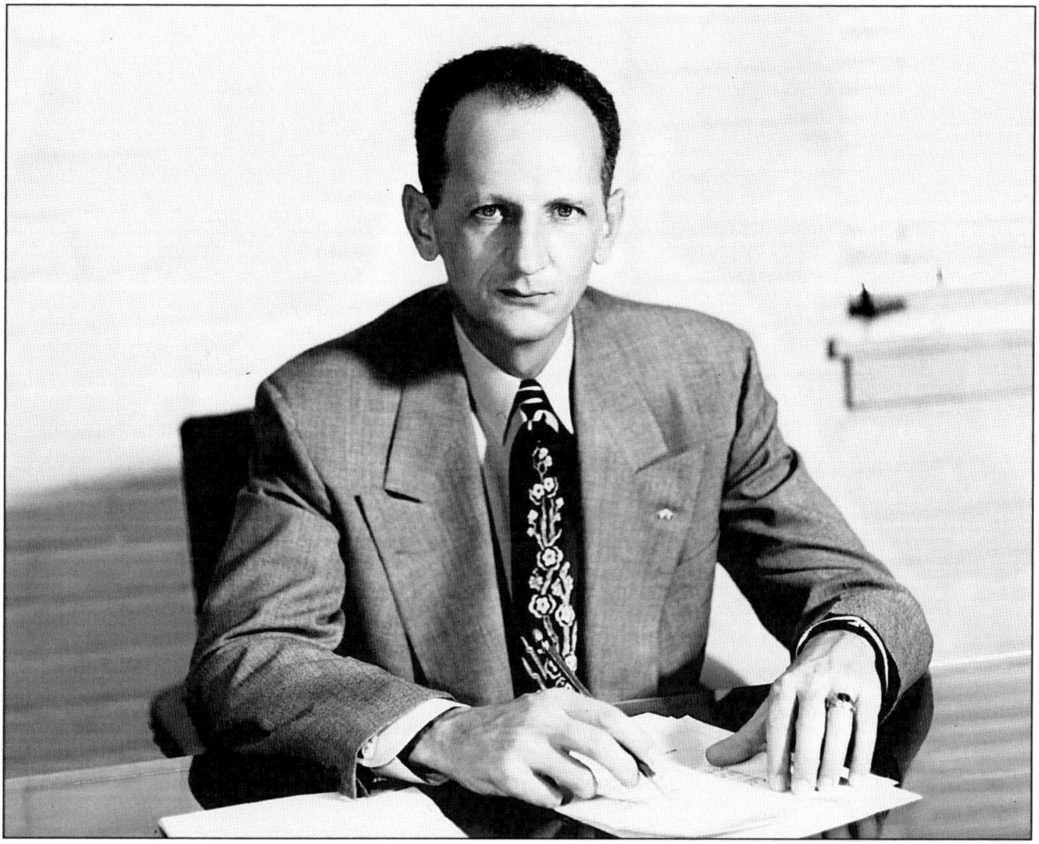

Lorne S. Hamme began his career in the accounting department of the Edinburg Citrus Association and later moved to the accounting department at Texsun. The general manager from 1949 to 1973, Hamme is credited with directing Texsun into the frozen concentrate market. (Yoder.)

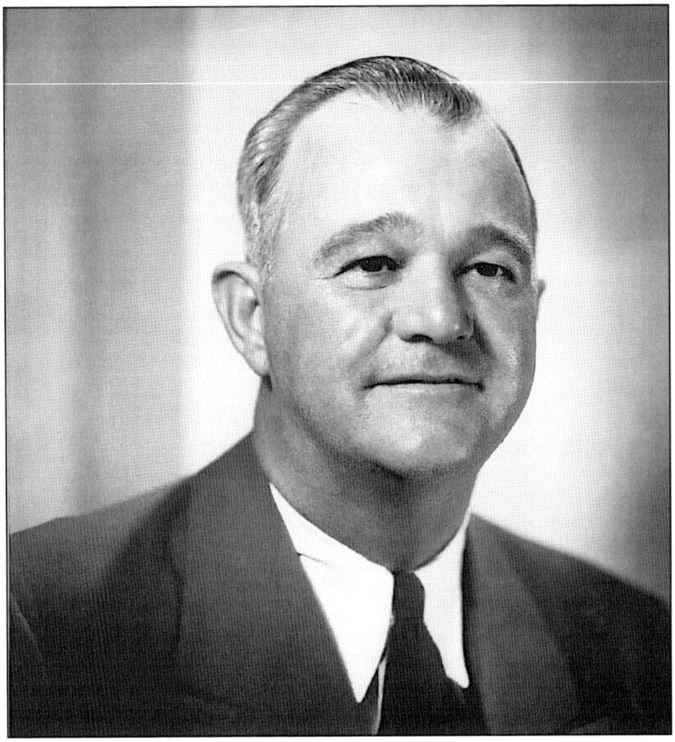

L.F. Martin, president of the Donna Citrus Association, served for many years on the board of directors for the Rio Grande Valley Citrus Exchange, Texsun Citrus Exchange, and Texsun Corporation.

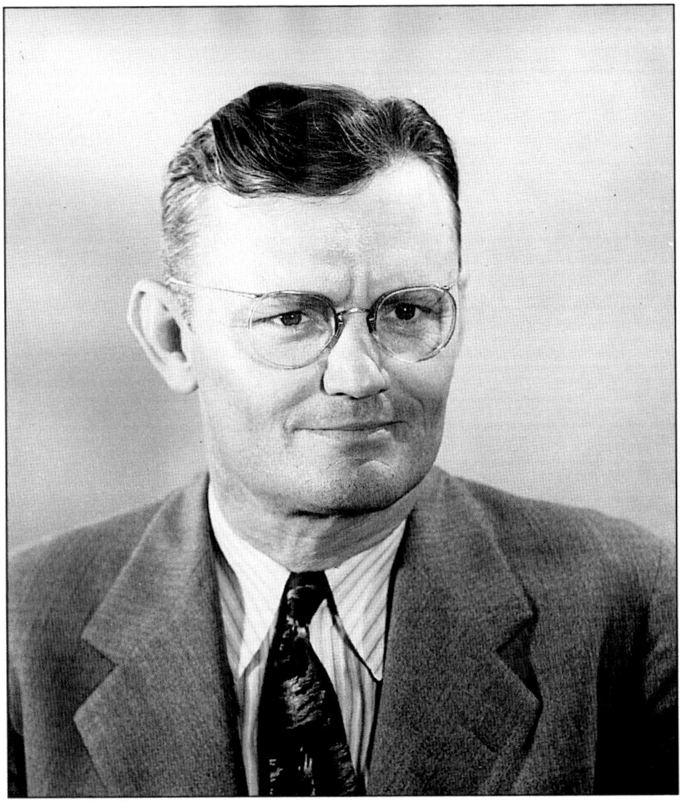

Graham Killough served as the general manager of the exchange from 1944 to 1945, as manager of the box company associated with Texsun, and as manager of the canning plant from 1946 to 1971. (Ken Snyder.)

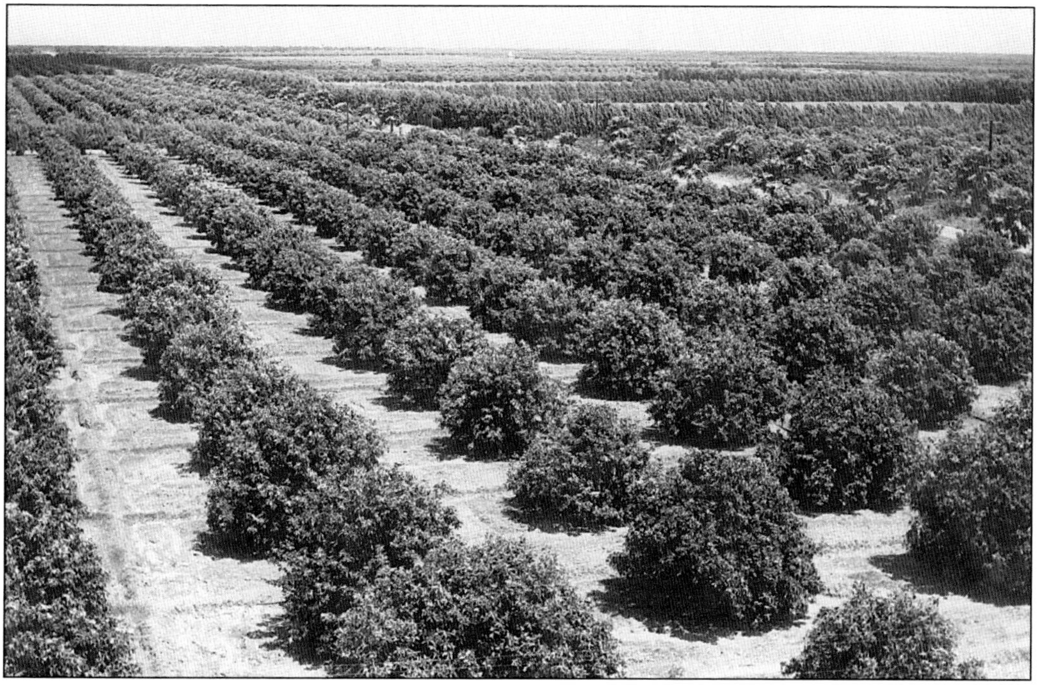

This is an aerial view of a large grove. Texsun contracted for growers' fruit and later owned two groves, one near Edinburg and one near McAllen.

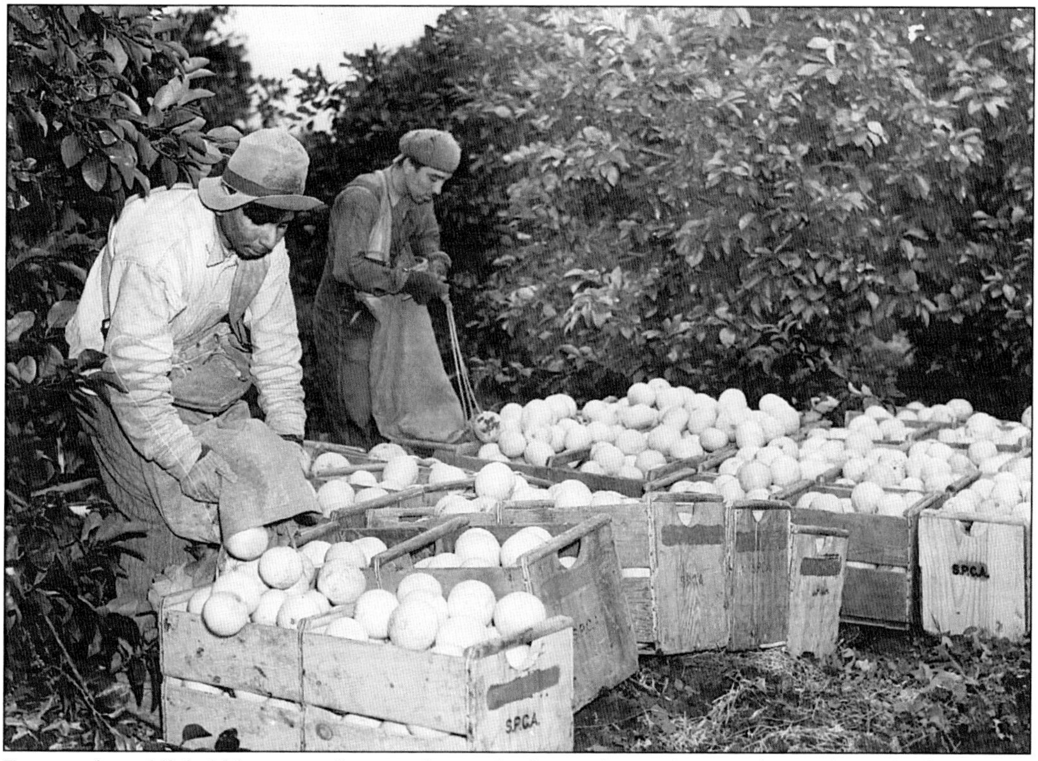


Fruit pickers fill field boxes with grapefruit, which are then taken to the packing shed.

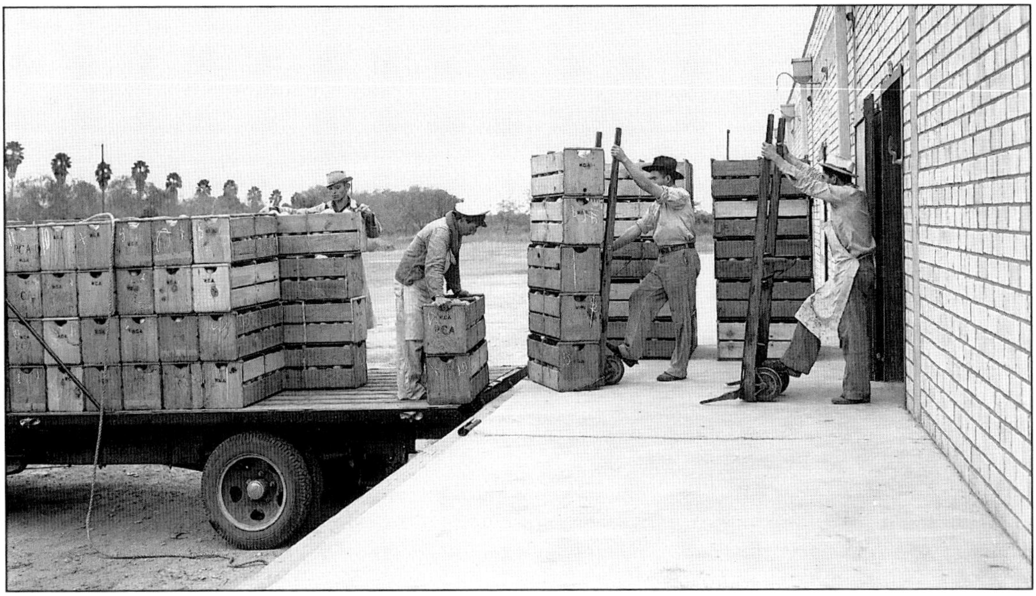

Here, the field boxes are being unloaded at the packing shed.

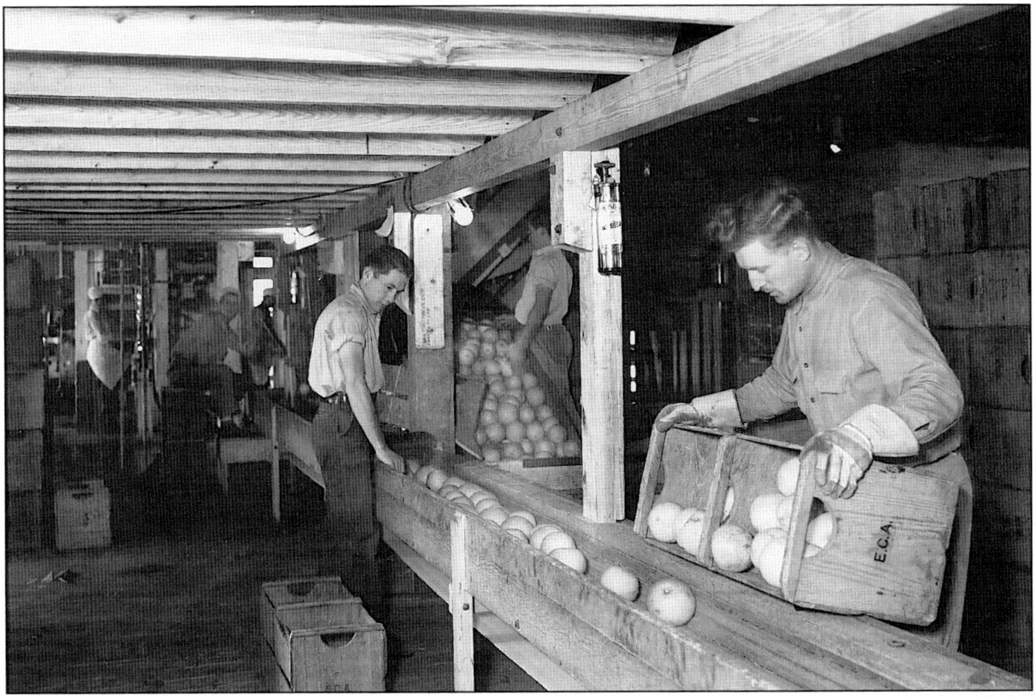


Next, field boxes are emptied onto conveyors at the packing shed. The grapefruit will be sorted and graded according to quality and will be sold as fresh fruit or squeezed into juice. (Edrington Studio.)

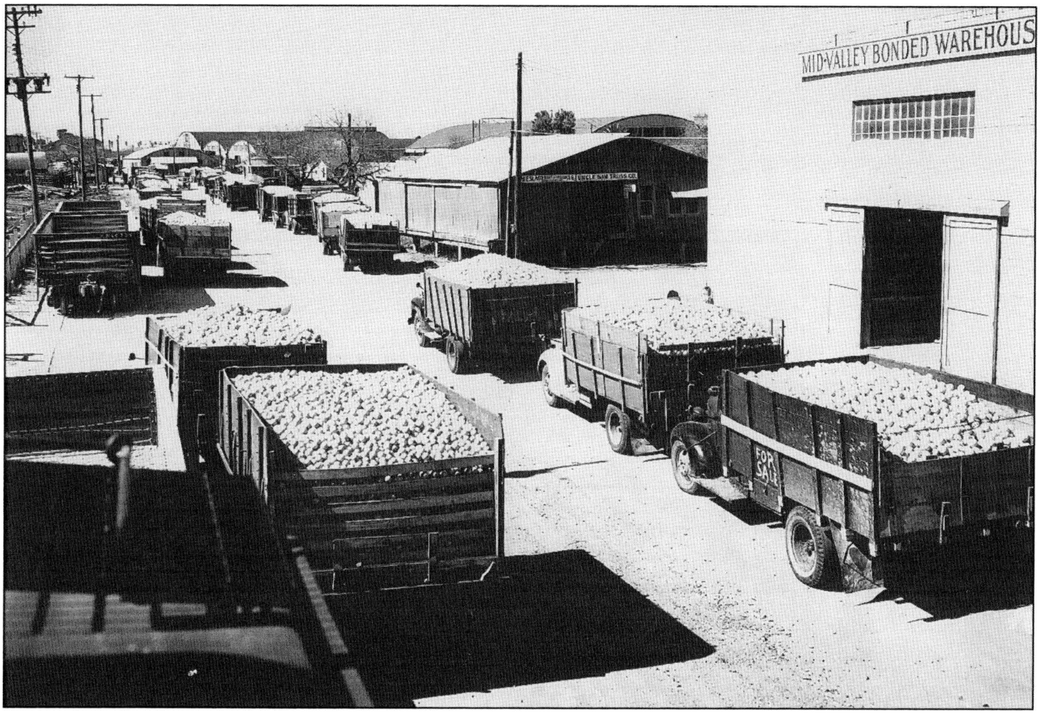


Truckloads of grapefruit are lined up for delivery to Texsun (at center in the background).

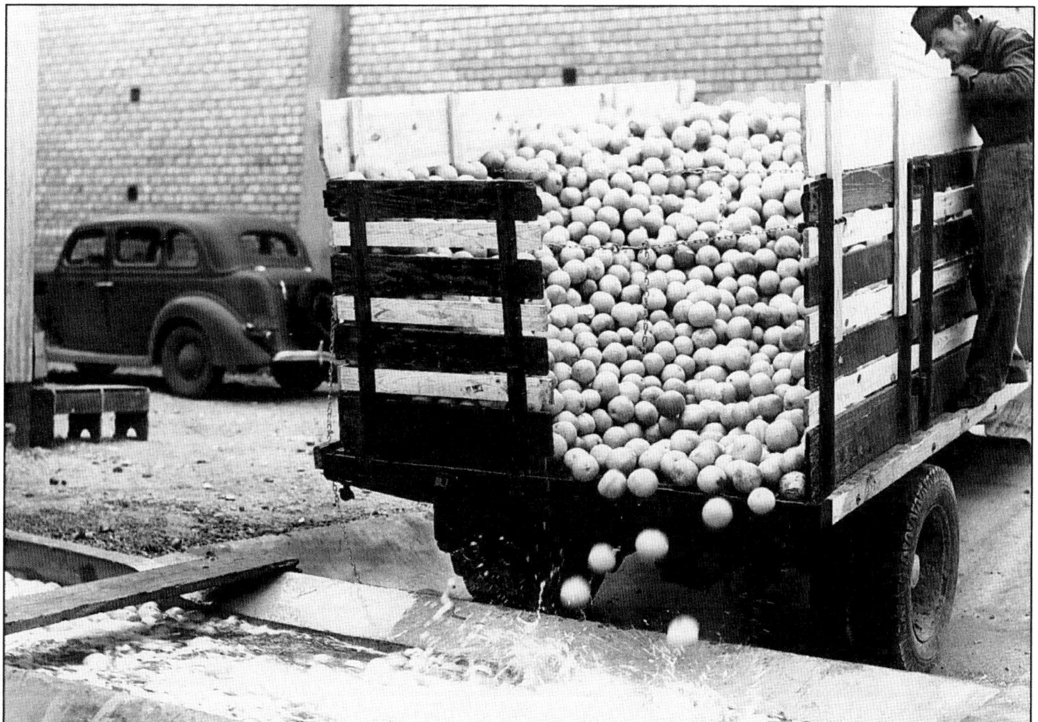

A truckload of grapefruit is being unloaded into a trough for initial washing.

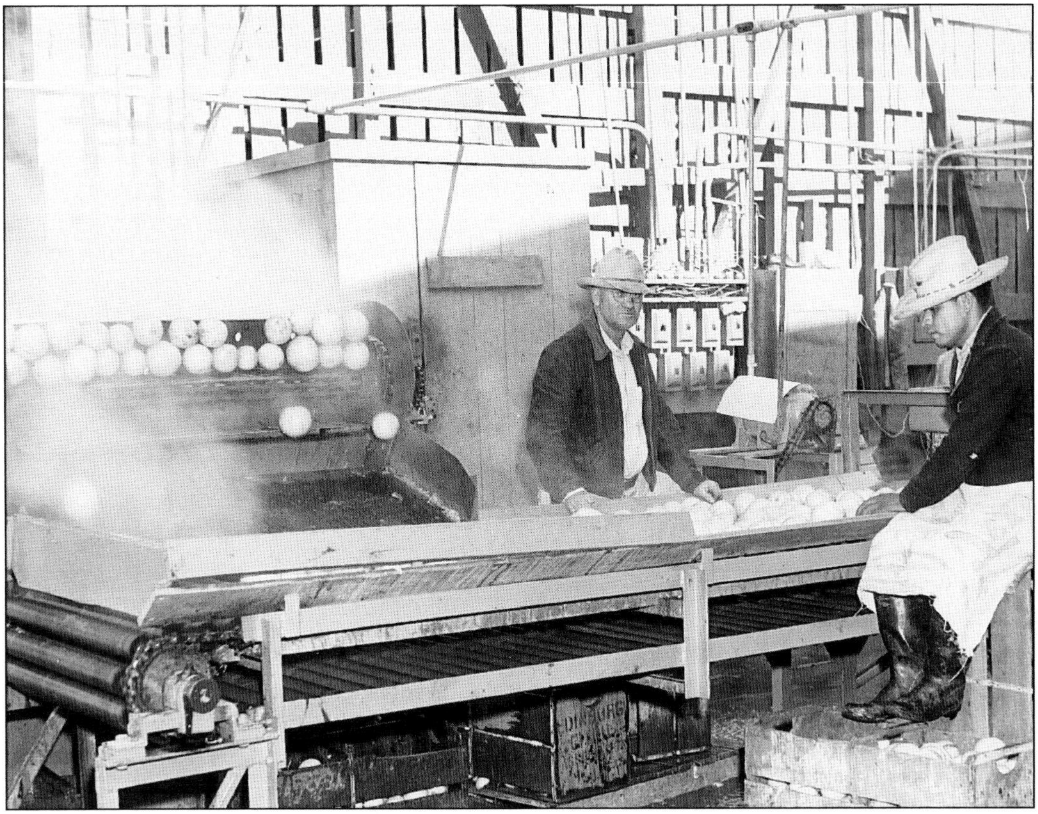

The grapefruit received a second washing and was moved by conveyor into the plant.

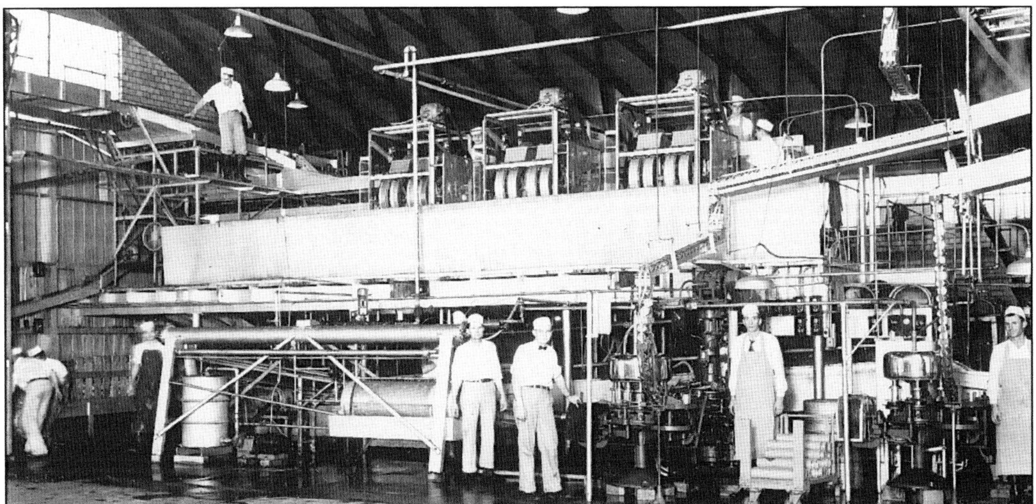

The exchange first rented a small tin building near the Missouri Pacific Railroad tracks and set up juicing equipment. Due to crop increases, the exchange built a larger facility in 1936, which opened on January 16, 1937. This image shows the ground floor of the new building. Grapefruit that was imperfect, due to size, shape, or other unusual features, was used for juice.

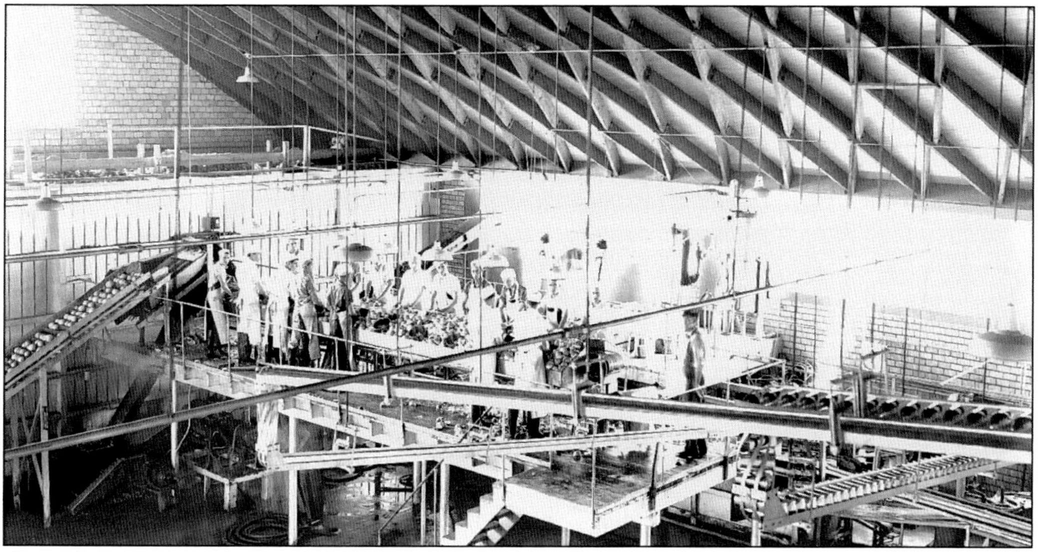

Grapefruit were moved by conveyor to a machine where they were cut in half, then onto a belt that carried the halves to the stainless-steel reaming table. (Edrington Studio.)

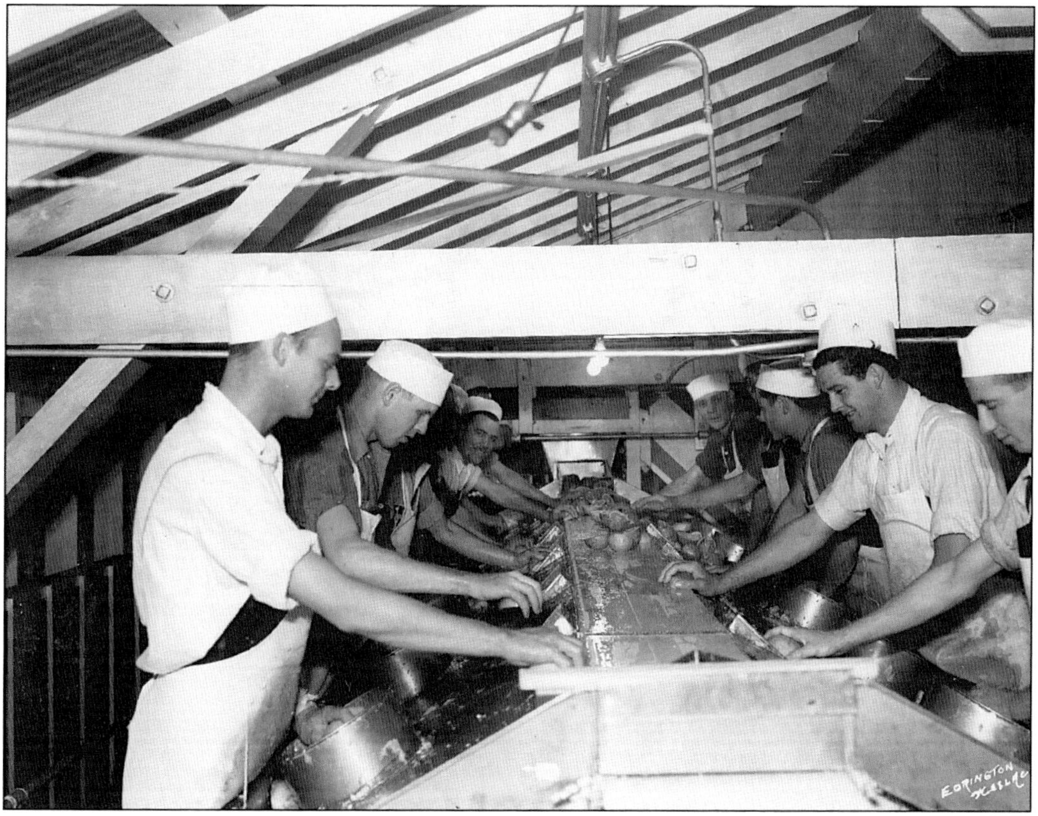

As grapefruit halves moved along a belt above the reaming table, men and women standing on either side of the reaming table pushed the grapefruit halves over the electric hand reamers and placed the peel on another belt that conveyed it to a truck outside the building. Mechanical reamers were installed for the next season. (Edrington Studio.)

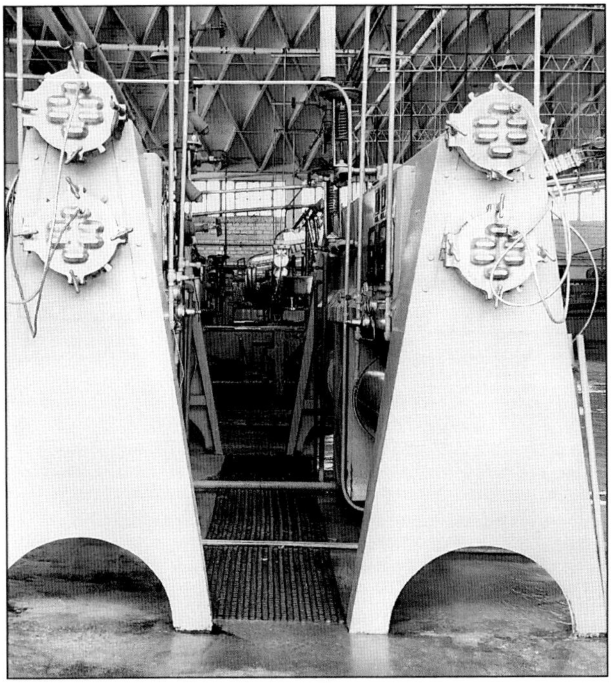

Sterilizers maintained the quality and flavor of the juice in the can for an indefinite period of time.

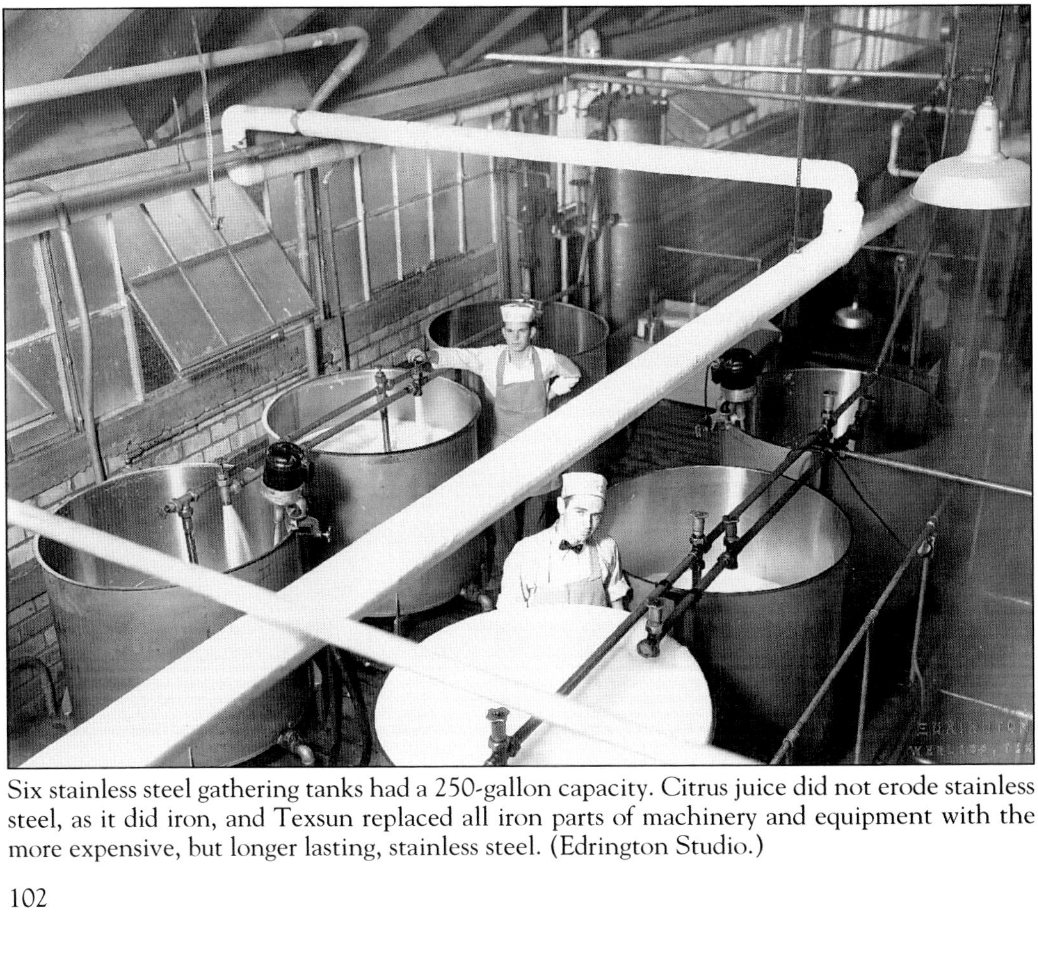

Six stainless steel gathering tanks had a 250-gallon capacity. Citrus juice did not erode stainless steel, as it did iron, and Texsun replaced all iron parts of machinery and equipment with the more expensive, but longer lasting, stainless steel. (Edrington Studio.)

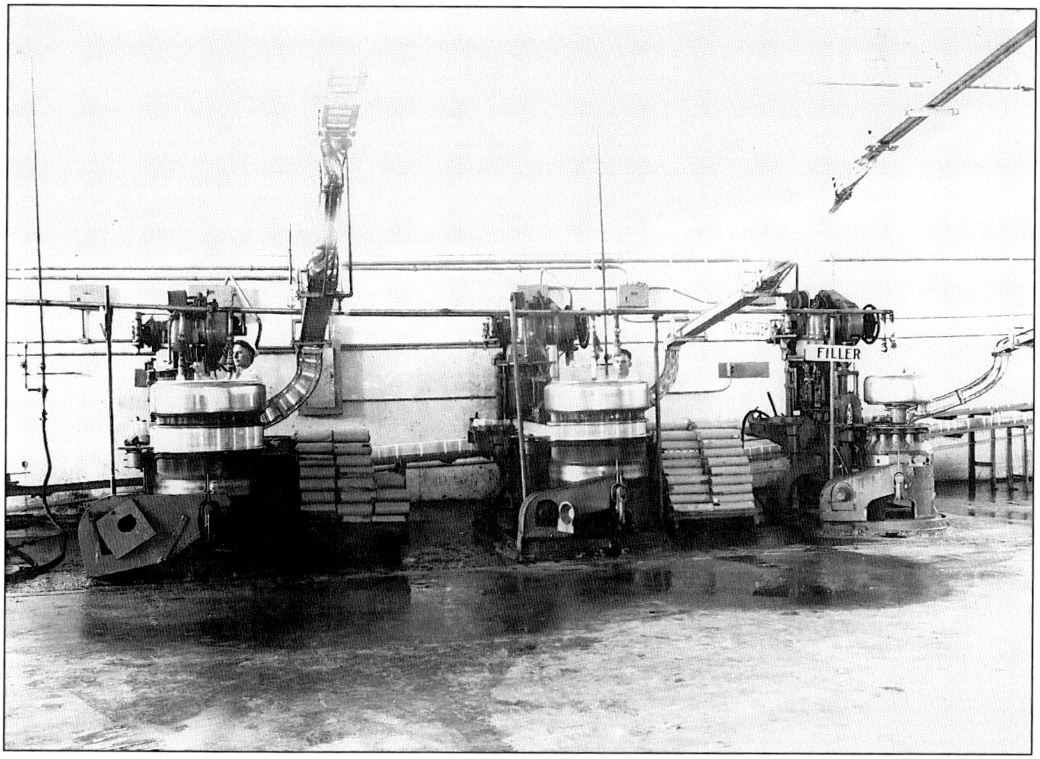


The cans were sterilized as well. (Brad Smith Photo.)

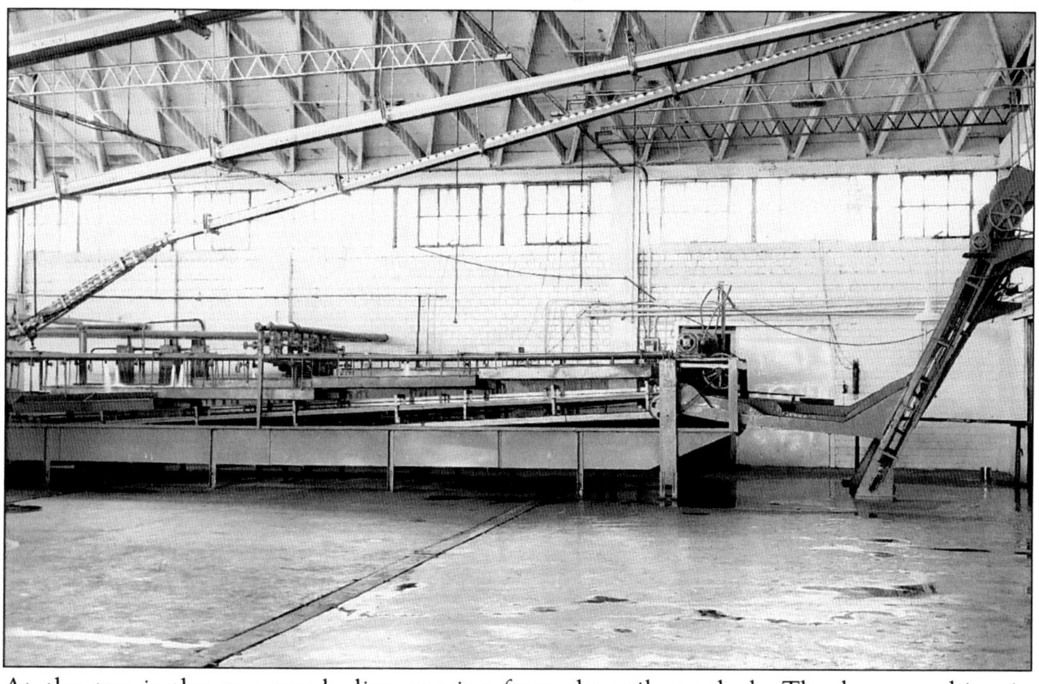

At the top is the can supply line coming from the rail car dock. The large machine in the center cooled the filled cans. The elevator on the right took filled and cooled cans to labeling machines.

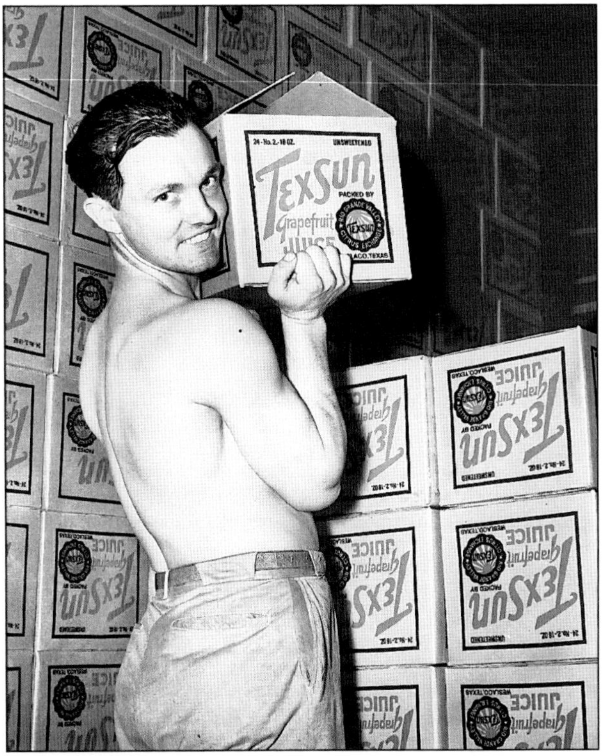


Cases of grapefruit juice were stacked by pitching the cases from one worker to another as the stacks grew higher. A few years later, Texsun began to use fork lifts and pallets, which reduced costs and damage to cans.

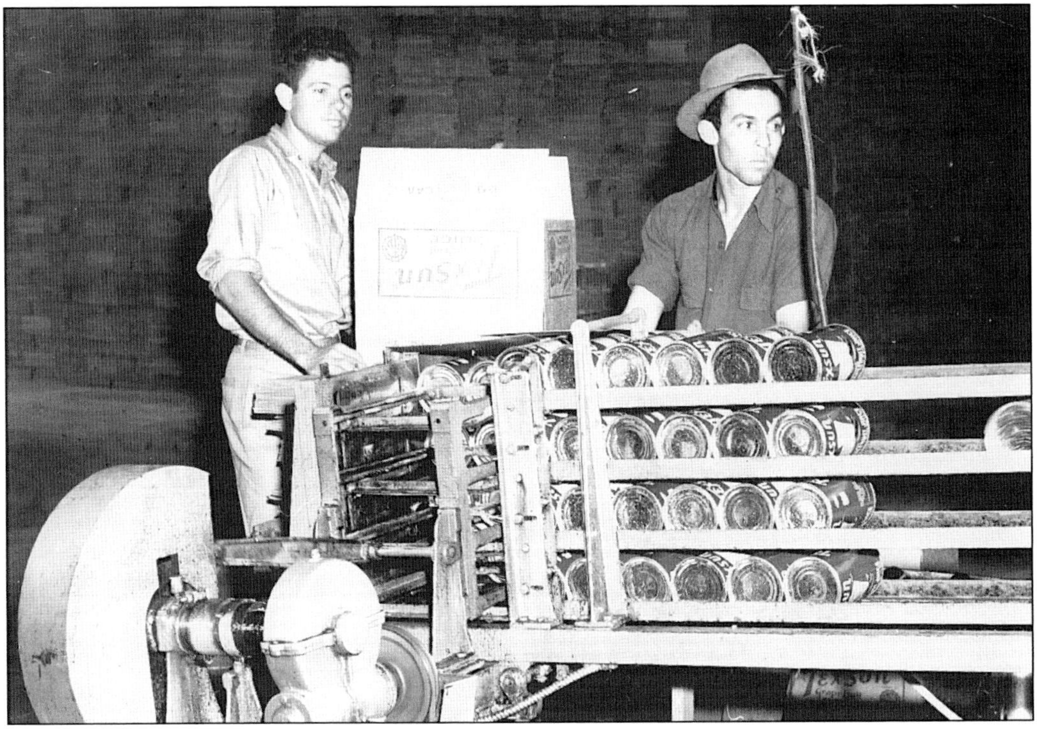

After being labeled, the cans were placed in cardboard boxes for storage and/or shipment. (J. Gilbert Hill.)

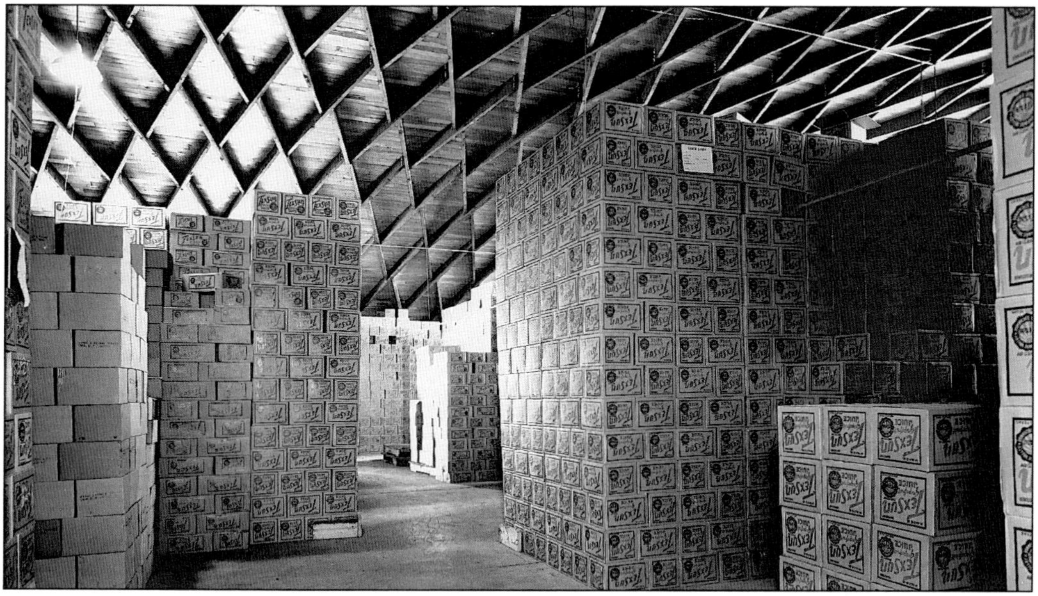

This warehouse, built adjacent to the canning plant in 1937, was large enough to store 750,000 cases of juice. During the mid-1930s and for many years thereafter, Texsun was the world's largest juice canning plant. From 61,000 cases produced in the 1935–1936 season, after expansion in 1937, Texsun produced 2,017,485 cases during the 1937–1938 season. (Edrington Studio.)

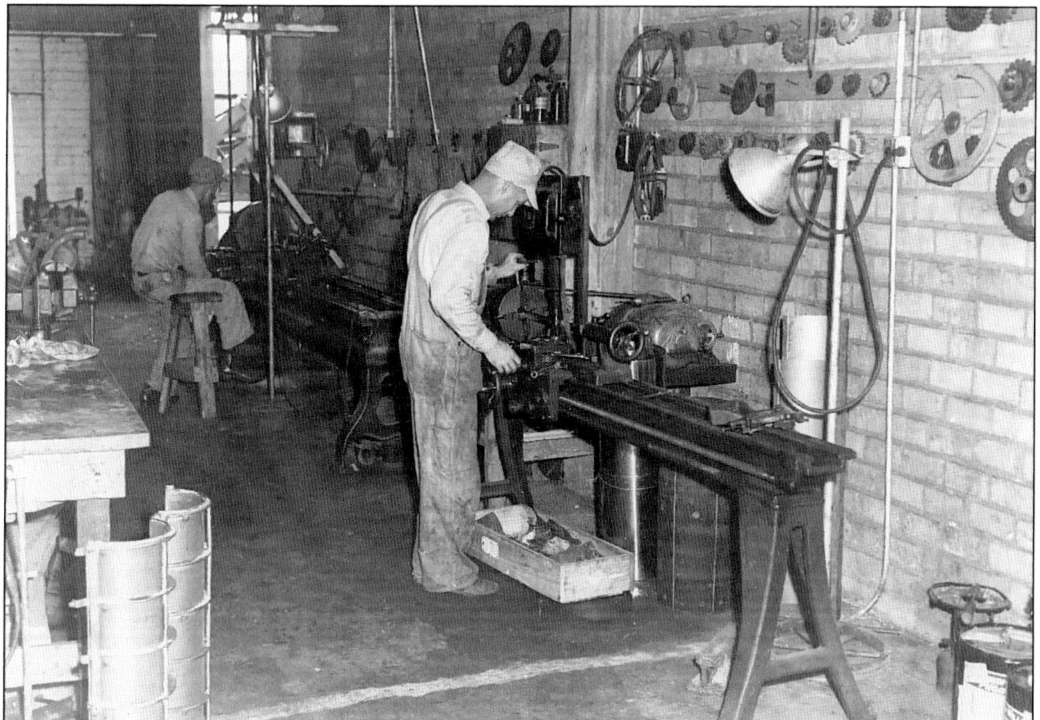

Efficient food processing required a great deal of automatic equipment, which had to be maintained. The machine shop was clean, well-equipped, and staffed by trained mechanics.

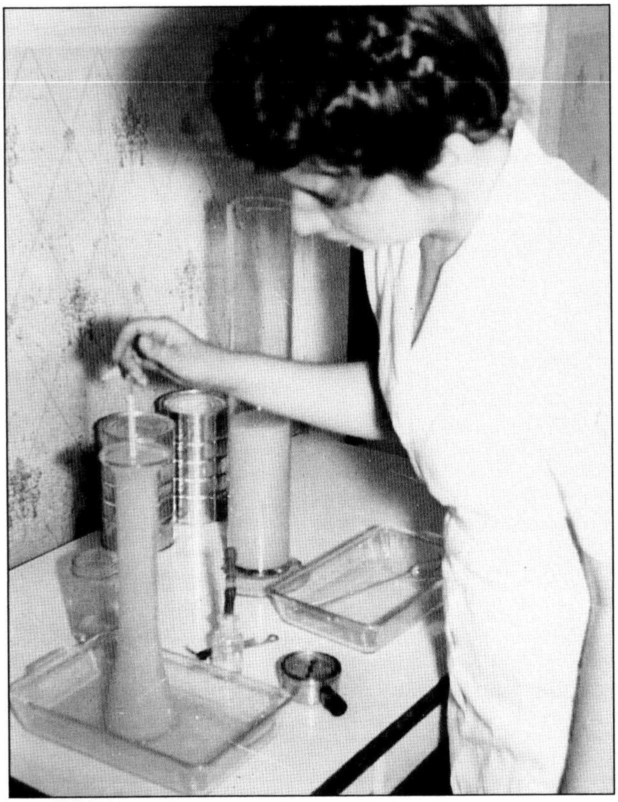

To ensure high quality, Texsun cooperated with the continuous inspection services of the U.S. Department of Agriculture.

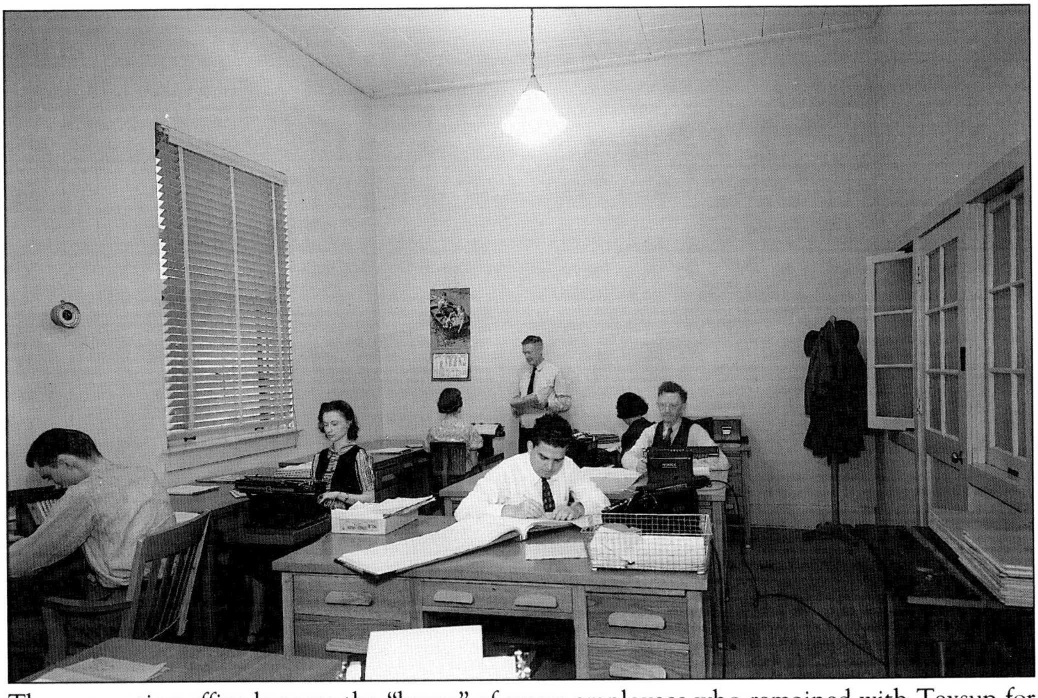

The accounting office became the "home" of many employees who remained with Texsun for decades and entire careers.

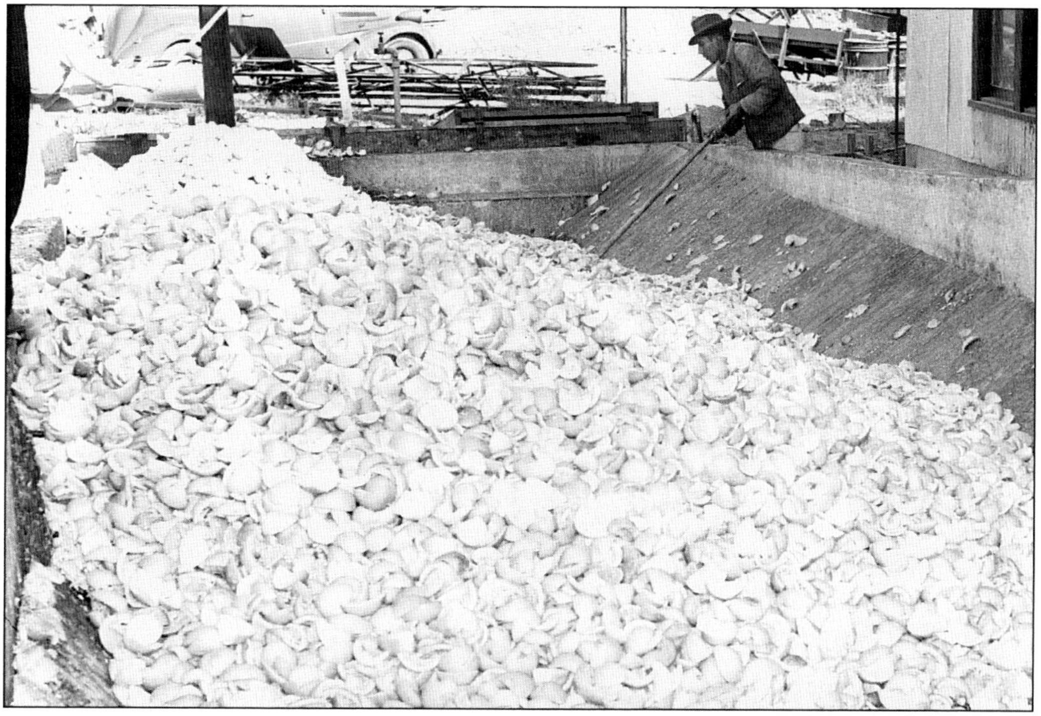

The juicing process discarded tons of pulp and peel. (J. Gilbert Hill.)

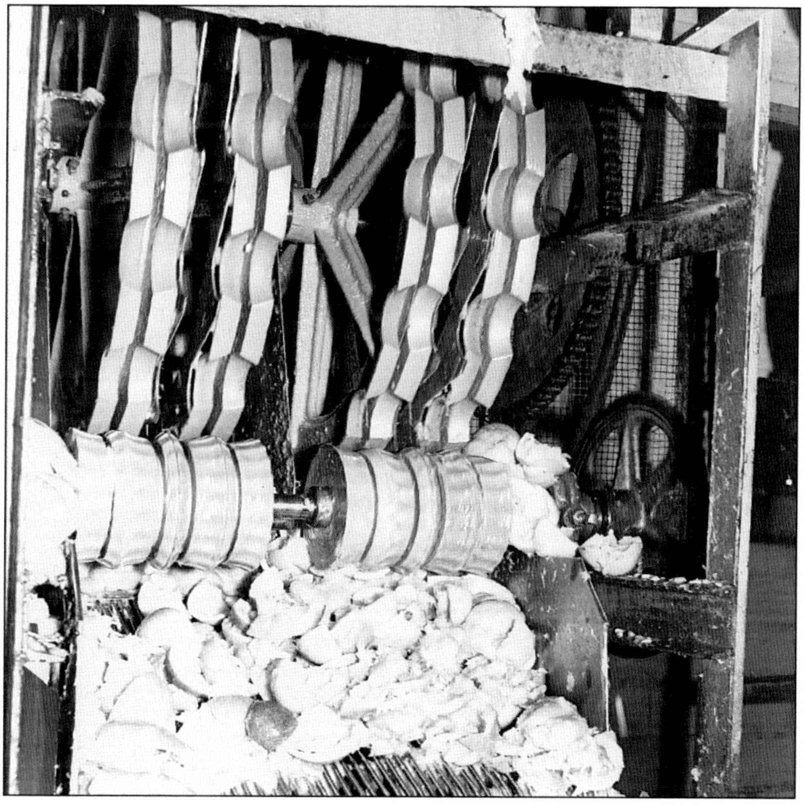

The discarded grapefruit halves were crushed. (Holbrook.)

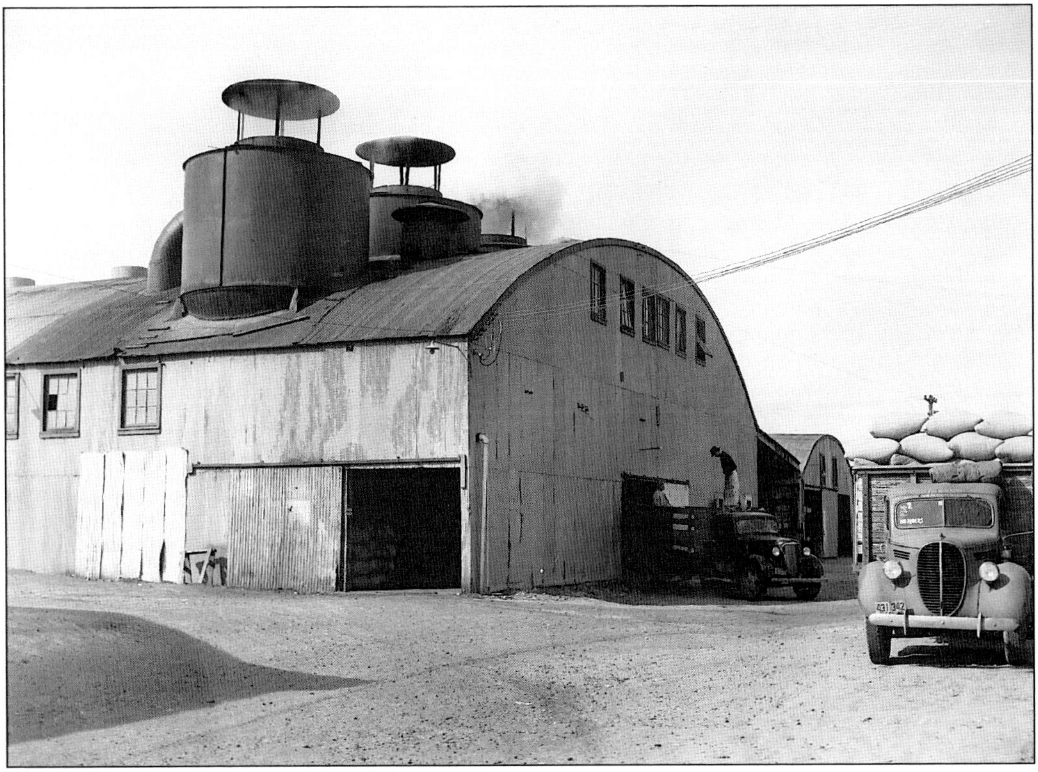

To use the tons of excess pulp and peel, Texsun built a four-unit dehydration plant next to the juicing plant during the winter of 1937–1938. The dried citrus pulp and peel were added to feed that improved milk production in dairy cattle and remained profitable as late as 1979. In this photo, steam rises from one of the stacks of the dehydration plant.

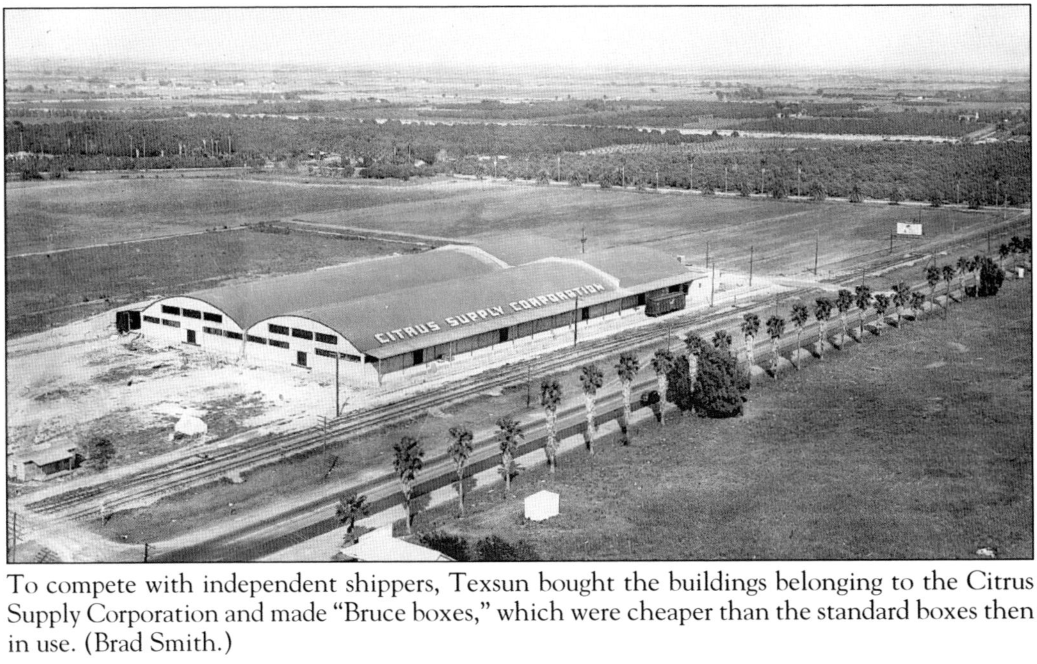


To compete with independent shippers, Texsun bought the buildings belonging to the Citrus Supply Corporation and made "Bruce boxes," which were cheaper than the standard boxes then in use. (Brad Smith.)

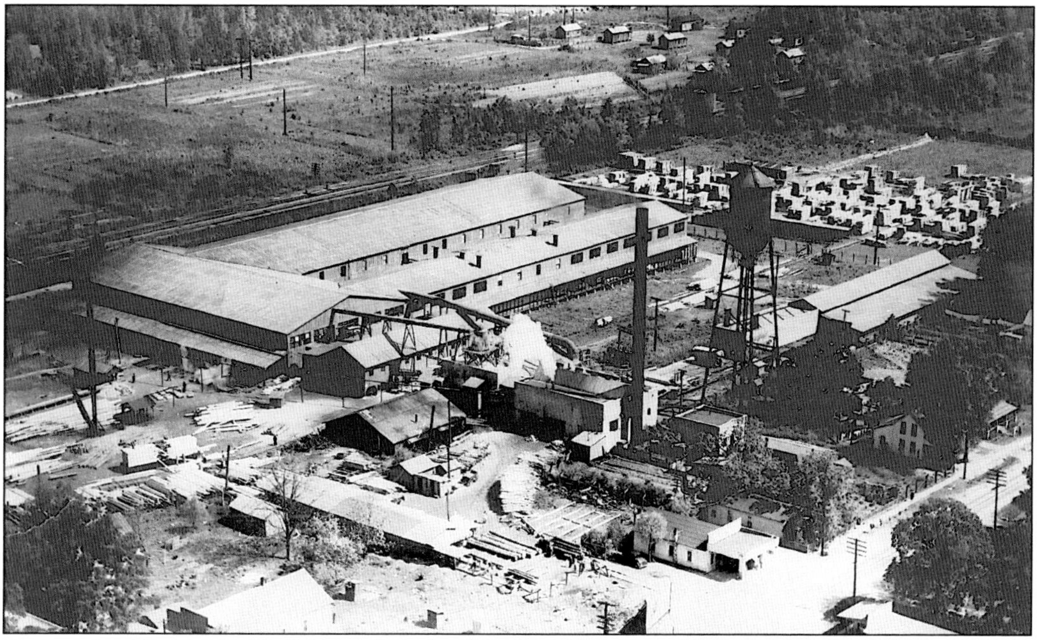

Texsun bought a veneer plant in Roseland, Louisiana, that would produce enough veneer for 4.5 to 5 million boxes per year.

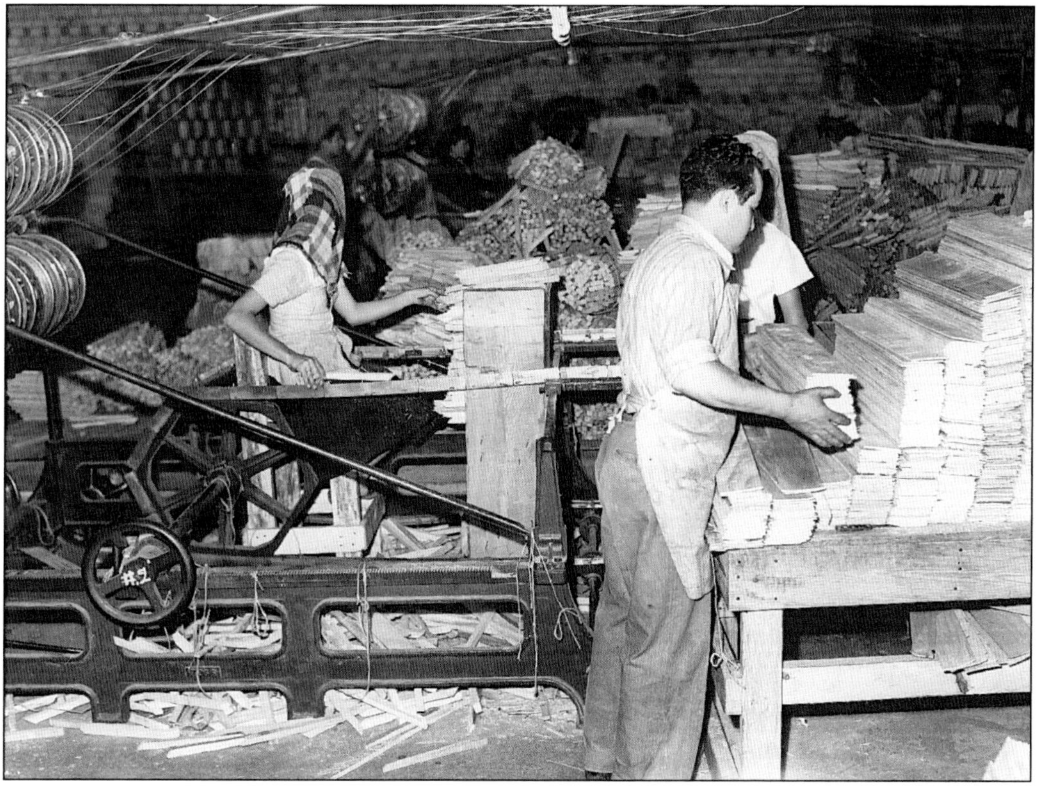

Bruce boxes were wirebound containers of veneer slats with solid ends. Here, stacks of veneer are being placed on a conveyor. (Brad Smith.)

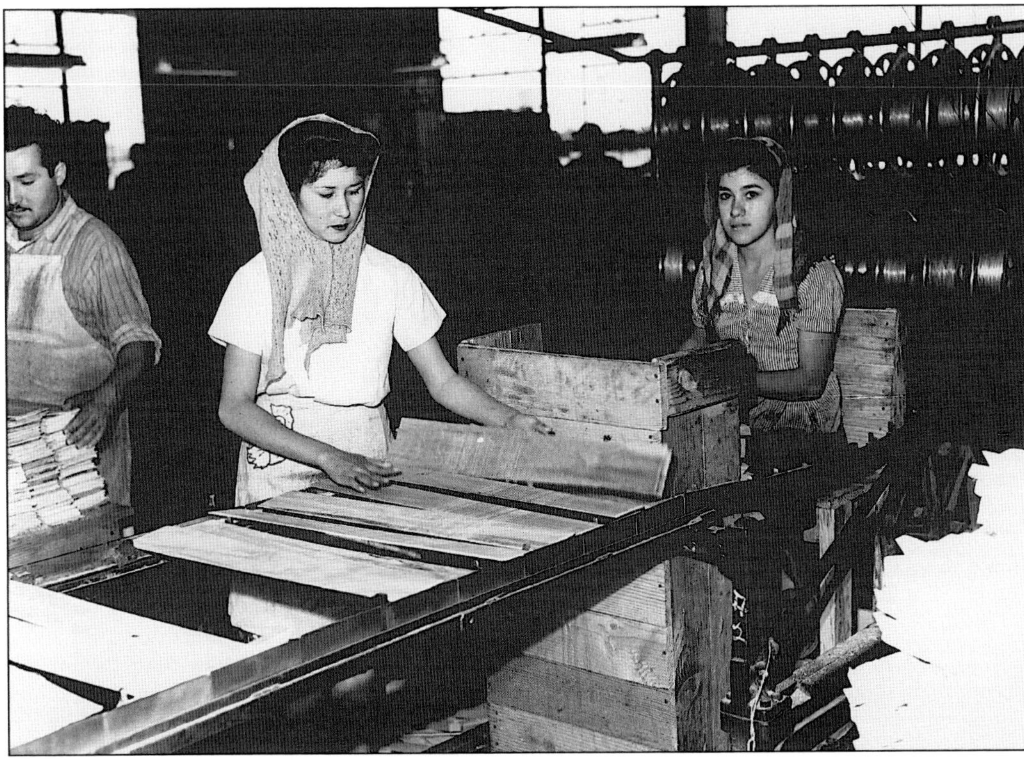

Veneer slats moved by conveyor to the wire machines. (Brad Smith.)

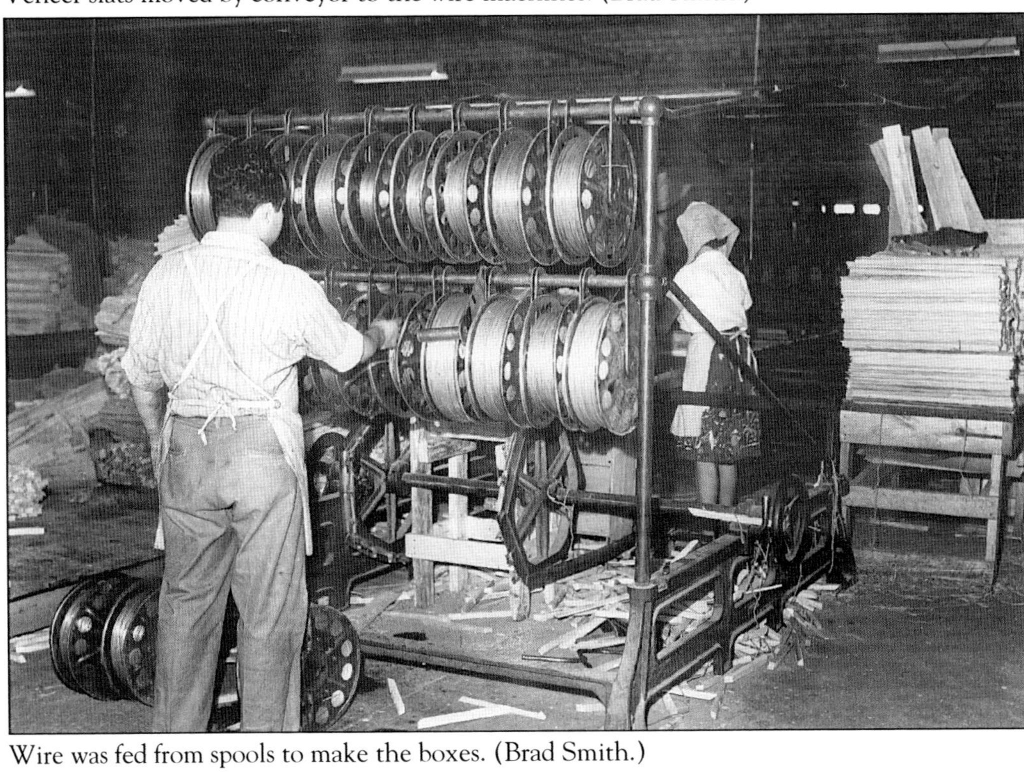

Wire was fed from spools to make the boxes. (Brad Smith.)

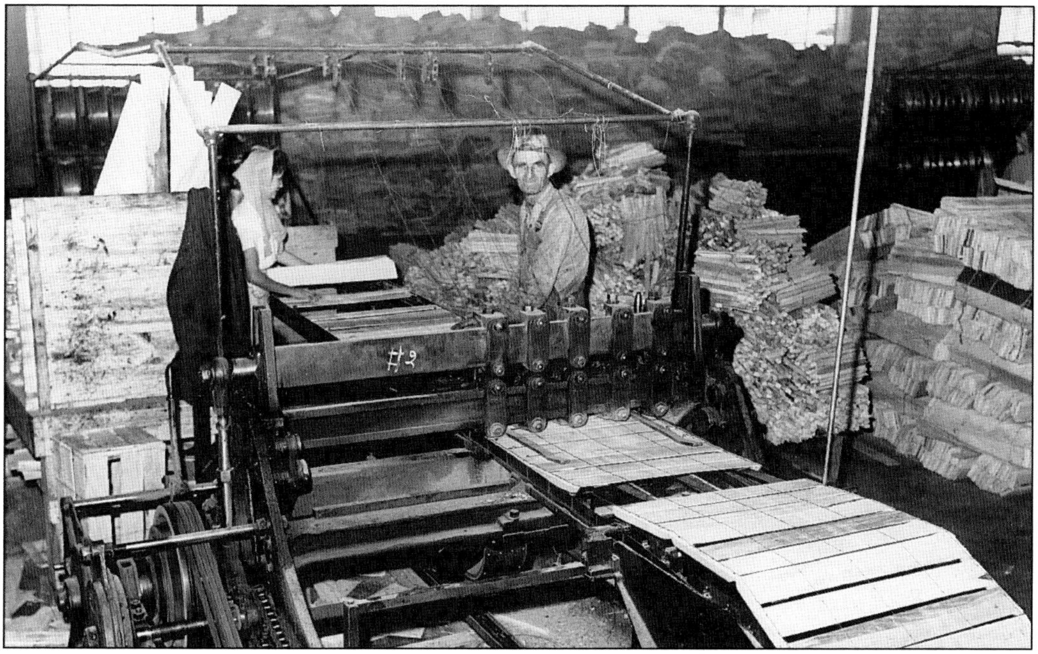

Five strands of wire connected the veneer slats. (Brad Smith.)

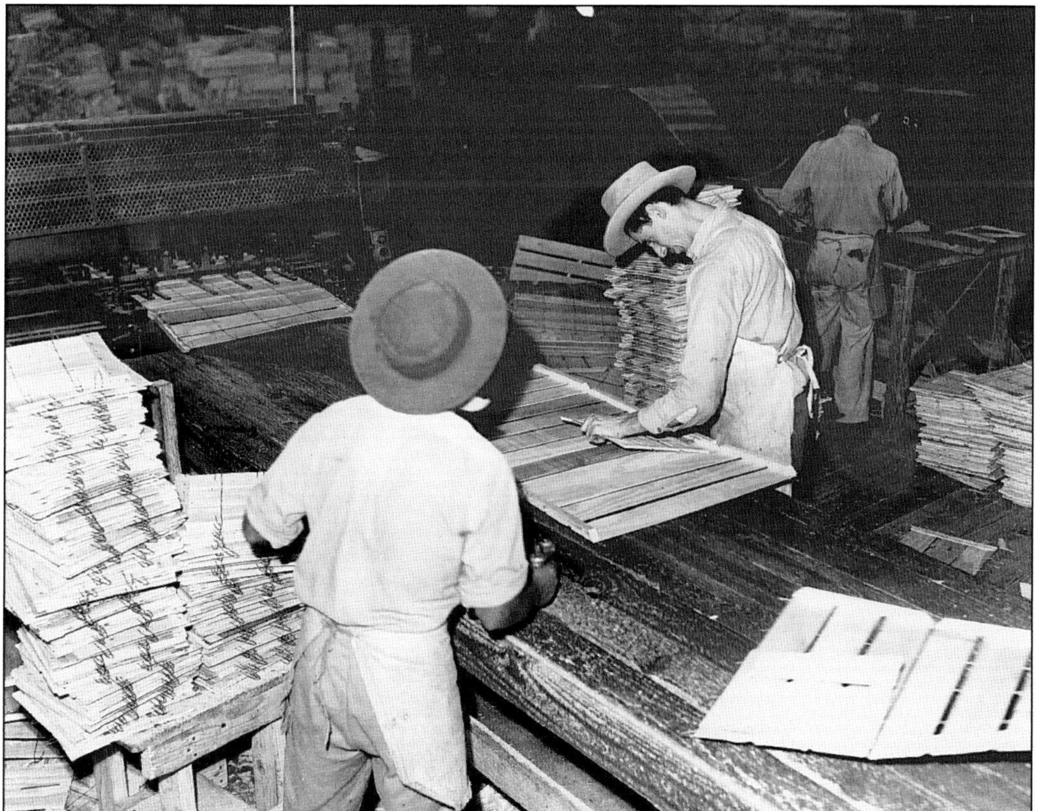

Solid ends stabilized each box. (Brad Smith.)

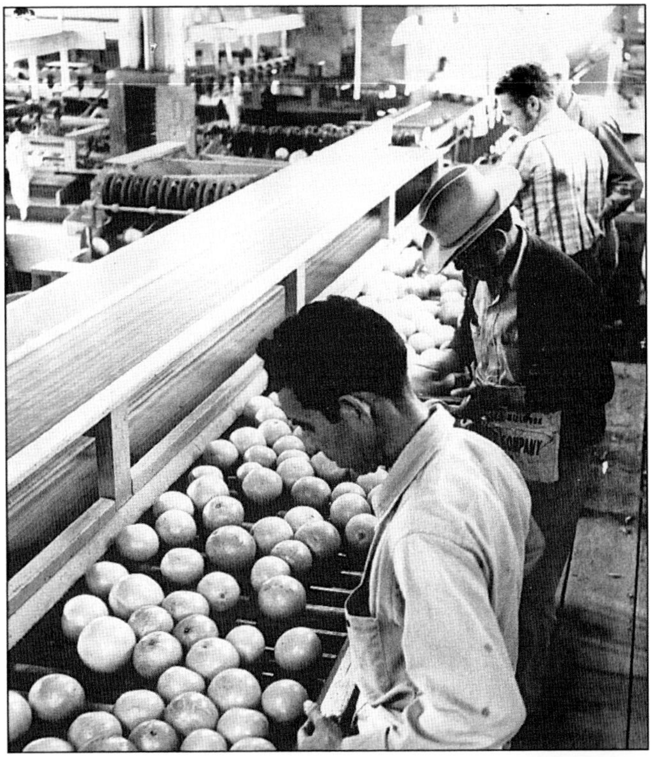

Prime grapefruit was sorted and graded by hand. (Shell Photography.)

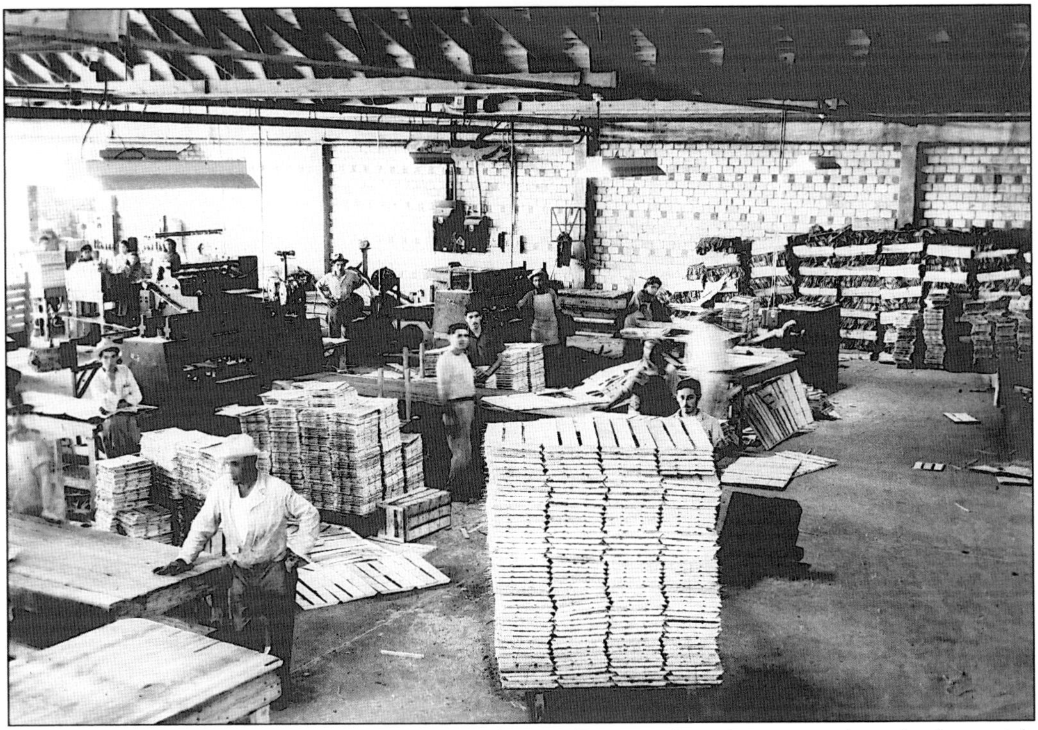

Veneer slats, connected by wires, were stored on pallets until ready to complete the box with the solid ends. (Brad Smith.)

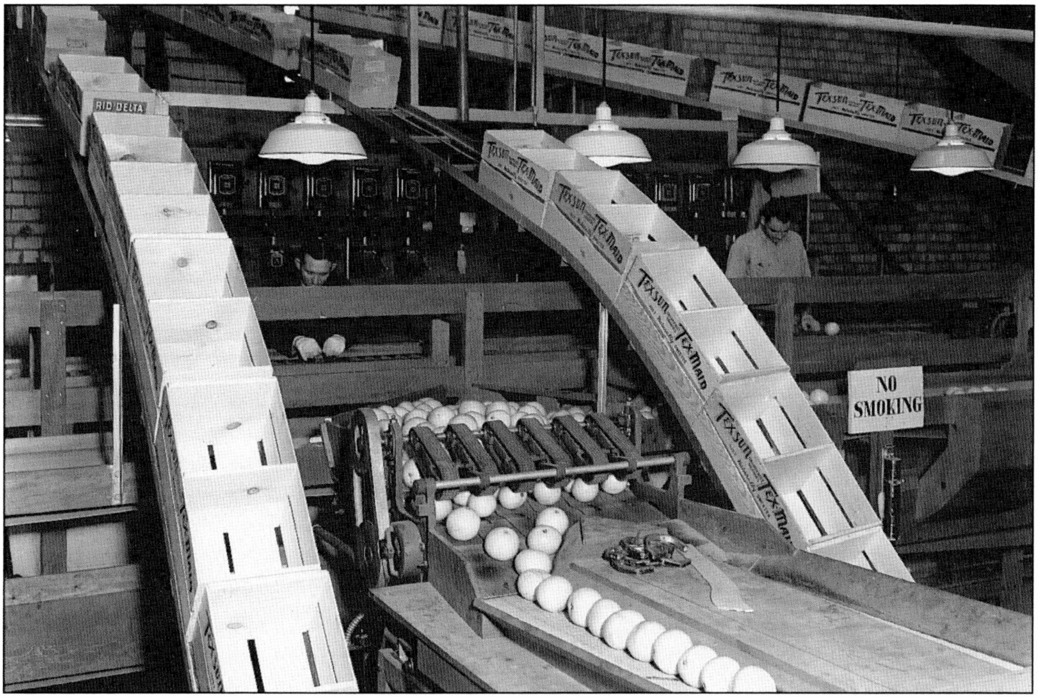


Bruce boxes, seen here on three conveyors, protected fresh grapefruit during shipment to market. (Edrington Studio.)

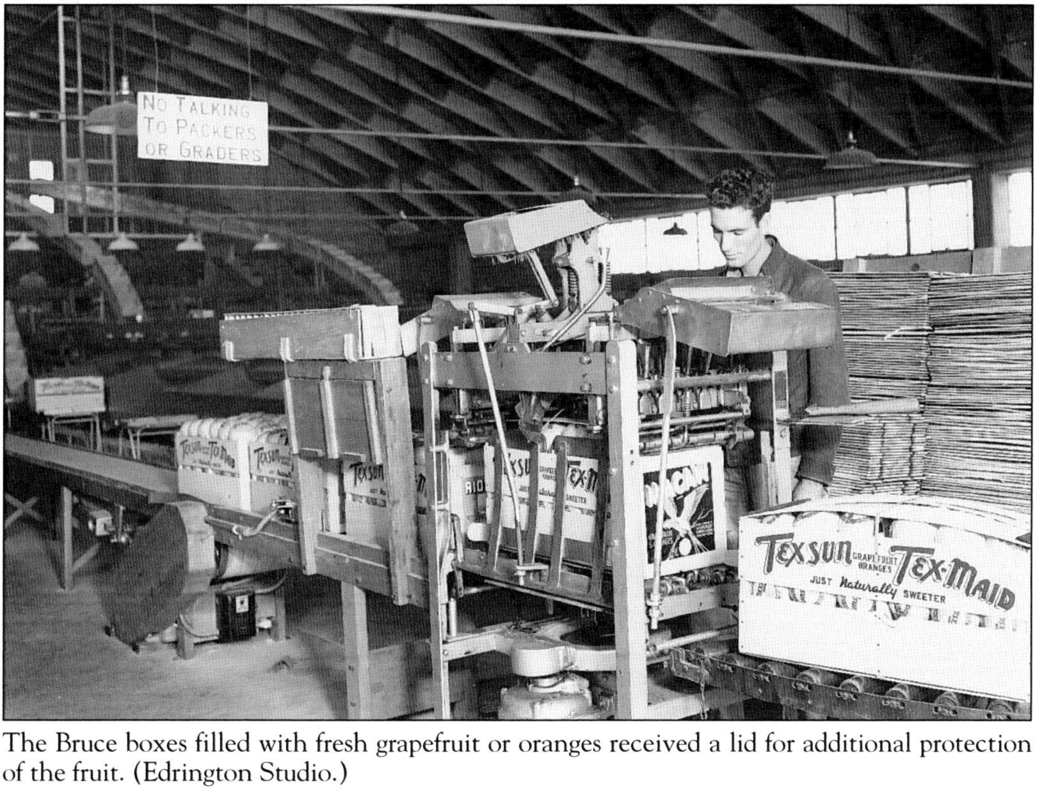


The Bruce boxes filled with fresh grapefruit or oranges received a lid for additional protection of the fruit. (Edrington Studio.)

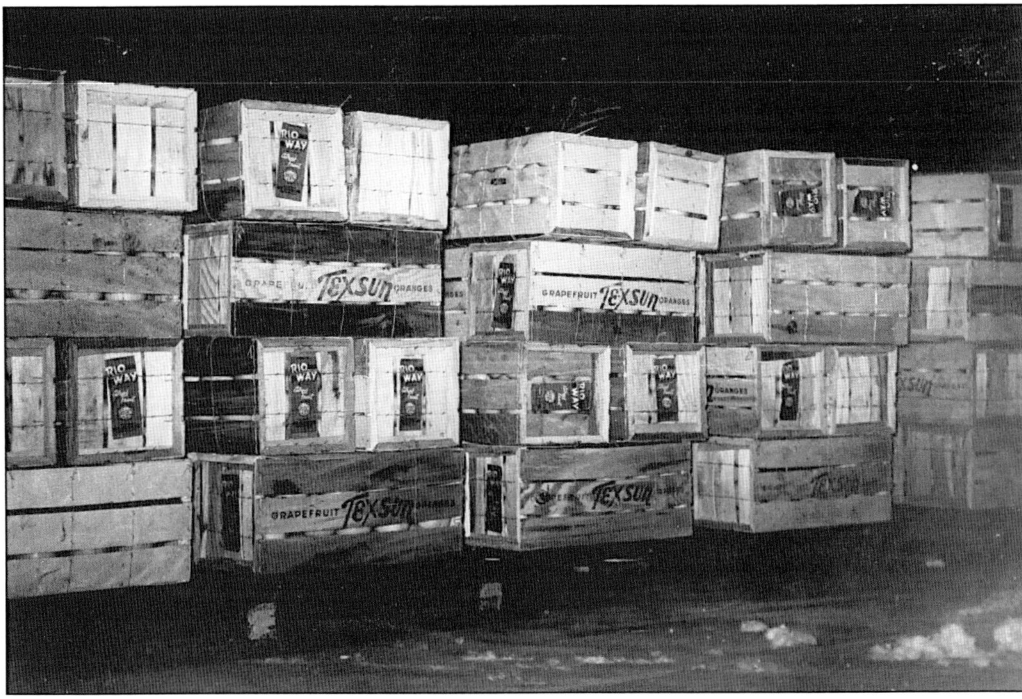


Boxed grapefruit were stacked on pallets for shipment.

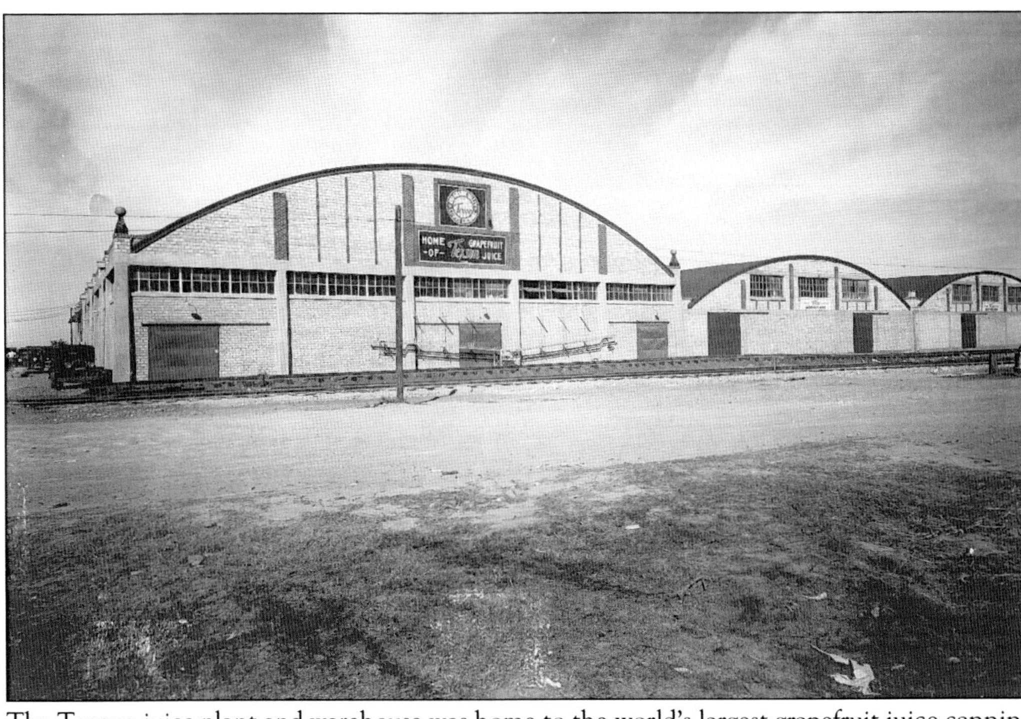


The Texsun juice plant and warehouse was home to the world's largest grapefruit juice canning plant for many years.

*Seven*

# Texsun Advertisements

Texsun advertised its many products throughout the United States and beyond. Over time, the advertisements reflected changing values even as they portrayed contemporary themes.

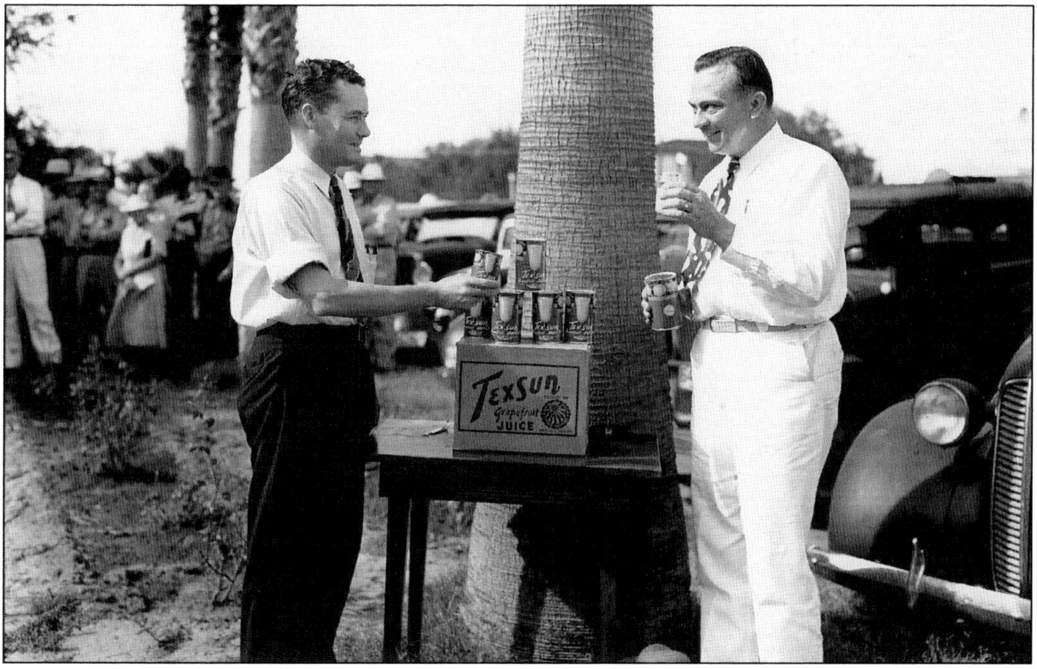


Texas governor-elect W. Lee O'Daniel drinks Texsun grapefruit juice, c. 1938. (Edrington Studio.)

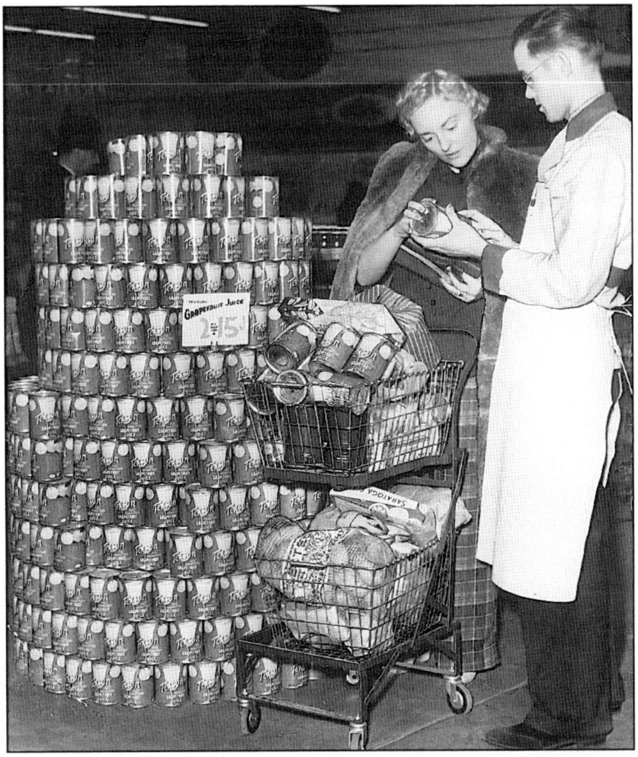


Texsun first opened a sales office in Chicago, then in St. Louis and Kansas City. This advertisement shows a customer buying juice in the supermarket of J.S. Dillon & Sons in Wichita, Kansas, on November 27, 1939.

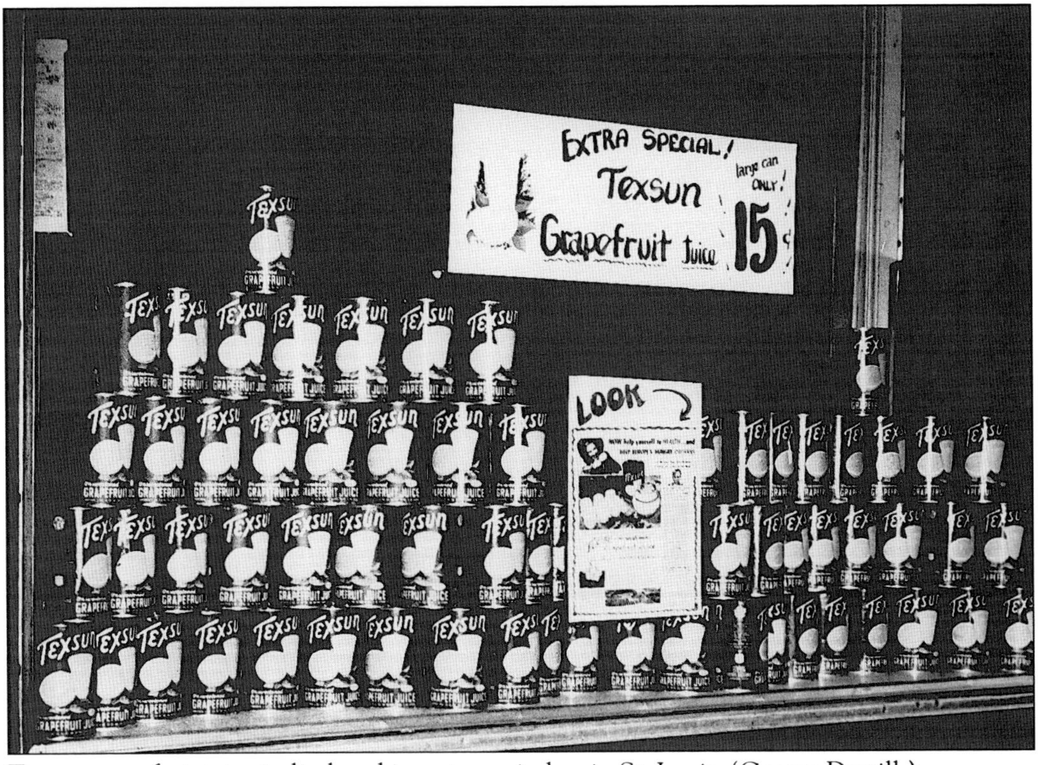


Texsun grapefruit juice is displayed in a store window in St. Louis. (George Dorrill.)

A Trans-Texas Airline stewardess is seen here with Texsun grapefruit juice.

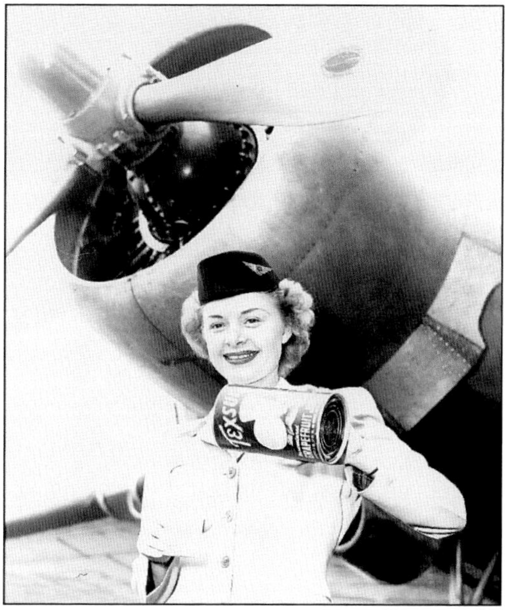

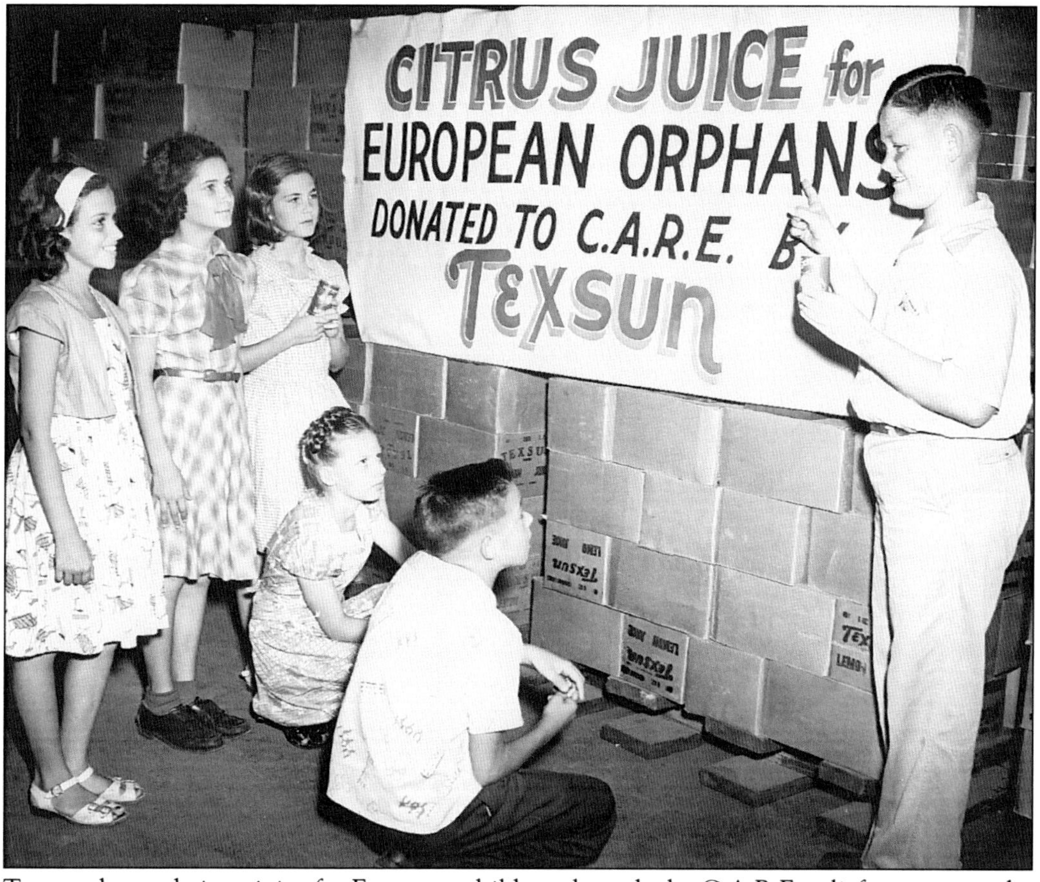


Texsun donated citrus juice for European children through the C.A.R.E. relief program in the post–World War II years. (Holbrook Studio.)

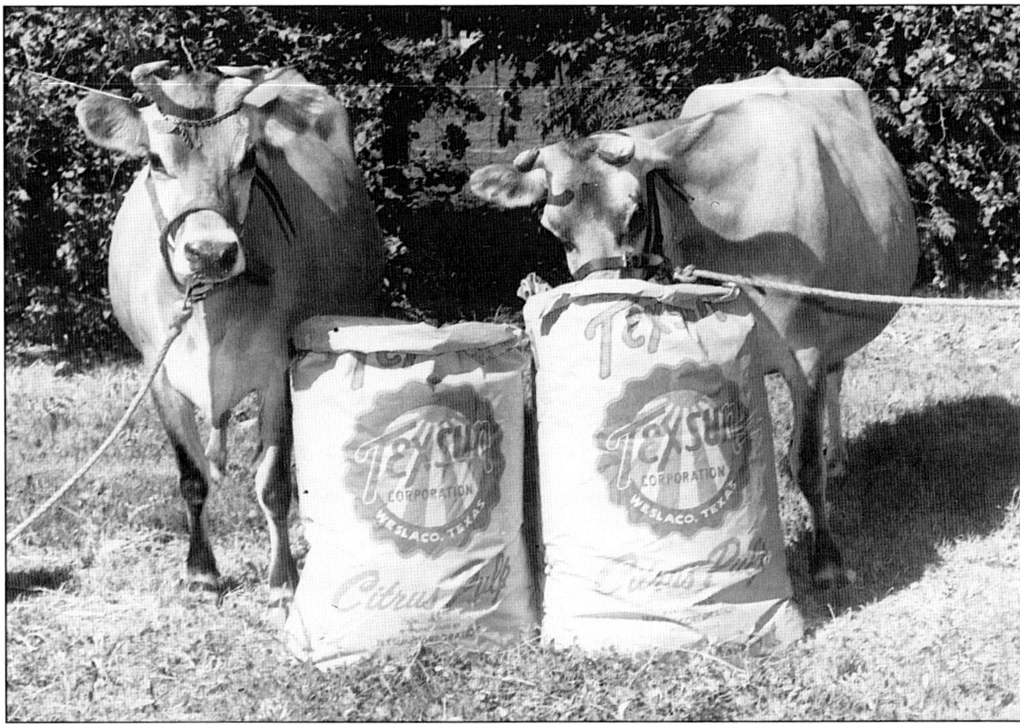

Texsun citrus pulp was used as feed for dairy cattle.

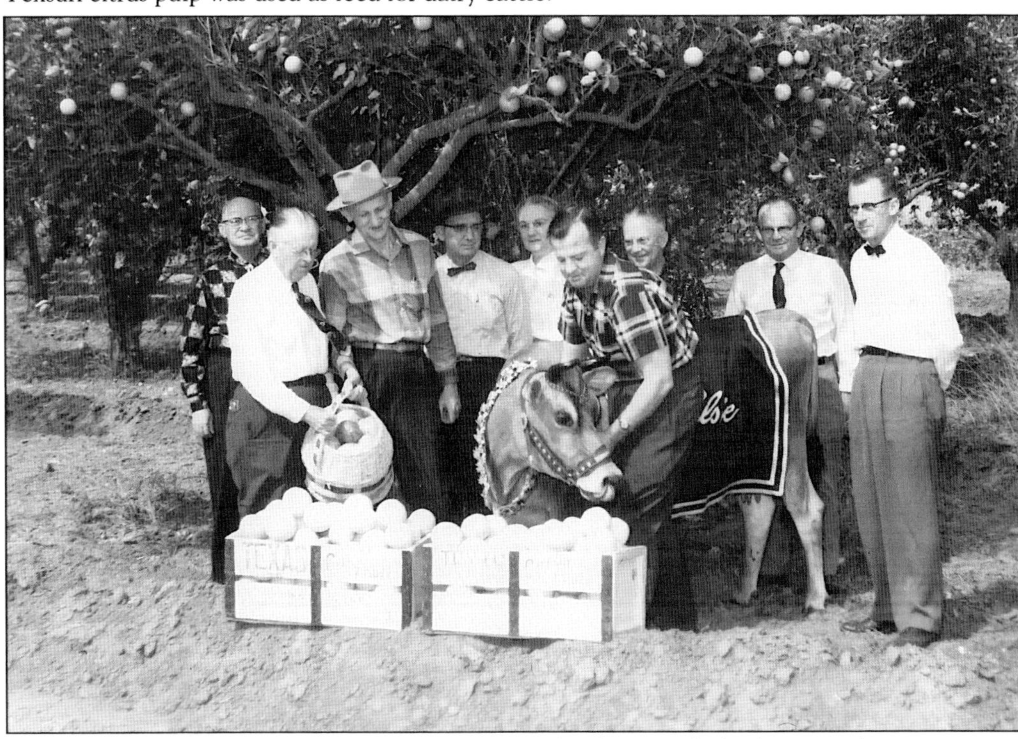
This advertisement promotes the use of citrus fruit for dairy cattle feed. General manager Lorne S. Hamme, in a plaid shirt and hat, is the third from left. (Brad Smith.)

Texsun advertisements are displayed at the Paramount Theatre in Cedar Rapids, Iowa, to promote the movie *It Happened on Fifth Avenue*, starring Gale Storm.

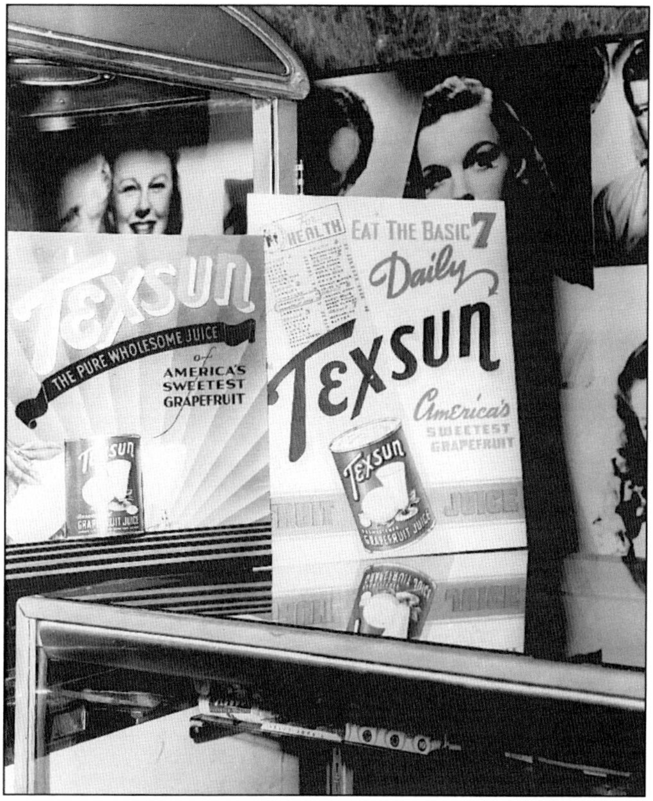


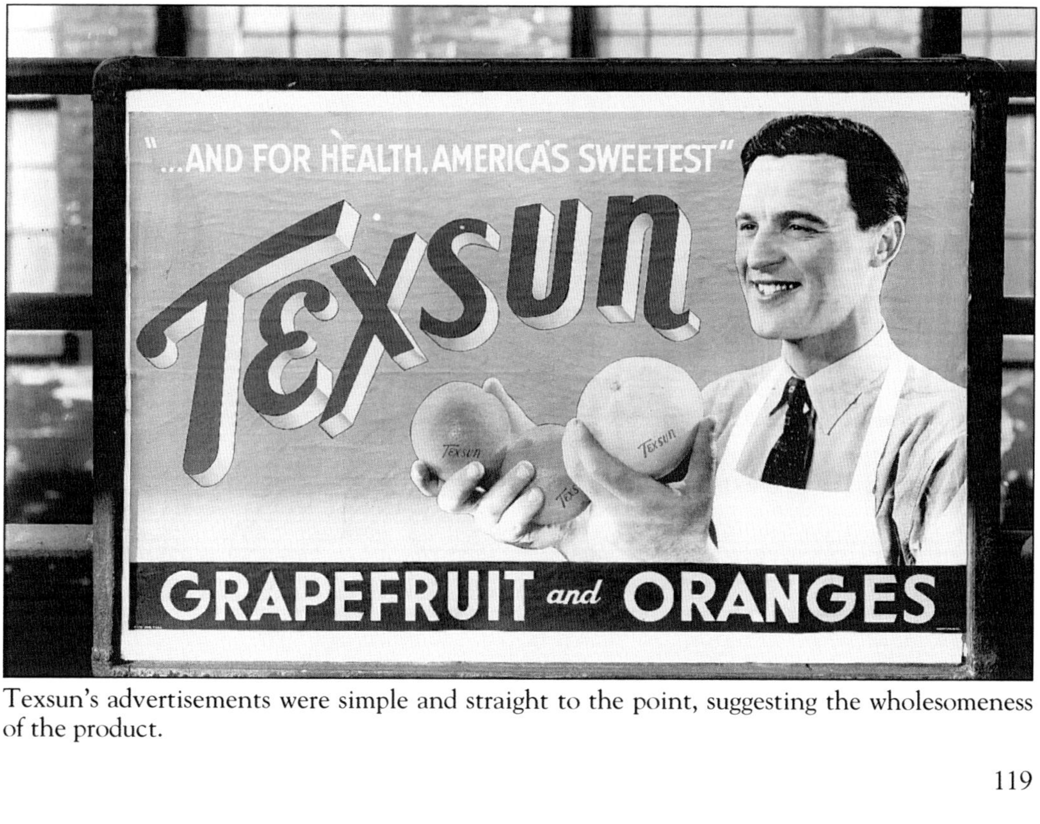


Texsun's advertisements were simple and straight to the point, suggesting the wholesomeness of the product.

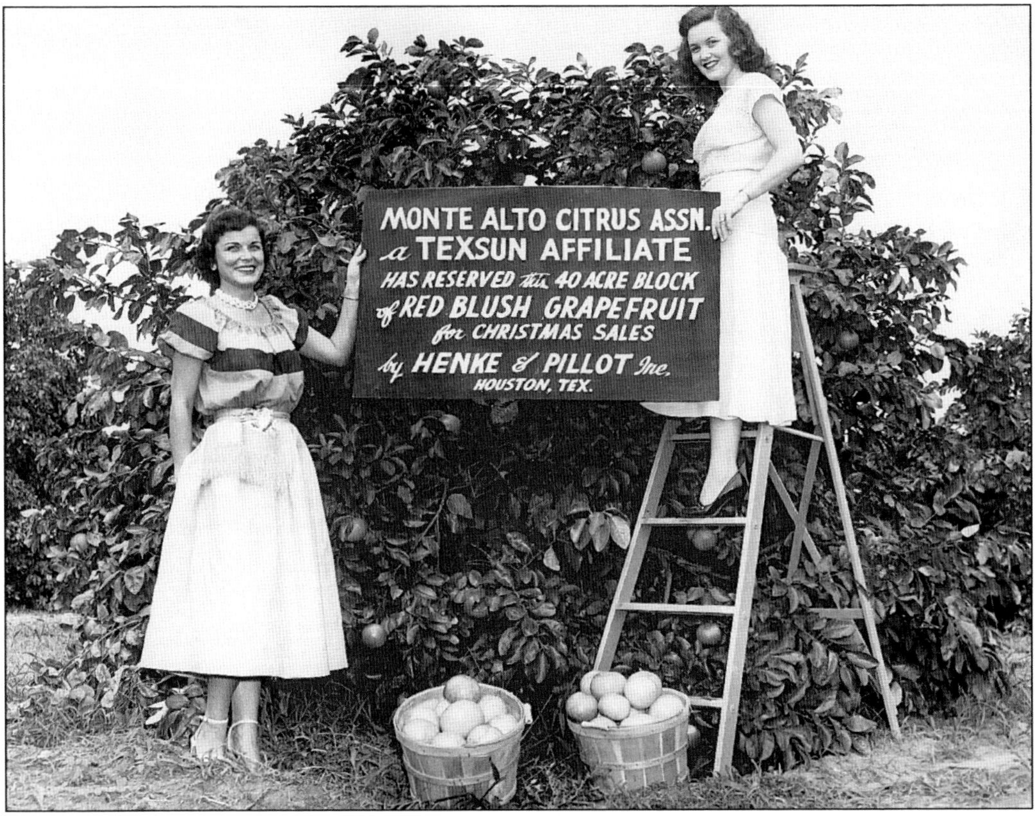


This Texsun advertisement features two young ladies of Mercedes. Henke and Pillot, Inc. was a grocery store chain in Houston.

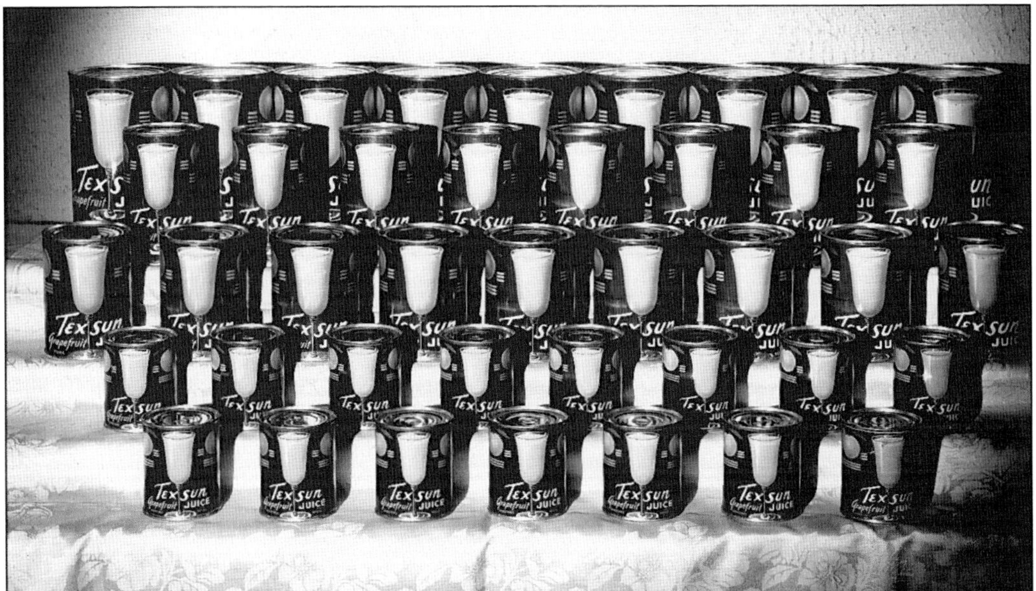


This Texsun advertisement was created by a commercial advertising agency in Dallas. (Parker-Griffith.)

Here is another advertisement by a Dallas advertising agency. (James F. Laughead.)

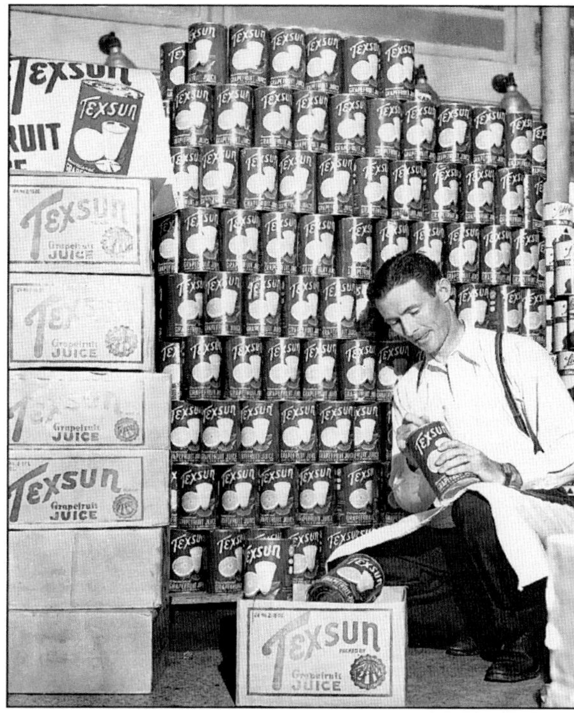


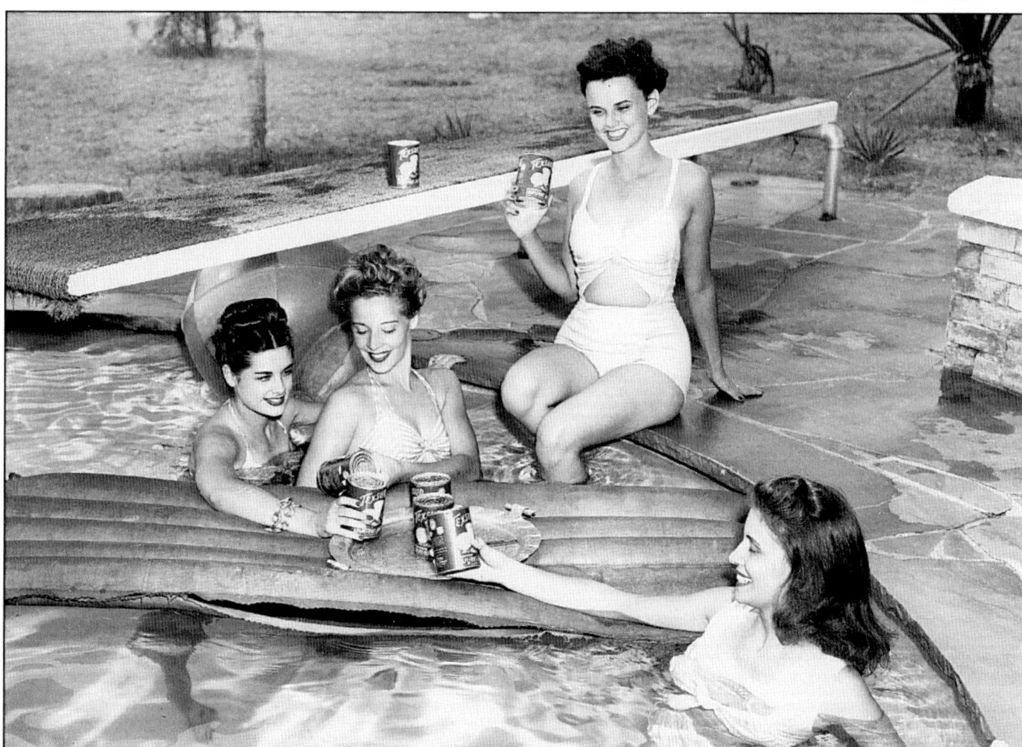

Texsun advertisement shows changing values after World War II. "Wholesomeness" was expressed in terms of beauty, leisure, and health. (Tom W. Collins.)

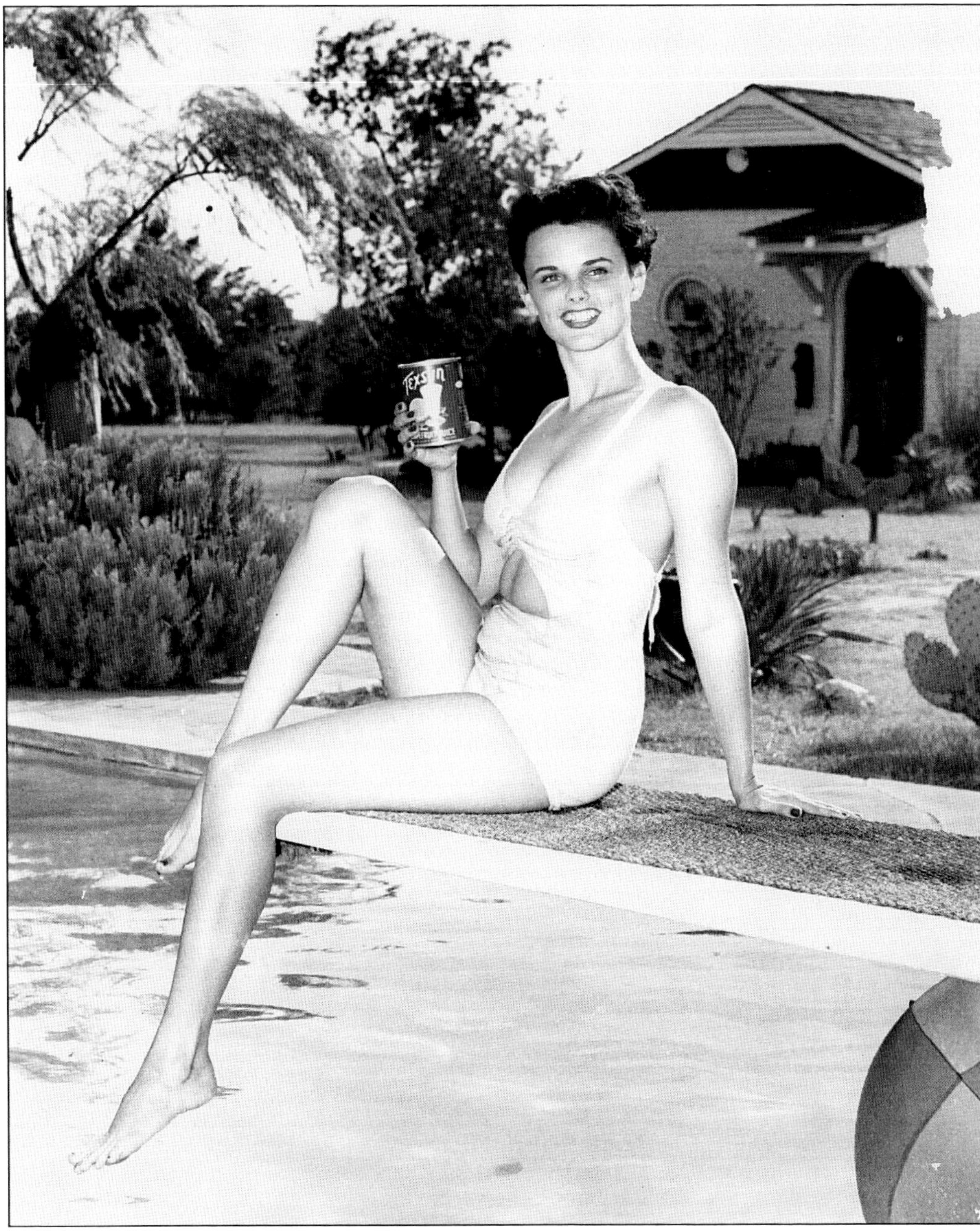

A Texsun advertisement uses a single model to symbolize product image. (Tom W. Collins.)

# *Eight*

# Changing Times

World War II brought America's strengths into sharp focus. No effort was unimportant. Weslaco citizens did their share and more to win. After the war, a return to what was normal was long overdue, but "normal" would never be quite the same as it was.

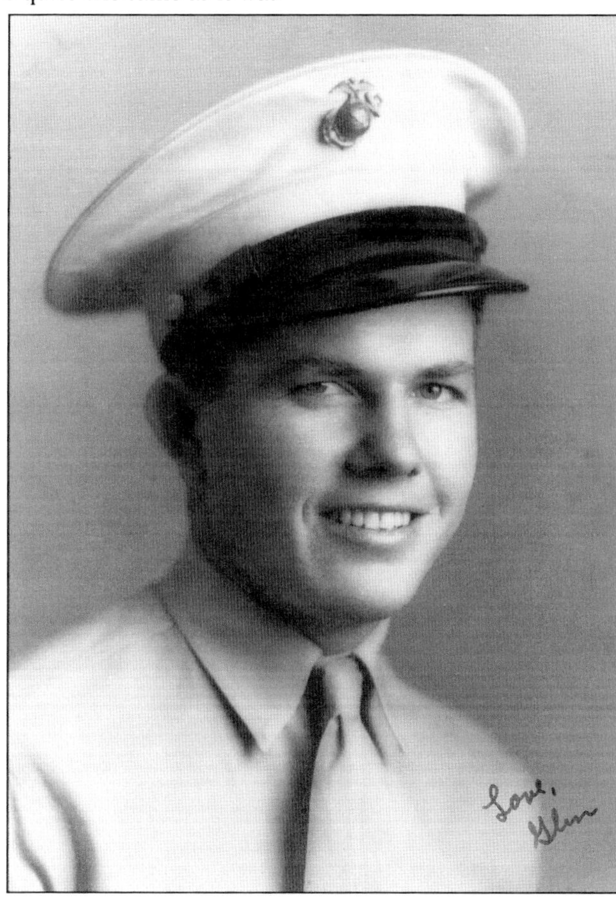


PFC Glen Cleckler joined the Marine Corps in February 1943 and served in the Pacific, Marshall Islands, and Iwo Jima. The photograph is dated December 1943.

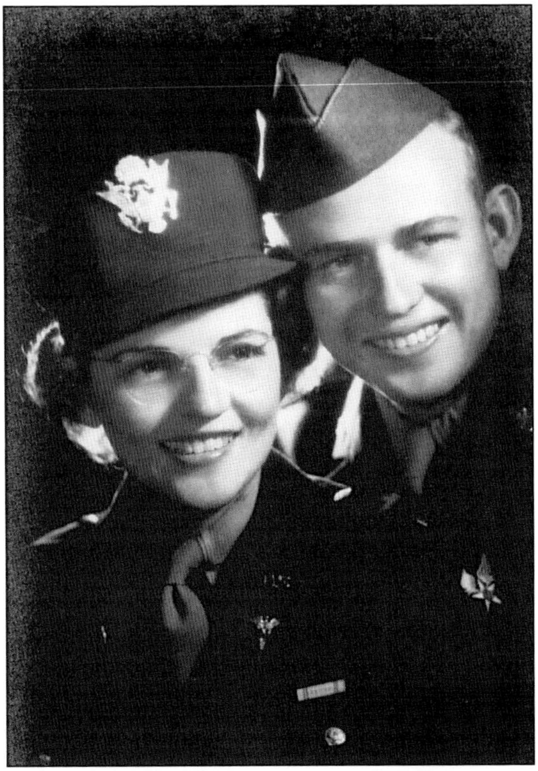

Lt. Verdie Pettit Todd of the Army Air Force Nurse Corps, April 1940–January 1945, is shown with her brother, Lt. Neal W. Pettit, of the 448th Bomb Group of 8th Air Force, June 1943–September 1945. The photograph is dated October 1943.

Pictured here are the mothers of eight Weslaco High School graduates who entered the war in 1943. From left to right, they are (front row) Mrs. Ryan, Mrs. Sooter, Mrs. Cleckler, and Mrs. LaDuke; (back row) Mrs. Guess, Mrs. Hall, Mrs. Block, and Mrs. Sims.

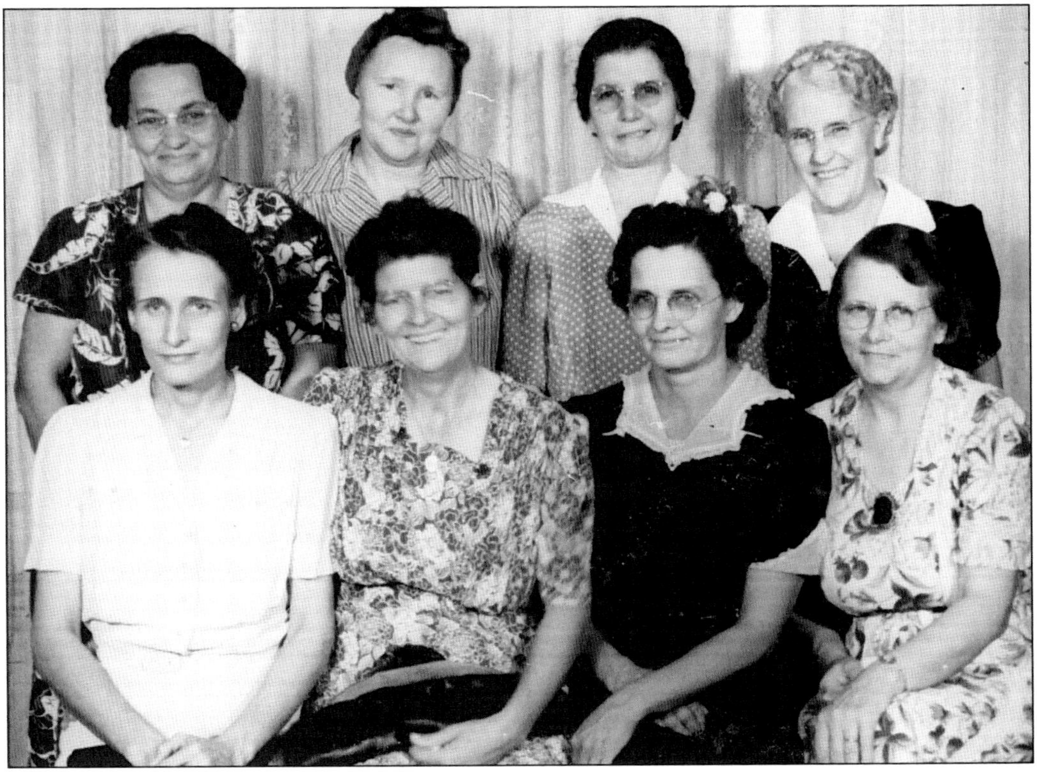

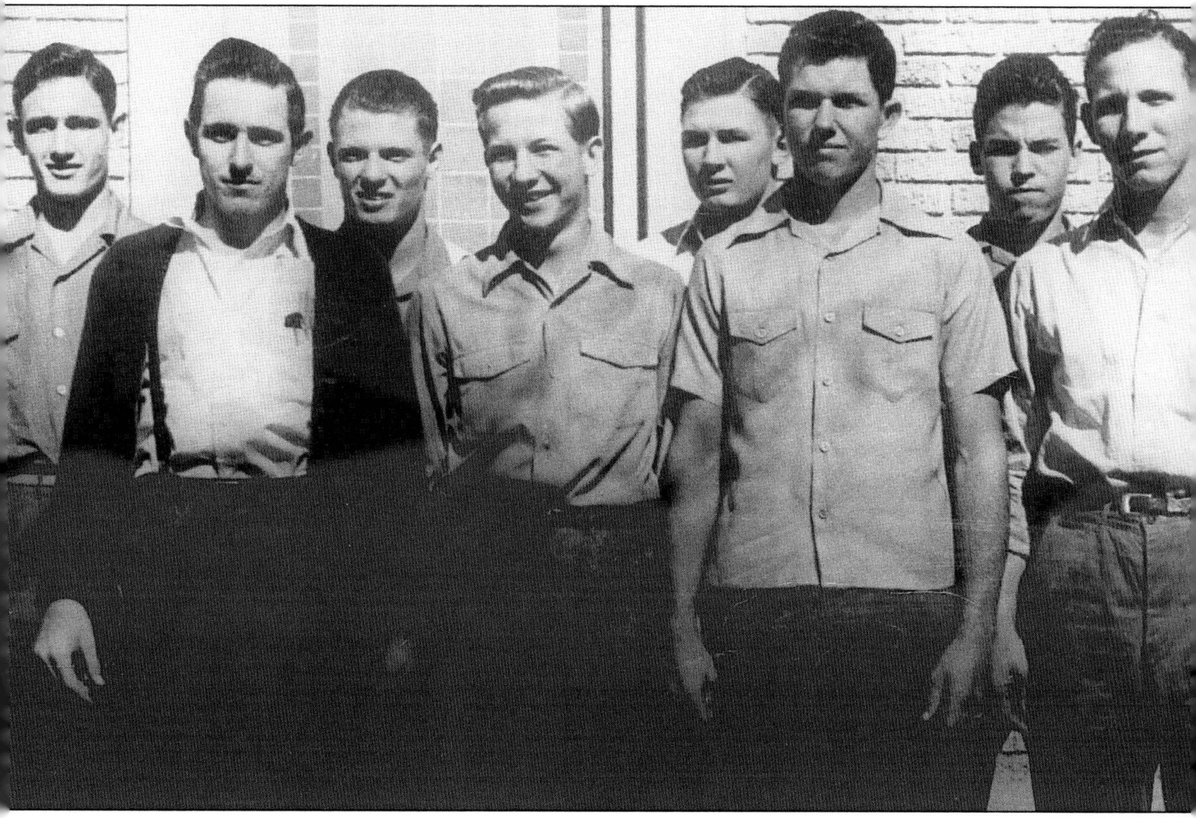

These eight senior class boys, members of the first string of the Panther football team, were graduated in a special exercise on January 25, 1943, because they were leaving for Marine Corps boot camp. From left to right are Leo Ryan, Carl Sims, Ben Guess, Leo LaDuke, Pete Hall, Glen Cleckler, Robert Sooter, and Harlon Block. Corp. Harlon Block trained at Camp Pendleton and Hawaii and landed on Iwo Jima on February 19, 1945. After the Marines took Mt. Suribachi on February 23, 1945, Block was among a group of five Marines and one sailor who raised the American flag. Associated Press photographer Joe Rosenthal snapped the photograph that became the symbol of the American spirit during the war and later earned him a Pulitzer Prize. Exactly one week later, on March 1, 1945, Corporal Block was killed in action as the Marines were attacking Japanese soldiers near Nishi Ridge. Corporal Block was first buried in the Marine cemetery on Iwo Jima but was returned to Weslaco for private burial in January 1949. All seven of Harlon Block's classmates served as pallbearers. Twenty Weslaco High School graduates and one teacher died in World War II.

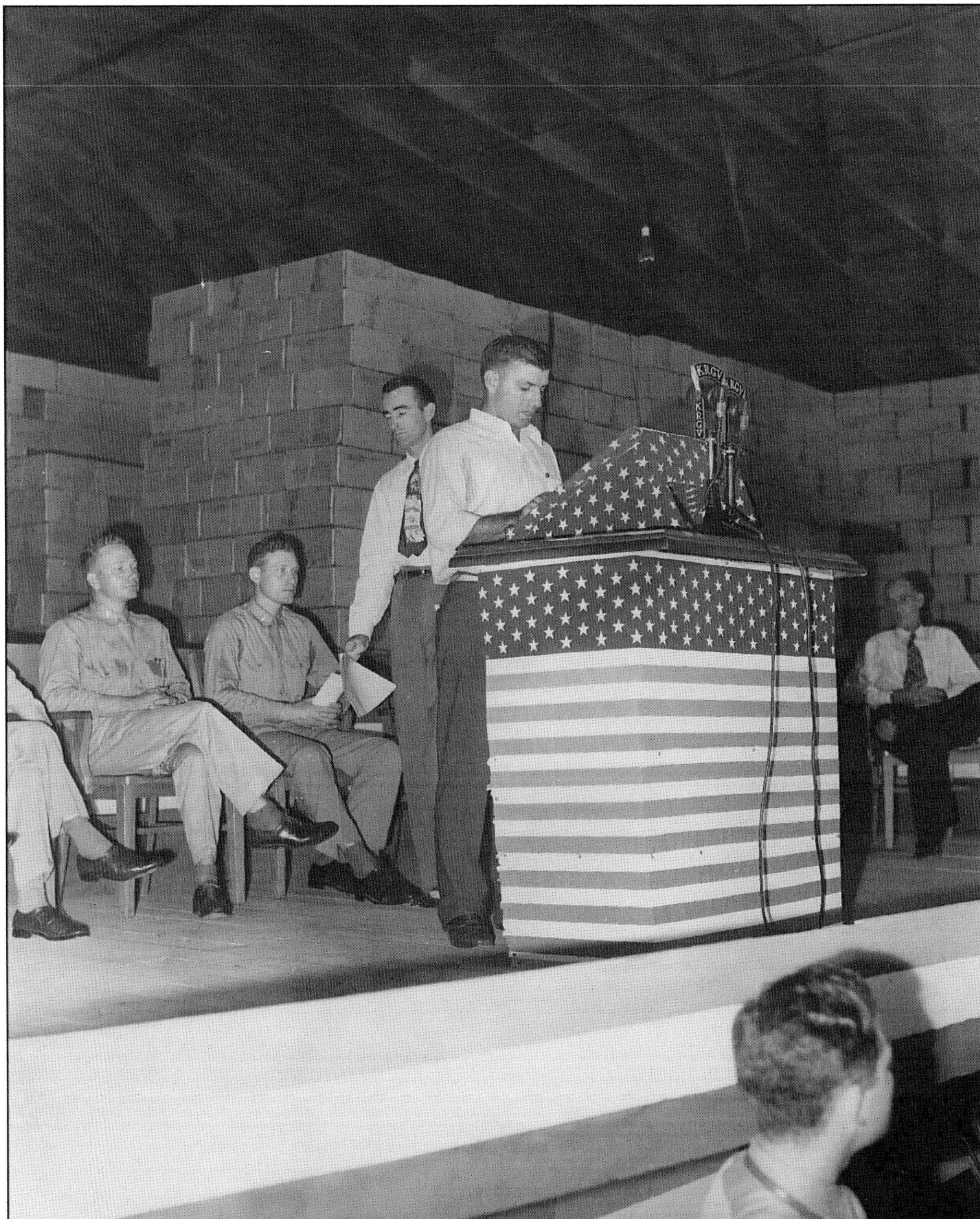


This ceremony honored Texsun for its contributions to World War II. By the 1940s, about 120,000 acres were in citrus cultivation. During the war, the military bought quantities of canned citrus juices. Texsun cans had to be painted olive drab so that sunlight would not be reflected off the cans and reveal our soldiers' position to the enemy. The cans were painted after the juice was sealed inside. (Brad Smith.)

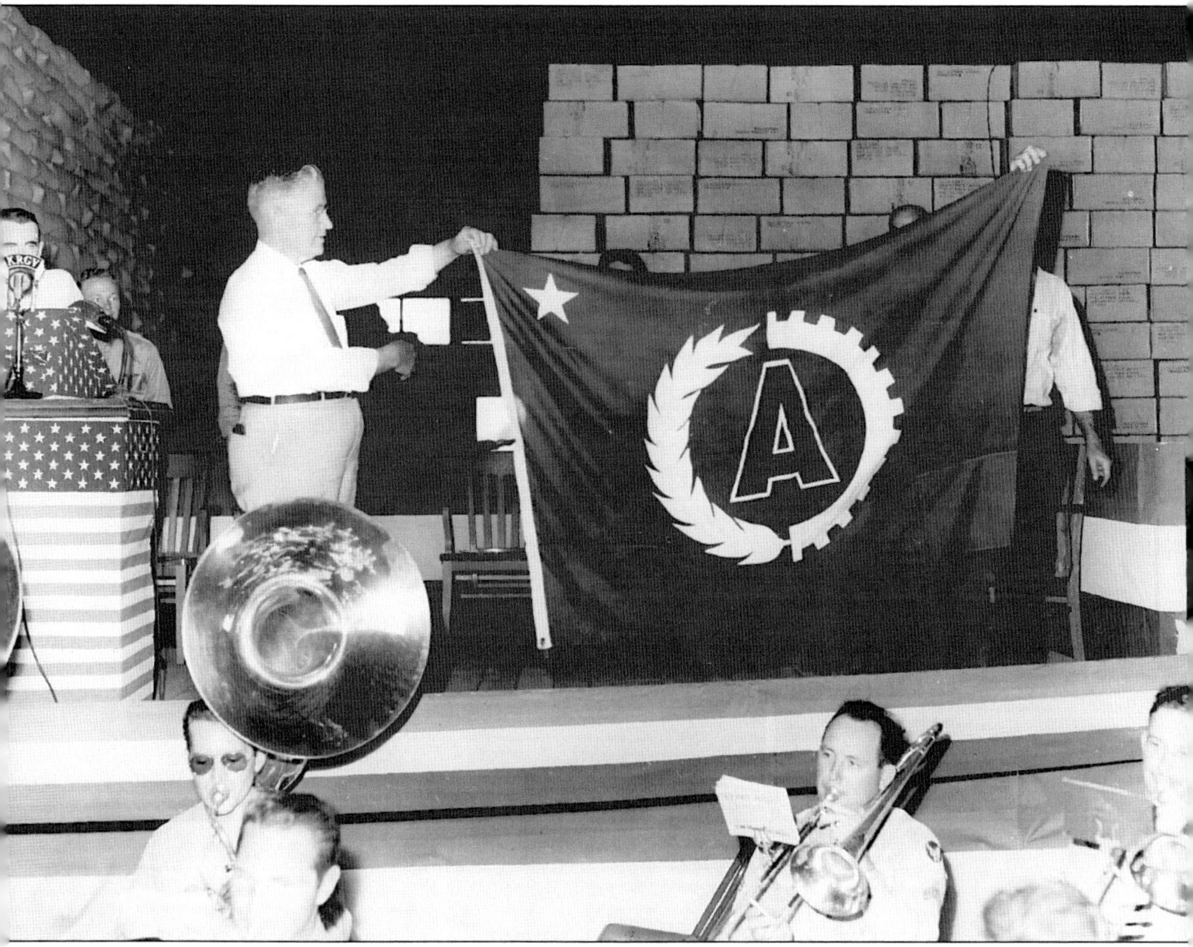

Texsun received the "A Award" from the U.S. government for consistent high-quality production. (Brad Smith.)

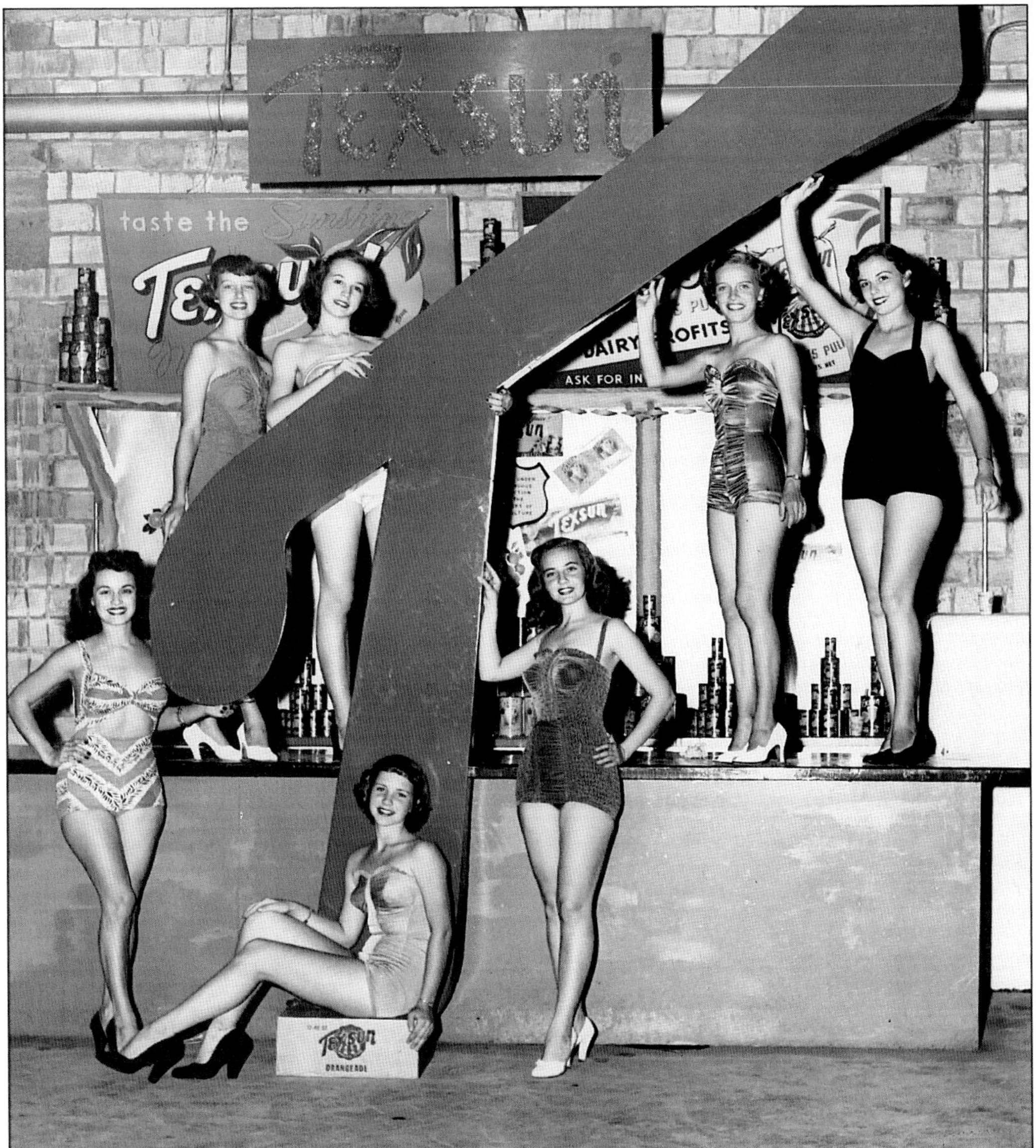


This Texsun advertisement featured young ladies from the Valley in swimsuit poses similar to those of the professional models. (Yoder.)